Cemeteries of Ambivalent Desire

University of Houston Series in Mexican American Studies

Sponsored by the Center for Mexican American Studies

Tatcho Mindiola

Director and General Editor

Cemeteries of Ambivalent Desire

Unearthing Deep South Narratives from a Texas Graveyard

Marie Theresa Hernández

Texas A&M University Press

College Station

Frontispiece: Gateway to San Isidro Cemetery.
Dedication Page: At the fence between San Isidro Cemetery and the prisoner/slave cemetery, a child's handprints and one footprint appear to have been made in wet soil, forming a mold into which concrete was poured.

Library of Congress Cataloging-in-Publication Data

Hernández, Marie Theresa, 1952–
    Cemeteries of ambivalent desire : unearthing deep South narratives from a Texas grave-yard / Marie Theresa Hernández. — 1st ed.
        p. cm. — (University of Houston series in Mexican American studies ; no. 5)
    Includes bibliographical references and index.
    ISBN-13: 978-1-58544-630-8 (cloth : alk. paper)
    ISBN-10: 1-58544-630-0 (cloth : alk. paper)
    ISBN-13: 978-1-60344-026-4 (pbk. : alk. paper)
    ISBN-10: 1-60344-026-7 (pbk. : alk. paper)
        1. Fort Bend County (Tex.)—History. 2. Fort Bend County (Tex.)—Ethnic relations.
    3. Ethnology—Texas—Fort Bend County. 4. Mexican Americans—Texas—Fort Bend
    County—History. 5. San Isidro Cemetery (Sugar Land, Tex.) 6. Sugar Land (Tex.)—
    History. 7. Fort Bend County (Tex.)—Historiography. I. Title.
    F392.F7H47 2008
    305.8009764'135—dc22
                                                                                    2007026394

For

José F. Hernández

and his *compadre,*

the late Esteban ("Steve") Flores

Contents

Acknowledgments ix

Introduction: "A Land Right Merry with the Sun" 1

Chapter 1   *Cementerios* 14

Chapter 2   The Manifested Destiny of History 35

Chapter 3   The Colonel 54

Chapter 4   River of the Demonic 85

Chapter 5   The Warrior 110

Chapter 6   Litigation 144

Chapter 7   Re-Membering in the Land of Oz 165

Conclusion: Monticello in Texas 185

Notes 195

Bibliography 219

Index 231

Acknowledgments

This book reflects the influence of a number of individuals. The most significant of these is my father, José F. Hernández, who began telling me stories of the history of Fort Bend County before I even began grade school. His experiences as a *mexicano* in a Jim Crow county came forth as poetic narratives. The interest, excitement, and drama in his storytelling were later infused into my own expressions. My children, Greg and Belen Tijerina, have also influenced the writing of this book because I wanted there to be something *in writing* so that they would know what life was like in Fort Bend County before they were born.

Hayden White and George Lipsitz urged me to continue the form and content of my writing, and I deeply appreciate their encouragement. Their unequivocal support, as well as their appreciation of the passion inherent in my work, made it possible for me to write this very difficult book. I am indebted to George Marcus for his continued interest in the "cemetery project," which we began discussing ten years ago when I wrote a small proposal on Sugar Land during his ethnography course at Rice University. As this book nears publication, I can appreciate his suggestion that this be a "second project"—after my first book. The density of tragedy and complicated relations embedded in this history required a seasoned perspective.

I also thank Shannon Leonard, Laura Helper, Brian Riedel, Naomi Carrier, Mariah Goselin, Maricela Villanueva, and Ana Burgoyne for reading and/or listening to my stories for this work. In addition, I greatly appreciate the institutional support provided by the University of Houston, especially the Center for Mexican American Studies and its director, Tatcho Mindiola, who not only championed the cemetery project but also provided me three precious semesters of paid leave to complete this book. While I was away from Texas, the Center for Cultural Studies at the University of California–Santa

Cruz, whose codirectors are Chris Connery and Gail Hershatter, graciously
welcomed me as a resident scholar for the 2004–2005 academic year, thereby
allowing me to work with UCSC faculty and resources.

My sincere thanks also go to Dean John Antel of the College of Liberal
Arts and Social Sciences at the University of Houston and to Marc Zimmer-
man, chair of Modern and Classical Languages, for their enthusiasm and assistance in recruiting me back to UH, which is an excellent work and creative
environment for me.

I also thank the following persons for their assistance in my learning
about Fort Bend County, Sugar Land, and San Isidro Cemetery: John de la
Cruz, Kathy Reyes, Jesse García, Marjorie Adams, Tim Cumins, Cata Arizpe,
Juan García, the late Linda Carrillo, and the members of the San Isidro Cemetery Association.

I thank my mother, María de la Luz Hernández, for her attempts to call
John de la Cruz when I was unable to find him and for relaying messages to
my father. I cannot adequately acknowledge the help of Tom Goselin, my
husband and life partner. His efforts at reading the manuscript, critiquing my
ideas, and supporting my research truly made *Cemeteries* possible.

As this work was nearing completion, my uncle Esteban ("Steve") Flores
died unexpectedly. For most of his adult life, he worked as a supervisor and
heavy equipment operator, and many of the streets in the new subdivisions of
Fort Bend were built by him.

Cemeteries of Ambivalent Desire

"A Land Right Merry with the Sun"

In 1903 W. E. B. DuBois wrote *The Souls of Black Folk,* in which he describes a "land right merry with the sun," where "children sing and rolling hills" are full of plenty. The highway of the King passes through this place of bounty, yet on the side of the beautiful road there "sits a figure veiled and bowed." The darkness of the character is uncomfortable for passersby. Their pace quickens as they walk past the bowed figure that seems so strangely out of place in this land of plenty.

This book is about an old Mexican cemetery caught inside a whitewashed suburban community. It is in a place that is "right merry with the sun," where "children sing." It is a bountiful area, home to the powerful and wealthy. Yet the cemetery is like the "figure veiled and bowed;" its dark history evokes an uncomfortable feeling in all who pass by.

Cemeteries of Ambivalent Desire is about a cemetery in Southeast Texas named San Isidro. Although known as a burial ground for ethnic Mexicans,[1] it was also a cemetery for prisoners and slaves. It is located in Sugar Land, a former company town in Fort Bend County, presently considered one of the wealthiest areas in the state and even the nation. Fort Bend was named after a garrison built in 1822 at the bend of the Brazos River. The area was called the Brazos Bottoms. In 2005 it was identified as Houston's wealthiest suburb; a place where the dividing lines between people and power create intense narratives. It is home to former congressman Tom DeLay and Clifford Baxter, the Enron executive who committed suicide in 2002.

Fort Bend is also the home of Texas history, where the first white people settled before Texas became an independent nation. Its nineteenth-century agrarian economic success—built on slave and convict labor—has transformed into a significant market for the twenty-first-century consumer. The county's economic development organization boasts that Fort Bend has more

master-planned communities than any other county of Texas, is the most diverse, and has a population plentiful with college graduates and homeowners.[2] The claims of diversity are valid, yet the people of color living in the
eastern part of the county (where the wealth is) are generally neither ethnic
Mexican nor black. Rather, they are Asian or South Asian.

In writing this book, I found a "land right merry with the sun," whose
striking and troubled history has left an unnamed ghost hiding behind a veil
that is yet to be removed.

Beginnings

The project began with my interest in an old Mexican cemetery located in Sugar
Land, on the eastern side of the county. San Isidro Cemetery was (and is)
the burial place for Latino employees of Imperial Sugar.[3] It is a place I often
visited as a child. From 1996 through 2004 I slowly learned the story of the
cemetery, the sugar company, and the county itself. The story of the county
seemed to come last. In this long overdue book I find myself going further
and further back past the stories of San Isidro Cemetery. As I reintegrate my
own history with these narratives, I realize that the veil DuBois describes also
covered my vision and experience of growing up in the county.

This book is about history and memory. As I write, the words of Houston Baker Jr. come to mind: "[M]y present work . . . revolves around re-
vision and re-visitation . . . and it begins for me with the inescapable fact of
the tightly spaced southernness I have long sought to erase from my speech,
my bearing, and my memory. But it has never really been possible. For . . . I
quickly discover I have not left the South, nor has the South left me."[4]

In this story of Fort Bend County the subjectivity of a memory is inexplicably tied to the perceived identity of a person. History is everything.
Thus the imagination of a preschool child who, because of her particular life
circumstances, was privy to the many stories that comprise "what it was like"
sometime in the past, enabled her to become a witness to what she saw. Decades later the child is now the ethnographer/writer. The imaginary enters
what she remembers. The relevance of her nuanced perspective is not clear, yet
she is aware that she is not the only one who imagines while she remembers.

Writing about San Isidro Cemetery and Fort Bend County is perhaps
a way for me to tell the stories that I saw and heard during the years of Jim
Crow. In an amalgamation of these narratives, those of people willing to speak
with me, and texts that have been written, I am attempting to create an im-

age of this space that during two centuries has consistently been central to the story of our national community. The spectrum from the personal to the political has the advantage of indicating how broader issues, events, and narratives affect the lives of individual people. I am not attempting to tell the truest or most comprehensive history. This is merely a recollection of stories and a musing on their meaning for a certain space and how it has moved back and forth through time.

These stories—threads that seem to travel disparately through two centuries—produce the fabric of my remembrance. I am like Houston Baker. The more I read, the more I write and the more I realize that I have not really left the place. It is inside me. It is in the moments of connection, when I remember something my mother told me that I think sounds like bell hooks. In *Yearning*[5] hooks writes that her grandmother Baba would often have white visitors, who in a respectful, yet familiar, way call Baba "Aunt Sarah." The visitors would talk for hours, the conversations seemingly intimate. Ultimately, some of these visits created connections that lasted Baba's lifetime. However, Baba never forgot history, slavery, and Jim Crow. "There was never any bond between her and a white person strong enough to counter that memory. In her mind, to be safe, one had to 'keep a distance.'"[6] When I was a child and later an adolescent, my mother would also tell me to keep my distance; white people could not be trusted. My relationships with them needed to serve a specific purpose that did not include friendship.

My mother's warning did not come from a woman who had experienced a lifetime of disenfranchisement. Her experience was not like Baba's. She had lived on the Texas-Mexico border, a place populated by people mostly like herself. Her family worked hard but lived a comfortable existence during the Depression. She had never been excluded from anything because of her race or skin color. Yet, her perspective was altered at the age of twenty-six by her arrival in a small town controlled by Jim Crow law and order. She learned quickly that not all white people were the same and that Texas, three hundred miles to the northeast, was a completely different world. And so, like Baba, who graciously entertained the white people who visited her home, my mother was also the gracious, well-bred, and socially poised wife of a small-town mexicano businessman. She never let on what she was really thinking. There was a purpose to every interaction with someone who was not family or a very close friend.

Similar to Baker, I am "re-visioning and re-visiting." I am seeing things now as they are revised with a complicated intertwining between the stories people tell me and the books and newspapers I read. I am again at this place in the South where I lived as a child. These new visions are blending with my memory, which is re-forming itself with the South that has risen up inside me again.

Identity

This book began with a story about an old Mexican cemetery caught inside a whitewashed suburban community. It is about identity constructed by stories. It is about narratives and perspective.[7] As in all constructions, many different components create the whole. It is necessary to present the historical narrative about the space in which ethnic Mexicans found themselves at the end of the twentieth century. Stories included about other people (powerful and disenfranchised) are necessary to the understanding of the space. While the book starts and ends with mexicanos, it considers their history inside a complex weave of narratives and experiences. Thus the emancipation of the slaves, Reconstruction, and the post-Reconstruction era, I believe, are as significant to this narrative as are aspects of the geography and current economy of the county.

A community formed by slavery does not transform itself completely. The ghost of bondage does not go away even when history is erased. It is malleable and transforms itself as needed while each era passes. Bondage catches each new generation in a different way. After slavery came underpaid freedmen, then contract prison labor, then the Mexican workers from Central Texas and northern Mexico. Tangible markers remain along with other imprints left on local culture. Everyone is affected, although in different ways. African Americans, ethnic Mexicans, new immigrants from Asia and South Asia, local whites, and the new corporate executives who have staked out Fort Bend County as their home live in a space where this shadow remains.

Producing the Nation

[T]o transcend this space of death requires a careful understanding of the trauma that in fact produced the nation in the first place and that, on the current evidence, is still pertinent to its understanding (Quayson 2003, 77).

*He [W. J. Cash] captured, that is to say, the mind of America in provid-
ing a comprehensive analysis of what he called the South (Baker 2001, 22).*

While it seems that the cemetery became a place where many of these unfortunate incidents laid the trauma to rest, the idea of *the South* remains in
this manuscript. The story of the cemetery is not enough. The space is where
events became embedded in memory in a tangible way—inside the graves of
the dead. Yet, the memories of those still alive flicker with each trace of remembrance. New encounters revive old ones. The old ones remain inside the
spaces where new ones appear.

The story of Fort Bend County parallels the metanarrative of American
life. White settlers, plantations, slaves, Mexican immigrants, Fordism, Jim
Crow, and late capitalism fall into the cadence of stories telling the history of
the county. Cotton and sugar hold much of this together. Quayson's premise
that trauma produces the nation in the first place resonates with the idea that
the cemetery holds the trauma. Here are the graves of people who died in the
fields, in the canals, in the bars.

The cemetery holds the secret to the metanarrative, while this Southern county holds the story of the nation. Houston Baker cites *The Mind of
the South*,[8] the work of W. J. Cash, in which Cash explains in painful detail
the narrative of the South, yet the context in reality is that of the nation. The
South's connection to the overall history of the United States is no longer so
difficult to decipher as it was when Cash's manuscript was published during
World War II. With recent disclosures regarding the black offspring of two
of our white national leaders (Thomas Jefferson and Strom Thurmond), the
secret is no longer private. The veil that camouflaged these "indiscretions" has
begun to move aside, revealing previously unspeakable information.

Whiteness: A Delicate Matter—The Affective Grid of Southern Politics

In *Carnal Knowledge and Imperial Power,* her magnificent book on sexuality and colonialism, Ann Laura Stoler proposes that "histories situated on
the peripheries of empire" have a "palpable obsession" with whiteness that is
focused inordinately on the "crafting of chromatic identities."[9] The conflict
and ambivalence related to these creations have caused havoc in the American South.

This fact may be related to my sense of discomfort in producing this manuscript. It comes with the feeling of telling secrets. As I speak to people and read books about Texas and the American South, I have come to believe that the foundational ideology of the South is based on the purity of race. The darkness of a Mexican cemetery is hard to bear inside a space known for its pristine whiteness. The incongruity between the public truth and the public secret lies at the heart of the matter. Throughout the history of the county, the ongoing quest for and statements about racial purity have been curiously accompanied by a silent, yet stronger, narrative. In an unofficial way, intimacy—sexual and otherwise—between all racial and ethnic groups was accepted and encouraged, especially between white men and women of color.

We know about the women of color who cared for the white children and prepared the family meals. The idea of sexual encounters between white men and their slaves (later domestic servants) has until recently been just a titillating thought. Biographies of great Southern men did not contain information about their intimate relationships unless it was in the context of marriage—that is, until Jefferson's secret was revealed. The polemic regarding the relationship between Thomas Jefferson and his slave Sally Hemings has made it possible for other stories to enter the mainstream of American belief. African Americans have told of these relationships in personal narratives and scholarly documents; they have not really been a secret.

However, most of white America does not see or hear these stories, even though they are clearly within "view." The details of most of these are not discussed in this book: proving the veracity of those narratives is not the focus of this project. However, I believe it is necessary to open the space so they can be heard. For those that still believe that the rape of slave women by slave owners was a rare occurrence, my response is to listen to the fact that these narratives exist. The awareness of their circulation is enough to justify their importance. Relationships in the domestic sphere are not subject to the same distinctions required in the outside world. During the era of slavery, the boundaries around the body were permeable. Feeding, bathing, and cleaning created intimate situations. Yet, it was the sexually intimate that was the most ambiguous and the most intense. Stoler proposes that the "domains of the intimate figured so prominently in the perceptions and policies of those who ruled" that they could be considered the "microphysics of colonial rule." They are "the affective grid of colonial politics."[10] As an aside, the term "colonial," for the purposes of this book, can easily be interchanged with "American Southern."

This affect is intensely represented in emotionally explosive encounters that occurred repeatedly in the history of Fort Bend County. These were usually, but not always, associated with race. Yet this intermittent violence "is legitimized by what it excludes."[11] The ghost of slavery is not visible in the twenty-first-century narrative of Fort Bend County. While the existence of slavery is acknowledged, there appears to be no conscious awareness of its atrocity. The violence of bondage is further compromised by the unspoken sexual liaisons between white men and black women. As Stoler's work indicates, "illegitimate unions between native [slave] women and European [white] men were woven into the fabric of colonial [Southern] governance."[12] The undetermined influence of these relations has produced a haunting that continues into the present. This is a place of exaggerated production and economic success, where the idea of civil society is not about civil rights. It is a city described by its mayor David Wallace as "laissez-faire capitalist heaven" with no public transportation, public hospital, or public golf course. It is the bastion of Texas Republican politics, created by "voters in the . . . suburbs who abandoned the Democrats over civil rights."[13]

Perspective: An Examination of Ethnography

Stephen Tyler, noted linguistic anthropologist, explains that ethnography is a "meditative vehicle" in which the anthropologist/writer reflects on what she has heard and seen as she proceeds on her "journey" through other people's stories.[14]

The writing of this ethnography encompasses a myriad of perspectives. Traditionally, it is our gaze that locates and documents the musings of culture. The myth of the participant observer forms the resulting text, yet I believe there is much more. In these times of postmodern ethnography, it is said that the work cannot be objective. Self-reflexivity is necessary. I propose that the influence of the ethnographic writers is much more pervasive. The identity of the ethnographer holds memories that upon initial observation may seem irrelevant. Yet the resultant study encompasses the identity of the writer holding memories that appeared long before her visit to the field site. It is the field site and ethnographic text that ultimately become containers for the writer's own reworked ideas and memories: old and new. The salient text emerges from the moment when these personal memories intersect with narratives emanating from others who lived in that space. It is an intertextual experience. The traces of history and memory that remain as the ethnographer proceeds through her work become words and phrases in the text. What evolves is a third type of voice, incorporating those who spoke and wrote about the place, as well as that of the ethnographer who gathers together the notion of the cemetery caught inside a world that erases and transforms almost everything it encounters.

This book has become more like a meditation. From the moment I first began writing about Fort Bend County and my memories of the place, the book continued to evolve into more and more of what seemed to be a dream. I began with stories of a cemetery belonging to Mexican workers (and their families) of the Imperial Sugar Company. As I approached the completion of the book I found disturbing narratives of slavery, violence, and a century-long backlash to Reconstruction. Even though I had a sense that something was missing, I pursued the original plan and pushed toward a complete monograph on the graveyard. Yet, I was not able to complete the manuscript until I decided to expand the base of study. There was more.

Poetics and Incompleteness

Aside from the specific story of the cemetery itself there are numerous aspects of this project that could each deserve its own unique treatment. These include the early history of Texas—including the effects of the civil war and the resulting Jim Crow years—which is central to Fort Bend County, since the first white settlers lived in the area; the assumed passivity of the ethnic Mexicans who came to the plantations in the twentieth century; the exaggerated affluence most recently located around the cemetery; and the "new" white-washed history of the county and its occasional implosions.

This particular history is not meant to encompass the details and in-depth analysis of these many significant historical events. It is a remembrance of what was seen by the author and others. It is also a musing on what it is and what could be. There have been other works on Texas cemeteries, including the recently released *Cemeteries: The Resting Places of Famous, Infamous, and Just Plain Interesting Texans* by Bill Harvey, a photographer and longtime employee of the Texas Parks and Wildlife Department. Harvey's work presents biographies of people buried in Texas cemeteries who "were significant figure[s] in Texas history or made a substantial contribution to its broadly defined culture."[15] Harvey describes cemeteries and their "interesting" inhabitants in addition to providing sixty black-and-white photographs. Twenty-one years earlier, the late Terry Jordan, a noted cultural geographer at the University of Texas, produced *Texas Graveyards: A Cultural Legacy*, a visually pleasing monograph on Texas cemeteries with 128 photographs.[16] While the brief written texts of these two books address culture and history, their perspective is broad, describing scores of cemeteries around the state. In addition, with limited exceptions, their visual and textual narratives do not provide a detailed sense of identity other than providing a paean to mainstream Texas history.

While not primarily about Texas cemeteries, a recent article published by Meredith G. Watkins provides an excellent model for studies focusing on the intersection between material culture and social history. Her essay, "The Cemetery and Cultural Memory: Montreal, 1860–1900," presents an in-depth cultural focus on the Mount Royal Cemeteries of Montreal.[17] She closely studies the intersection of various ethnic groups buried at Mount Royal during a forty-year time period. Watkins concludes that people disappear from the cemetery landscape if they are not "important," that "the common conception of the cemetery as a site of memory for all is false." I agree that people disappear, just as the slaves and prisoners disappeared in San Isidro Cemetery. Stretching the concept of "memory" further, I believe memories continue even if the material remains of a person or gravestone do not exist. What is left are disqualified memories that are said to lack detail, relevance, or logic amid the large, more materially substantiated memories that have been incorporated into narratives about "significant" figures in "history."[18]

Cemeteries of Ambivalent Desire is distinct from the work of Watkins and other scholars in its inter-disciplinary perspective. *Turning South* by Houston Baker[19] served as the structure for the present work. The author of this book is an academic who is "looking back." This book is an attempt to incorporate my own memories with the history I was told to read in school and the history I was told by people in my ethnic Mexican community.

A close look at the county's past produced so many complicated narratives that I had to leave a number of areas unexplored. These include accounts of the systematic extermination of the Native Americans I found in numerous texts regarding the Republic of Texas; the relationships between Mexican troops and county residents during the Texas Revolution (most of the Mexican Army camped either at Fort Bend or at what is now Kendleton on land owned by a Spanish-speaking quadroon named Elizabeth Powell); the systematic banishment of ethnic Mexicans from the county and other nearby areas after the Texas Revolution; lynching and other forms of violence against freedmen and the development of the local Ku Klux Klan; a more thorough investigation into what Kendleton residents call the "Turkey Creek Feud," which resulted from monthly raids in which white men from Fort Bend County went in groups to Kendleton for the purpose of raping black women; a detailed analysis of the documents available regarding the prison farms and their frequent reports of torture and murder; a broader understanding of the lives of ethnic Mexicans, especially the role of the thousands of migrant workers who traveled through the county from the 1930s to the 1960s. Most important of all is the legal case *Terry vs. Adams et al.* (1954), which reached the Supreme Court, along with *Brown vs. Board of Education*. Called the "last of the white primary cases," *Terry vs. Adams* finally ended the county's manipulation of the primary voting system, which was disenfranchising black voters. Each one of these subjects merits an entire project.

This book contains narratives about the people of Mexican descent who lived in Fort Bend County—their stories about life and work. In consideration of the type of world it was, it is necessary to delve into the days of Jim Crow in the area, and how people of different colors were affected by these racial rules. The life of the cemetery is translated into different mediums as I speak of the county, its communities, and its farms. It means many things. Finally, what has surrounded the cemetery is presented as a continued expression of the interrelationship between the present, the future, and the past. These three have an ambivalent relationship. At the level of concrete necessity, slaves and prisoners were desirable as a source of labor. Black women were desired for labor, sex, and at times affection. The ambivalence creates an awkward situation of holding/desiring yet pushing away—hiding, burying in graves that may eventually be washed away by Oyster Creek. The tight hold around the cemetery, with its tall fence, locked gates, and no sign, can be read as protection, or alternatively, as delimitation of detritus. The desire for history and barbarism to be contained in those five acres has kept San Isidro functioning like a secret space full of unexplained and undocumented events.

Borderlands between People and Disciplines

It may be easy to create a dichotomy between the affluent and the working class in the study of Fort Bend County or between Anglos/whites and blacks and ethnic Mexicans. The history of slavery and Jim Crow provides numerous opportunities for criticism. The hierarchies of living spaces (subdivisions) situate economic wealth in such a striking manner that all other forms and ways of living seem miniature in comparison. The reality is that there is a bit of affluence in every sector, even the areas (and there are still a few) that do not have full utilities (running water). Since most of Sugar Land is—or at least used to be—considered "new money," affluence is associated more with tangible wealth than with sophistication and high culture. Yet this is not a study to classify and contain. Instead it is meant to be a treatise on the linkages between what we see as different—from wealth to poverty, from life to death. They are all connected, most often in ways that are less visible and naturally less acknowledged in our present day of quantifiable necessities.

This text seeks to focus on the cemetery within cultural and historical spaces and how it has become the container for the unfocused past. It also examines the boundaries surrounding scholarship and scholar. What is the position of the author? Who has defined her authority? Is her position affected by her "nativity?" As the narratives are told and examined, I also wonder about the genre of the text. Is this ethnography? Is this memoir? Is this critique? Perhaps it is all three (and more). My intention in this trajectory is to use non-ordinary avenues to understand the importance of the cemetery and the county. This is particularly necessary because of the paucity of archival records concerning the laboring classes who lived on the plantations both before and after the Civil War. My concern that archives can be destroyed, manipulated, or misread leads me to search for other forms of discourse. This study is more about people's views on the world and each other, past and present. The impossibility of finding great amounts of information (especially in a place where so much history has been erased) that can be absolutely proven encourages me to indulge in the existence of the narratives—where they have been and where they are going.

Methodology

The research for this book began in 1996 and was completed in 2005. Living near Fort Bend County for most of this time, I met regularly with my interlocutors. Conversations with persons involved in the history of San Isidro Cemetery comprise a significant amount of the ethnographic work, in addition to the information provided by my father, as well as my own recollections and experiences.

Textual references from scholarly works and newspaper articles provided a foundation for the stories of everyday life my informants provided. The archives of the *Dallas Morning News* afforded a glimpse into the violence that permeated the prisons of the County. Last of all and perhaps most insightful was my visit to the archives of the Congregation of Saint Basil in Toronto, Canada. There I found numerous letters and reports written by Basilian priests

At San Isidro Cemetery, this metal sign is placed over what is now the parking lot. Before 1993 it marked the entrance from the bridge over Oyster Creek (1998).

who had lived in Fort Bend County in the 1930s and 1940s while establishing what they called the "Mexican missions." Four missions were set up in the county, including one in Sugar Land named for Saint Teresa. The Basilians' writings gave me a better understanding of the intense poverty experienced by ethnic Mexican sharecroppers. The priests' experiences as educated white men who were not from the South and did not have that "Southern mentality" illustrated for me how the different ethnic and racial groups viewed each other. Their combined emotions of caring, empathy, and revulsion toward ethnic Mexicans are revealing, as are their more paradoxical "Southernized" views toward African Americans. Their writings instructed me in the pervasive ambivalence between the different ethnic and racial groups in the county. While the Basilian documents are not often cited in this book, the images in their letters and journals deeply influenced my perspective while I wrote about Fort Bend County history.

The methodology of this type of scholarly writing, which incorporates a somewhat visceral response to each new piece of information, may appear somewhat excitable or innocent. It is actually a form a writing that incorporates a subtle irony. Barthes's idea that narrative "is simply there like life itself' is similar to the trajectory of this text, which encompasses stories that are life itself."[20] Regardless of our awareness of other contested sites (e.g., the slave cemetery in lower Manhattan; the entire Native American nation, which was eliminated by westward American expansion, or even the Southwestern United States after the Treaty of Guadalupe Hidalgo), people often believe that this type of "contestation" could never happen *here*. Texas is supposed to be the place of the Wild West, horses, and cowboys. When I mentioned the cemetery book to an academic at Cambridge University, he was surprised to hear of plantations in Texas. This book is about the surprise we encounter when things are not what we believed them to be.

Chapter one

Cementerios

What is encased in the tomb, grave, or monument stretches from the individual who has died to the descendants of those who buried her. Stories of their relationship parallel the larger story of the land that holds the cemetery itself. The dead do not exist in isolation. They remain not only in their graves but also in the imaginary of all those connected with that piece of land—from long ago to well into the future. This imaginary forms memories and expectations that guide those associated with the cemetery.

Cemeteries contain the desire and imaginary of the past. Under six feet of earth, each buried body is made invisible to the living. Some bodies are secretly preserved in modern-day chemicals. Others have been reduced to the pieces of soil that firm up their graves. Those walking above them cannot see. Bodies inside their caskets appear merely to be sleeping. Things stay the same in the metal caskets, with expensive, airtight vaults creating an artificial boundary between the deceased and the continuously transforming outside world. The artificial boundary surrounding the unchanging body of the deceased holds tenaciously to the technologically constructed reality that projects permanence and strength. The semantics of power continue to affect those who are alive; they do not change the dead. Those uncorrupted bodies remain as sleeping people who, if they came above ground, would appear pale and still, with enough semblance of life that they could confuse whoever saw them. Such is the power of death and burial. What is buried reaches back over and over to relay the rules of before. The dead have stayed artificially bounded to the space, deceiving the living into thinking that what they said as living people is still valid and proper.

We fool ourselves about those whose bodies and tombstones have disappeared. Crediting only what exists in the material world, proves us scientifically correct. In our twenty-first-century minds, power lies in what can be proven, touched, seen.[1] Even then, the proof can come only from those authorized to validate such information. Genealogy has been the criterion for authority in the case of the cemetery and its surroundings.[2] The stories that lack authorization are not written with the ease of those enclosed in legacy. They become like a secret lover, simultaneously cherished and despised, intensely desired yet not worthy of a public presence. Their silence indicates a false disappearance that belies an intensity that only magnifies over time.

This book is about those invisible narratives and their relation to an old *Mexican cemetery*. It is a textual exploration into the life of a place and its relationship to an event of national importance. The invisible stories inflect and flavor the continuously evolving history. The cemetery I write about is located on land once owned by Stephen F. Austin. In 1823 it was part of the first "official" colony of Anglo settlers in what was then the Mexican state of Coahuila y Tejas. Two centuries later this same piece of land lies within one of the wealthiest and most conservative areas of Texas and the United States. Former Congressman Tom DeLay, once known as "the Hammer" on Capitol Hill, heartily represented the area for twenty-two years. It is the home of corporate power. Houston executives favor the area for its whitened environment and gang-free suburban schools. The chief financial officer of Enron Corporation committed suicide in his Mercedes on his tree-lined street not far from the cemetery.[3]

This is a text about the relationship between the particular and the collective; geography links the two. There is a seemingly improbable relation between a child's narrative about a forty-year-old memory and newspaper reports on the highest-profile suicide of 2002. Yet, the fabric of the intertwining narratives connects one story to another. The physical distance between the cemetery and the Enron executive's home is not more than two miles. This work is about the space and time in between these two points. What remains between is not constant. The chronological and socioeconomic distances contract and expand sporadically, disallowing the standard categorization of space and time. The past and the future are affected by an imaginary history that conjured a "place of origin" that persistently seeks to cleanse and strengthen the fabric of its constitution.

Re-Membering: The Poetry of the Past

The project began with the story of an old Mexican cemetery that has been in continuous use since the mid-nineteenth century.[4] San Isidro Cemetery is located on the original land grant of Stephen F. Austin, which later became part of the Imperial Sugar Plantation; it is now surrounded by an affluent, master-planned suburban community in a city named Sugar Land. The cemetery, named San Isidro, is located on two and a half acres of land, fifteen miles southwest of downtown Houston. Before the city grew around it, San Isidro was located in fields owned by the Imperial Sugar Company in an area one mile from town. The five-hundred-year-old pecan trees continue to bear fruit every fall.[5] In 1950 the cemetery was so beautiful it could have been a visual poem. The area was well shaded, green, and lush, often overgrown with carrizo (reed grass). Oyster Creek ran between the cemetery and the company's Mexican encampment, Gran Centro. The creek brushed the edge of the cemetery. The water has always been high, even in times of drought.

It is said that the cemetery was originally intended for Mexican laborers working for Imperial Sugar in the early part of the twentieth century. Their descendants are still being buried there. The San Isidro Cemetery Association coordinates the burials and visits and tends the existing graves. *Separated from San Isidro by a chain-link fence is an overgrown area known as the black cemetery. No one has been buried there for more than fifty years.*[6]

Oyster Creek: *Tierra Ajena*—Land Belonging to Another

> *San Isidro . . . protector de la holgazanería;*
> *San Isidro Labrador: quítame el agua y ponme el sol.*
> *San Isidro: por la mancero que nunca tu mano tocara;*
> *San Isidro: quítame el sol, a cuya luz se espulgó la*
> *Canalla; quítame el sol y ponme el agua.*
> *Si por los cabellos arrastras la vida,*
> *como arrastra el hampón la querida.*
> *Ella trabajará para ti*
> *San Isidro . . . deja que los ángeles*
> *Vengan a labrar . . .*
>
> *Alfonso Reyes, "El Descastado" 1918*

San Isidro, Protector from Laziness
San Isidro Labrador: protect me from the water and give me the sun
San Isidro: for the plow that your hand never touches
San Isidro: take away the sun in whose light the decadent were removed
Take away the sun and give me water
If you drag life by her hair, as the brute drags his woman
She will labor for you.
San Isidro: allow the angels to come
Work the land . . .

This statue of San Isidro Labrador, brought from Santiago, Nuevo León, Mexico, in 1999, stands in a gazebo at the center of San Isidro Cemetery (2004).

El labrador working on the Sugar Land plantation was not in bondage per se.[7] His body did not have a certificate of ownership belonging to someone else. If he ran away, a slave bounty hunter would not drag him home. If forms of labor can be described in generations, el labrador in Sugar Land came three generations after slavery. Once the slaves were emancipated, the planters attempted to hire them to work the land. From 1888 to 1914 the Sugar Land plantation used prison labor. When this was banned for humanitarian reasons, the plantation began looking to Mexican laborers who were migrating to Texas en masse because of the Mexican Revolution.

The name San Isidro comes from the Spanish saint, San Isidro Labrador.

He lived in twelfth-century Spain and is the patron of agricultural workers. Although no one could specifically remember who named the cemetery, the connection to San Isidro Labrador is always acknowledged. Those who decided on the name must have been thinking about the land and the fact that it belonged to "someone else." In the eerie world of Sugar Land's history, the idea of ownership, whether of human beings or the land, remains alongside every thought and action. While San Isidro protects the laborer from nature's violence, his presence is a validation of the Spanish term *ajeno*. If the title to the land had belonged to the men who worked it, their patron might have been Saint Joseph, Saint John, or Saint Francis. Isidro is there because, in the hierarchy of the plantation, el labrador unfortunately had minimal status. As Isidro demonstrates in words penned in 1598 by the Spanish writer Lope de Vega, "Hermano, Él me ha de enseñar que una hormiga de la casa de Dios tiene gran valor, yo soy pobre labrador" (Brother, He will indicate to me that an ant from the house of God has much value, I am a poor farm laborer).[8] If the owner and overseer do not recognize the value of *el labrador*, it is God who acknowledges the laborer's merit.

Isidro gives dignity to the labor. The hagiography of San Isidro presents a holy man who is continuously poor. He is known for his labor on land that is not his. The magic of his faith sustains his hope. Similar to sharecropping in the southern United States, in medieval Spain the lord of the manor allotted a small parcel of land to his *criados* (workers) for their own planting. There is a folktale that San Isidro's parcel was so productive that his *amo* (overseer) became envious. Isidro responded by telling the amo to take all of the grain because the husks would be enough for him. To everyone's surprise, the traces of grain left in the husks multiplied, leaving Isidro more than enough for his family.[9]

San Isidro protects the farm laborer, who is at once vulnerable and privileged. His vulnerability is directly related to his relationship with the amo, the plantation overseer. The privilege of those in Sugar Land was the stability provided by the company. Workers always had a house to live in and enough food for the family: the company provided for the bare necessities. Work was steady as long as the men were productive. Yet, the vulnerability was constant. The world surrounding the plantation was depriving and dangerous. Mexican families living on other large farms in Southeast Texas seldom had adequate housing or enough food. The laborer in Sugar Land was vulnerable to his own productivity. Reyes's poem points to the vulnerability: the laborer has to produce, and needs protection from the risk of laziness. The sugar company easily sent away workers who were not highly productive. His work was fruitful

"A man who works with his hands . . ." Relief paying homage to the laborers buried in San Isidro Cemetery. San Isidro Labrador is the patron saint of laborers (2004).

if there were enough sun and water, yet not too much of either. The workers acknowledged that their life was brutal. If they were forced by the amo or by circumstances, they worked for the company. Reyes' verse, telling of the force of labor, explains: "If you drag life by her hair, as the brute drags his woman, she will labor for you." It was the company and the world of the South that dragged the laborer by the hair. El labrador had no choice but to work. Ultimately, the wish for magic remained, and there was always hope that an angel would come and tend the plow.

In the representation of Isidro, the cemetery is the place of protection for the Mexican laborer. His worth is significant in God's realms. Thus, over the decades, Isidro's cemetery has become the embodiment of celestial materiality. It is the space of the sublime, where the graves hold the history of the land. The tight boundaries that follow the edge of the cemetery are filters of desire. The sumptuous lawn and towering pecan trees whose branches reach across like a mother's arms are enclosed in this space of the *réel*.[10] The shade covers what it needs. There are many heroes in the stories and the texts that tell about the land. Isidro's cemetery contains the stories that are not quite there, not quite real, and possibly imaginary. They are about what the truth cannot tell.

Image and Imagination

I often lie here until late in the evening, feeling time roll back
(Sebald 2001, 119).

Imagination is a central aspect of memory. Anything remembered is subject to the priorities inside a person's mind, especially when the person remembering is a small child. Memories may be variegated by other bits of information that come in response to the event we are remembering. These may be a word, a sigh, or an expression on the face of a companion. These added experiences, in their minute way, become embedded with what we remember. Although this could be construed as a lack of clarity or accuracy, I believe it is actually an integration of the different stimuli associated with a certain event. Information provided before or later, in a different time and space, embeds itself into the memory, re-forming it and creating its own subjectivity.

Privilege is a central aspect of this narrative. The non-privileged people buried in San Isidro served those with privilege. The county is known for being the site of Texas' first Anglo settlement. In a varied form of privilege, I came to see the workings of the county in the mid-twentieth century. My father traveled from South Texas to the farm town of Rosenberg, in west Fort Bend County. In 1950 he began managing a funeral home, later purchasing the business. I was his only child (for eight years, until 1961, when my brother was born).

My father came from a town that did not know Jim Crow to one that people called "the hellhole of the Brazos." His own grandfather was powerful politically and taught him how to communicate and negotiate with men of power. My father—with his own demons of poverty after the onset of the Great Depression—placed his greatest value on my person. My nice clothing seemed out of place among the sharecropper's children in the town. I was placed in first grade at the age of four. I did not speak Spanish, while most of the Latino children (and their parents) did not speak English. In the surreal position of observer, I traveled about the county with my father. I stood alongside him while he spoke to judges, attorneys, and sheriffs. I attended political rallies. I was present a rally where John Kennedy spoke when he was running for president. My father received a signed letter from Kennedy after the election was won, along with an invitation to the inaugural.

The awkward place of privilege in a Jim Crow town created many instances where the positioning of my identity was totally dependent on my father's presence. Emotionally distanced from many realities, I was told so many stories, but they seemed to have no endings or conclusions. People were poor, they were sick, and they died and left behind families. Truckloads of migrant workers made their way to Rosenberg in the 1960s during the cotton season. These were narratives about adults experiencing tragedy. It was confusing. I struggled to keep from thinking that there was something wrong with Mexican people (like myself?) that kept them in such poverty. The darkness of my own skin also caused me concern. I already knew that whiteness was elemental to the problem. Only later did I begin to understand that a cultural obsession with whiteness had intertwined with the whole idea of labor—work—farm labor. The farmworkers, considered another stream of "dark people" in a county where at one time there were two slaves to every free white person, were considered a painful phase in the history of the area, whose whole existence and success had for so long depended on free or cheap labor. The funeral home saved my father and me from picking cotton. Yet, I often felt confused about why I was not allowed to go to the cotton fields (would I get too dark?). Why did my father not let me sit in the balcony at the movie theater (would people think I was black?)? Why did my mother refuse to live on the "other side of the tracks" (would we be seen as lower class?)? In the company of my father I was "passing," so to speak. Camouflaged by his presence and dressed in presumptuous clothing, I traveled into the zone of safety. In a place where the requirements for "passing" were so significant, I often reflect on the existence of this boundary. It became important to understand the division between safety and danger.

After 1956 our family lived in an apartment on the second floor over my father's funeral home. The presence of the dead was a central aspect of my life. I heard the crying at the wakes, attended funeral masses, and accompanied my father to different cemeteries. Our trips to San Isidro were unique. In an area where the landscape is flat and uneventful, crossing the boundary into the cemetery produced the sensation of an entirely different space. We crossed an old wooden bridge over a creek into a canopy of gigantic pecan trees. Questions that remained in my mind found imaginary answers on the gravestones. The dates 1950, 1940, 1945, and 1925 provided a text from where I could begin my imaginary musings on what lay behind people's desperation about the boundary of race and danger. Thus I began to imagine that the laborers buried in San Isidro knew the answers because they had lived long before I was born and knew many things that I did not know. They knew how to "make do" in a world where they were almost strangled by Jim Crow; surviving by making "something else out of" the rules, "subverting them from within."[11] They understood well the problems and advantages of passing into forbidden spaces and forbidden identities. In many ways they were trapped in their own living and work spaces and in the identities designated for them (that of passive but hard workers). Yet they knew that their white bosses and supervisors for other reasons could traverse legal, geographic, and racial/ethnic boundaries, often without consequence. This book is an attempt to understand the nature and consequence of these different types of passings.

Oyster Creek 1958

There was a rusted black water pump at the center of the cemetery, the kind used in movies about the Old West. I first remember the pump from when I was six or seven years old, although I believe I was taken there as soon as I could walk. When I went to the cemetery with my father, I would immediately go to the pump. Wanting water to come from the spout, I would crank for what seemed a long time but would get only a few drops of water. The old pump was important to me because in those days I was constantly watching movies with Roy Rogers, John Wayne, and Gary Cooper. The *old* seemed much more important than the *new*.

The drive from our home in Rosenberg to the cemetery was usually uneventful. We drove north on U.S. 59, past the prison farms, and turned right on State Highway 6. It was all coastal prairie—flatland. From Highway 6 we turned left on a dirt road past the village of Gran Centro. We drove by the barracks where the laborers lived with their families, and past the farm equipment. By the time I remember going to the cemetery, they were no longer using mules and plows (although they did into the 1950s). We took another left turn after Gran Centro, and this road led us to the wooden bridge. Probably constructed in the nineteenth century, it was so old that the wood had turned black. It hovered low over the creek, with two-foot railings on each side. The bridge and the creek were so close together it seemed the water almost brushed the wood as it flowed down toward Galveston. Only one car could cross at a time. No one seemed to know when the bridge was built. My father says that people used to fish from the bridge. Sometimes in cold weather they would build fires on the bridge itself, and indeed there were markings of old fires here and there. No one knew how important the bridge would become forty years later, when the continued existence of the cemetery depended on the integrity of the structure and the motivation of its owners to repair or replace it.

Once we crossed the creek there was a narrow path, just wide enough for one car, which ran between gigantic pecan trees. We soon reached a chain-link fence with an arched metal sign that had once been painted white. It said "Cementerio San Isidro." We drove in and parked our car on the right side of the burial ground. Although far from accurate, my impression of the space was that it was in fact an island on Oyster Creek. I was so sure of this that, when I began writing about the cemetery forty years later, before I actually returned to see the place, I described it as being surrounded by water. The idea of this type of enclosure came from the limits of its accessibility.[12] We could enter only by crossing the creek. For more than a century there were only fields on the far side of the cemetery, yet there was no road that could take us there—only the wooden bridge, full of marks from old fires, that let in one car at a time.

It felt like an island. Once my father drove past the gate, the landscape actually created a different sensation. During summer days when the temperature in Fort Bend County was one hundred degrees, inside the cemetery it was ten degrees cooler. The change in temperature intensified the surreal nature of the space.

As I waited for my father to finish his business, I would wander through the place. I would always go to the black water pump first. Then slowly I would walk by each grave, especially those of infants and children. I read their names carefully and studied when they lived and died. I tried to imagine who they were. I connected these small monuments with the small caskets that had lain in state in the chapel of my father's funeral home. They were always white. The babies were pale, with pink cheeks, eyes tightly shut, and looking unhappy, as if they had fallen asleep while dissatisfied with their mothers. The babies in the caskets haunted me for a long time.

I often asked myself: Who were these children? Who were the adults? Why did they die? What was the context of their presence at the cemetery? What remained in their bodies? Were their spirits still there, overlooking their graves? Were they aware of my presence? The answers were simple. What else could I

Virgin Mary next to a gravestone in San Isidro Cemetery (2004).

believe but that the people continued to exist in some form, living out their lives as spirits inside the boundaries of the cemetery?

Construction and Destruction: 1970

"Suddenly the land was attacked by hordes of earth moving equipment. Levees sprang up around the property, the lands were leveled and drained by an elaborate network of drainage ditches; pumping stations were installed. Many miles of wide streets were created and attractively landscaped as they were finished" (Armstrong 1991, 168).

The land surrounding San Isidro was sold to Jake Kamin and the Nassau Bay developers' group for the construction of the Sugar Creek subdivision. Robert Armstrong, a long-time manager of Sugar Land Industries, writes of the company's owners: "The Kempners felt confident that this group [Kamin's] could be depended upon to build a high quality residential suburb which would set the tone for the future development of the remaining 7,500 acres of Sugar land Industries' farm lands in the neighborhood."[13]

Large homes began to appear outside the fence bordering San Isidro. Previous to this time, few places in Fort Bend County could provide this type of living environment. All of the houses were two stories high, large, and most were at least 3,000 square feet in size. I would stand inside the cemetery fence and carefully observe the construction. The houses seemed so big; they had so many bedrooms. I imagined the opulence of living in this type of environment. It was so distant from the homes of the people who were buried at San Isidro.

The farmland surrounding the cemetery was transformed into a huge construction site. A number of small villages nearby had been populated for decades by company employees who worked the fields; The villages were all destroyed. As Armstrong describes it, "the land was attacked." Fields were torn up, trees were uprooted, and the trucks came in as if they belonged to an army. In one big move, a whole world disappeared. In his text Armstrong makes no mention of the laborers' homes or villages. Yet, I was later told that the people who lived there experienced the entrance of the construction equipment as a great, obliterating moment. Houses that had stood for decades, with the same families living in them, totally disappeared.

The Bridge: 1989

"The possibility of a collectively animated worldly memory is articulated here in that extraordinary moment in which you—who never was there in that real place—can bump into a rememory that belongs to somebody else" (Gordon 1997, 166).

Years after I left the county, I met my father and my son at the cemetery. It was a summer day. My son had spent a few days with my father. There was a funeral at San Isidro. By that time I was living in downtown Houston. Sugar

Land was a halfway point to pick up my son. We planned to meet at the cemetery.

Coming from the north, I drove down the freeway that had been completed in the early 1970s. I took the exit into Sugar Land and drove up a new street called Lexington. The new houses and young oak trees led me to Oyster Creek. At the edge of the new subdivision (named Settler's Way) I encountered the old bridge. There were a hundred or so people parking their cars on the southern bank of the creek, near the new tennis court next to the bridge. The hearse came as close as possible to the creek. People were walking across the bridge. The funeral procession moved toward the gate of the cemetery. The bridge could no longer hold the weight of so many cars.

A few years later a *Houston Chronicle* reporter, sensing a story that would catch people's eye, wrote about the cemetery. When she asked cemetery association member Rudy Cruz about the bridge, he told her: "I had to carry my uncle across [the bridge] after we couldn't drive it anymore. . . . It was raining. We had to go through all this mud and his son is walking beside me saying, 'Don't drop my daddy, Rudy, don't drop my daddy.'"[14]

There was something stunning about watching the people walk across the bridge. I stood for a moment, watching. The event felt so immediate—the casket being carried across the bridge over the water of Oyster Creek. It felt like something out of time and space. Here in suburbia, amid the SUVs and the generous six-figure incomes, was a group of people walking in a funeral procession across a bridge to a cemetery—a defiance of suburban reality.

It was a space of neither here nor there. I watched but did not belong. It was not my story. Yet I felt the impact of something beyond my experience. In the words of Avery Gordon, I fell into the space of someone else's "rememory."[15] There had been countless funeral processions before the 1950s in which the families carried their dead to the cemetery. The village across the creek, no longer in existence, had been home to numerous families. It was a center of movement for the entire plantation, with railroad tracks that allowed trains to nestle close to the loading docks that carried away vegetables and cotton. No wonder the village was named Gran Centro—the great center.

It was as if the families from disappeared Gran Centro were again walking their dead across the creek. The funeral I was observing was actually retracing the steps from Gran Centro to San Isidro. It was uncanny. In this moment I was thinking of something I had never seen, yet I was certain that it was a real experience. Gordon continues: "You think, 'I must be thinking it up, making it up.' Yet in this moment of enchantment when you are remembering something in the world, or something in the world is remembering you, you are not alone or hallucinating or making something out of nothing but your own unconscious thoughts. You have bumped into somebody else's memory; you have encountered haunting and the picture of it the ghost imprints."[16]

Return: 1996

"A man becomes haunted by a woman who is barely there. He is searching for her, for knowledge, for himself. She is haunted by something else it takes him a long time to figure out. The search is everything to him. What does he find when he goes looking for the woman who has become an apparition? The knot of the ghostly and the real" (Gordon 1997, 70).

It was a Saturday morning in September 1996. It had been at least seven years since I last visited San Isidro. I had recently entered a doctoral program in cultural anthropology at Rice University. In a class on ethnography we were asked to write a proposal for an innovative project. Creativity was most important. After floundering with some abstract projects, I remembered the cemetery and an old dance hall a few miles away. Using my own memories of these spaces, I began writing about going back into history and making sense of people's stories using the lens of the present. The dance hall had long been demolished; in its place now stood an auto body shop. The cemetery, however, still existed; in fact, it was more vibrant than ever. A new cemetery organization president, Vietnam veteran John de la Cruz, had reorganized the association. He spent almost every day at the cemetery. Organization members became more involved. As a result, when I relocated San Isidro that Saturday morning in 1996 I found it had evolved into such an entrancing place that it bordered on the sublime.

Entering First Colony subdivision again, I was fairly sure the landmarks had remained the same. My father had told me some years before that the bridge was gone. Distinctly remembering my regular trips through Sugar Land, I drove through the subdivision, certain I would find San Isidro. I found myself at a dead-end road next to the tennis court facing Oyster Creek. As I had remembered, the cemetery was across the water.

Disconcertingly, I saw no sign, no evidence of a cemetery. I stepped out of the car and walked toward the creek. Sitting in the grass was a blonde mother with a toddler. Nearby was an Asian woman in her sixties practicing tai chi. I looked across the water and saw more trees and large homes with decks. I questioned my memory. Had I gone the wrong way, made the wrong turn? Was it a different exit off the freeway?

I then drove to a nearby fire station and asked about the cemetery. The EMT told me there was no cemetery in the neighborhood. He had lived there for ten years but had never seen one. How could he attend to people in the neighborhood who were in crisis but not know this? Did it still exist? Eventually I called my father, who insisted that the street leading to the cemetery was called Snearles and that I was right around the corner. Later, when I was driving down Searles (without the *n*), I thought about the EMT and not knowing where this space was. To me it seemed to have evaporated. To the EMT, it had never existed. Yet the street without the *n* in the name did lead me to the cemetery. It was in the middle of the subdivision, with a large fence on one side and Oyster Creek on the other.

At the gate of the cemetery is a wrought-iron door locked with a combination lock. A Mexican American man, Mr. Belasco, about seventy years old, is sitting in his van, waiting for someone to come by and open the gate. I call my father again, who says the combination is 2323, 3434, or 4545. None of these numbers work. A few minutes later an older man and his son arrive. This is Mr. Zamora. He is 86 years old. He looks through his wallet for about 15 minutes and finds a scrap of paper with the number. He works on the lock for another five minutes and is able to let us in. The numbers are 2323, but the lock needs to have the dial almost into the next digits to open. Mr. Zamora raises his hand into the air, holding the lock. I think to myself: The cemetery is not clearly visible to local people, the combination is known to only a few, and very few of them know that the lock has a trick to it.

The fence surrounding the cemetery is expensive. It is wooden and about eight feet tall, and every fifteen feet there is a square brick column. When I first saw it I thought it was the backyard fence of one of the big houses. The entrance we use is new and actually brings us to the back of the cemetery.

The wrought-iron gate serves as an entrance point to a space in my memory and that of Mr. Zamora and his son. The place feels enclosed: by the fence, by the creek on the other side, by the very large pecan trees that drape the sky over the cemetery. It feels protected, separated, and hidden, reminiscent of the enclosed space of a home. In my mind, San Isidro creates the image of a body: warm, covered, and protective. It is covered with memories, spirits, and dreams, realized and unrealized. It is interwoven with my

Statue of the Virgin of Guadalupe next to a gravestone in San Isidro Cemetery (2004).

childhood memories and my imagination and connected to the times I accompanied my father on his frequent trips to the cemetery. The inner spaces of these enclosed areas are secrets, told only to those initiated: Mr. Zamora, the undertaker, and those who have been intimately connected to the space for a long time.

Once inside this protective space, I feel as if I have entered a memory. The textures are sensuous and multilayered. The trees are gigantic, and their green pecans are all over the grounds. There are ancient gravestones and modern ones, graves covered with artificial flowers, ribbons, and toys. The land is bumpy, perhaps suggesting graves that are no longer marked. The rows are somewhat uneven. The remaining gravestones have their own individuality. There is a twenty-foot statue of Christ near the original entrance, which is crowned by a string of letters reading "Cementerio San Isidro." Also near the statue is the *descanso*—the canopy. The original dates to 1950. Under this canopy, even in 2004, every casket is laid to rest briefly before it is taken to the open grave. Throughout the cemetery are small shrubs, frequently surrounded by natural or artificial flowers.

Bachelard's description of how childhood remains alive in the realm of daydreams is reminiscent of the sensations and memories surrounding San Isidro and its enclosed, half-hidden space. My experience upon entering the cemetery reminded me of *The Secret Garden,* a novel by Frances Hodgson Burnett.[17] In it, a young boy and girl find a hidden garden that was locked away after the death of the boy's mother. His father had ordered it closed and now does not allow anyone to enter. Through their adventures the children find the gate and the key. Even in its wild state, the garden is beautiful beyond imagination. In secret, they begin to visit the garden daily, planting new flowers and pruning back the overgrown shrubs. Eventually it is restored to its original state, yet for a long while their efforts remain a secret to the boy's father. Similarly, the tall fence that made San Isidro look like the large backyard of a Sugar Land estate made the cemetery invisible to many. The Sugar Creek Homeowners Association does not allow San Isidro to have a sign at its gate. The place has become a secret, in a sense. In *The Secret Garden,* the grieving widower locks the garden away because he does not want to remember, leaving me to wonder what Sugar Land would want to forget.

When I returned to San Isidro in 1996, I was struck by the concealed quality of the space. It was hidden, inaccessible, locked away so that certain memories could be forgotten. After it was restored, it remained a secret. The memories it would evoke were unthinkable to the rest of Sugar Land.

The Fire: 1939

Ike Kempner, the owner of Imperial Sugar, sent word to Cosme Galván that he would visit the cemetery the following morning. Galván was in charge of San Isidro and was concerned that the grass was too high. The owner would think Galván had not been taking care of the cemetery and would want to take the land away. The night before the *patrón* (boss) was to arrive, Galván decided to burn the grass. He forgot that the markers of the graves were all wooden crosses, including the one marking the grave of his own son, Isaac, who had died that year.

Wanting to know about the history of the cemetery and details of the burials, I asked John de la Cruz if there were any people who might remember San Isidro before the 1950s. He suggested I speak to Guadalupe Galván, the widow of Cosme Galván. It was she who told me about the fire. People had told me it happened in 1920. Guadalupe was not sure of the year, except that it occurred around the same time her child, Isaac, had died. The flames had destroyed the wooden cross that marked his grave. She remembered, however, that Isaac was buried near the south boundary of the cemetery. She said the fire had been an accident.

There is no story of how Kempner reacted, although it is known that throughout most of the 1950s the cemetery was overgrown with grass and weeds. Oftentimes funeral processions were led by a man with a machete who cut the tall grass and created a path for the mourners. Starting a controlled fire would have been a logical response in 1939. Since there are no documents mapping the gravesites, the fire placed those buried in San Isidro further into obscurity.

Guadalupe Galván was in her nineties when I visited her in 1998. She was one of the oldest surviving members of the San Isidro community. Her home was on Guadalupe Street in Stafford. The small frame house had a statue of the Virgin of Guadalupe in the front yard. Mrs. Galván was inside sitting in a wheelchair. Her daughter was also present.

Of the numerous people I asked about the fire, no one could remember a specific year. Somewhere between 1920 and 1930, they said. The only one who could make a connection was Mrs. Galván; after all, it was when her son had died so soon after being born. The death records at the Fort Bend County courthouse gave the final date, yet her connection was what led me there. Remembering is often about birth and death. It took Isaac's death to set the time in place—January 1939.

In the process of searching for Isaac's death record, I wondered how necessary it is to "set time in place." If we want to follow a strict chronology, the archives are most relevant—that is, if they are accurate. Yet, it is also worth studying the varying years that were given for the fire. No one else could connect it to something concrete; it was in the past; a difference of ten years or more was not a problem. Perhaps it would be for some historians, yet for the people of San Isidro it is part of its multifarious past. Academics have a need to set concretely the moment something "happened." Yet, it is important to remember that we are serving only our own needs. No one from the San Isidro group was asking to find the specific year of the fire. It was I, as ethnographer, who was looking for a secure date. Mrs. Galván's recollection of her son's death tells us that the loss of a child from pneumonia at two months of age is far more significant than all of the wooden crosses standing in an old cemetery.

The Mediation between Life and Death

"In . . . [a] story from Lac Court Oreille . . . Kukukuu, the Great Owl, says, 'I shall come and sit by the burial place of the dead to see that their resting place is not disturbed'" (Pomedli 2002, 54).

On several occasions I have been at the cemetery in the evening with Kathy Medina Reyes and/or John de la Cruz. Kathy and John have been president of the cemetery association at different times.

It is almost sunset and the owls begin hooting. The towering pecan trees hide them as they call out to us. I ask if it is common to find owls in the area. Neither Kathy nor John have seen or heard them anywhere else near Sugar Land. Kathy says they are telling us to go home. The voice of the owls, in Kathy's view, is a reminder that San Isidro is, after all, a space of the dead. The living are allowed inside to keep the cemetery in order to be close to loved ones who are buried there. Yet at dark, the owls gently tell us its time for us to go to our own homes, and the dead remain alone in theirs.

Several conversations later, John explains that the owls guard the cemetery. The cemetery needs protection from the living. In his essay on Native American folklore, Pomedli describes owls: ". . . as protectors of the dead, but even more than that they are the very ancestors who have passed to the spirit world." In an oddly haunting passage Pomedli writes of the "paralyzing and haunting effects of an owl's gaze. An owl presents a double mirror with life on one side and death on the other. This is akin to the Mide mediation between life and death, with its healing lodge erected near water, thereby presenting ways not only to ensure life, but also a death or ghost lodge."[18]

The owls that inhabit the cemetery are illusive. On the evenings that we heard their calls we looked up to the trees but could never see them. They sit on the branches near the creek, an embodiment of the ancestors and their ghostly stories. They are themselves the boundary between the dead and the living.

A Social Figure

The ghost is not simply a dead or a missing person, but a social figure, and investigating it can lead to that dense site where history and subjectivity make social life (Gordon 1997, 8).

Kathy Reyes tells me of ghosts. Her sister has seen their late brother sitting in a chair at their home. In early May 2001 I awoke at 2 A.M. and found my daughter watching the History Channel on cable television. The program was titled *Haunted History.* The particular sequence she was watching described a photograph taken at a cemetery. Although the photographer had seen only a few gravestones when he took the picture, the printed image showed the translucent image of a woman in a robe kneeling over a headstone. The photographer researched the background of the grave and found that the deceased had died a hundred years to the day the photograph was taken. Cause of death was complications of childbirth.

The next morning I received a telephone call from Kathy Reyes. She was calling to give me her new phone number and tell me about the upcoming weekend cleanup at the cemetery. I told her that during the night I had seen the television image of a ghost at a cemetery, which had made me think of San Isidro. I had thought that, in the four years I had been conversing with the San Isidro group, no one had spoken of seeing ghosts at the cemetery. I told Kathy of my wonder regarding the presence of ghosts. I said, "Does it ever happen?" She responded, "Of course, it does." "Where?" I asked. "It happened at my mother's house. We recorded sounds of railroad trains. We photographed empty walls, and when the pictures were developed, one of them had a plantation house, like from the movie *Gone with the Wind.* There was a woman dressed in white with two children by her side." "How did that happen? Is the house an old one? Is it haunted?" Kathy responded, "My mother moved into the house when it was new. It was built over a private family cemetery." I asked her, "Where are the graves?" "They are still on the property," she told me.

The stories of ghosts in my conversations with Kathy Reyes are situated in what Avery Gordon terms the polemic between the "experience of reality" and what "we then decide to call knowledge."[19] The ghost of Kathy's brother sitting in a chair localizes the idea of ghostly reality. He is not a remnant of some distant past. He is as easily sitting in the chair at his mother's house as he is buried in the cemetery. Distinguishing fact from fantasy is not necessary in this conversation. The idea is not to prove that ghosts exist but to elucidate the existence of their narratives.

It is, however, the ghost standing in front of the plantation home that is the most telling. The plantation has left its imprint upon the cemetery and its environs. A way of life that revolved around slavery has remained in the background. The social figure of the slaveholding woman, standing in front of her plantation home, dressed in white, next to her two children belies a status and an identity. Her position provided the status of lady, "the highest condition [in plantation society] that a woman could aspire" to.[20] The domestic arrangement that relieved her of the usual duties expected of wives and mothers was alleviated by the presence of slaves, ultimately affecting the "relationships, roles, and identities" between and among the plantation woman and her servants.[21] Most significantly, the plantation lady, with her honor, virtue, and purity, coalesced with the idea of maintaining whiteness at all cost. As Pauline Yelderman describes the Reconstruction-era planter class in Fort Bend County, "The purity of a lady" was even more important than a man's honor.[22]

In November 1998 Lori Rodríguez of the *Houston Chronicle* described the black cemetery this way: "Next to it [San Isidro], [is] the now-fenced, overgrown and long-inactive African-American cemetery."[23] Beyond the rows of infant graves is a chain-link fence that guards an acre or so of overgrown brush. Underneath the trees and shrubs are graves and scattered tombstones. It is a section where African Americans are buried, and that is all that is known. It remains anonymous. Some speculate that slaves and prison laborers are buried there. Every few months the cemetery association goes beyond the fence and clears out another foot or so of brush. *I ask John de la Cruz about looking inside. He discourages me, saying there are rattlesnakes.*

Chapter two

The Manifested Destiny of History

Michel de Certeau explains that, before we can know what a "history says about a society," we have to study how "history functions within it." The "historiographical institution" (which in Texas could be the Texas State Historical Association or the Institute for Texan Cultures) permits "one kind of production and prohibits others"; it "makes history." The institution takes on the role of collector and/or censor with regard to contemporary analysis of socioeconomics and political history and practices. The collection of documents that provides the information on the history of Fort Bend County and of the state has been elevated to a higher status because they were transcribed, copied, photographed, or placed in vaults. They "modify a received order and a social vision," creating a narrative for Texas that assumes its manifested destiny.[1]

Making History

In 1897 the state of Texas, in an effort to organize and disseminate its history, established the Texas State Historical Association. The mission statement of the organization declares that its purpose "is to foster the appreciation, understanding, and teaching of the rich and unique history of Texas and by example and through programs and activities encourage and promote research, preservation, and publication of historical material affecting the state of Texas."[2] The association sponsors the publication of books, a respected journal, and educational outreach to Texas public schools. A second Texas historical institution, the Institute of Texan Cultures, was created in 1968 as part of San Antonio's HemisFair. The event, described as a "Confluence of Civilizations in the Americas" was a World's Fair that used ninety-eight acres of urban renewal space. Sixty historic buildings were torn down to make room for HemisFair.[3]

In this atmosphere of celebration and historical erasure, the museum gallery of the Institute of Texan Cultures first opened as the "Texas Pavilion." The institute was mandated by the state to "investigate" and present its "ethnic and cultural history." More than 220,000 people toured the institute's exhibits in 1999.[4]

Nineteenth-century Texas history is documented and circulated by these organizations. While academics may study the more detailed nuances of Texas narrative, these two institutions direct and form the nature of regional historiography. They are the patrons of many Texas storytellers.

The history of Texas reproduces myths that are formed by an originary transgression, or what de Certeau would call "a murder of an originary death." Traces of a "dead past" are faintly visible, yet undecipherable. There is something in the story of Texas "that is as impossible to recover as to forget."[5] The originary moment that is emphasized occurred when three hundred settlers came to Austin Colony. The year was 1823. The attempt at erasure contains a number of faint allusions to the savage nature (and people) that were eliminated or expelled in order for the colony to survive. More significantly, the colonists' denial of their own mark (or admittance) of savagery created an inconclusive rupture between the past and the imperial future of Texas.

The leagues of land once owned by Stephen F. Austin contain narratives that explain the social vision of Texas. San Isidro Cemetery, in particular, provides a junction that simultaneously holds what was once desired, yet ultimately censored. It exists as a dreamlike heterotopia that contains, among other things, what is ejected from the twenty-first-century everyday life of the county. Its existence alongside Oyster Creek makes it a witness to the chaotic birth of the governmental institution now known as the State of Texas.

The narrative of the cemetery has focused on an ongoing dispute between the cemetery association and the surrounding subdivision. A front-page *Houston Chronicle* newspaper article noted that the cemetery represents "Hispanic heritage."[6] As a cemetery originally established for farm laborers, the facility of assigning it a heritage less valued in the overall history of the state obfuscates its importance to the larger narrative. The parallel between the diminishing importance given to the slaves and laborers who built the grand plantations and the diminishing importance of the cemetery itself gives way to the overblown, heroic story of the grand republic.

The insistence of this history is embedded in almost every person living in Texas. As students are entering adolescence their imaginaries are instructed in an entire school year of Texas history, as required by state law. Classes memorize the story of Austin's Colony, the first "authorized" white settlement in what was then Mexico's Coahuila y Tejas. They already know about the Alamo; a 2003 re-make of the film had enough Spanish-speaking characters to seduce a considerable audience.[7] As the students are entering the most rebellious phase of their youth, they are taught good citizenship by learning of the early Texians (a term used for residents of the Texas colonies), mostly immigrants from the upper South (Tennessee, Kentucky, Virginia), who settled in what is now Texas as lawful immigrants to Mexico, yet later became insurgents who formed their own Republic of Texas. In the twenty-first century, textbooks are nominally respectful of the state's racial and ethnic diversity, yet for many scholars, whether they are conscious of the fact or not, the history of Texas—and more specifically, the battle of the Alamo—continues to represent a binary struggle between the righteous democracy of America's Manifest Destiny, and dark, archaic Mexico.[8] In 1898, Leroy Bugbee, a political science professor at the University of Texas, published his essay on Texas slavery. He credits the ". . . energetic pioneers from the United States and the development of the rich bottom lands of Texas [that] marked the beginning of a new era, not only in the history of Mexico, but in that of America . . ." Bugbee is specifically talking about the Colorado and Brazos River Bottoms.[9]

Mythohistory: The Seat of the Future Empire—Oyster Creek, August 1821

In Robert Caro's fascinating biography of President Lyndon Baines Johnson he writes of Texas history's beginnings when, in 1830, overlooking what is now Austin, Texas "the dashing President-elect of the three-year-old Republic of Texas, Mirabeau Buonaparte Lamar, hunting buffalo on the edge of the [Texas] Hill Country, looked out to the beautiful hills and exclaimed: "This should be the seat of future empire!"

The mythohistory begins on the banks of Oyster Creek, fifteen miles southwest of what is now Houston. Stephen F. Austin first saw Oyster Creek as he approached the Brazos River in 1821. He was traveling to San Antonio to proceed with negotiations regarding his first settlement of colonists into Coahuila y Tejas. He noted in his diary that the land reminded him of the Red River in northern Louisiana. The soil was dark and rich, especially in the Brazos river bottom.[10] Austin reserved five leagues for himself. Five nineteenth-century Spanish leagues were equal to 34.6 square miles or 22,140 acres.[11] Wharton notes a "legend" that Austin was planning to locate his homestead here, on property that was crossed by Oyster Creek on the north and bounded by the Brazos on the south. Austin ultimately located the headquarters of his colony in San Felipe, forty miles away. He passed his land on to other colonists, with the area around Oyster Creek going to his secretary, Samuel Williams.[12]

The mythohistorical origins of Texas are lodged in the larger context of national identity and nation building. As he was traveling through the American South, raising funds for the Republic of Texas, Austin told audiences that "The emancipation of Texas will extend the principle of self government over a rich and neighboring . . . country. . . . It . . . will open a door through which a bright and constant stream of light and intelligence will flow from this great northern fountain over the benighted region of Mexico."[13]

A recent biography of Stephen F. Austin by Gregg Cantrell attests to the connection between state and nation, by which the "Texas Revolution and the establishment of the Lone Star republic" were foundational in the United States' "drive for mastery over the North American continent."[14] Austin's speech in Louisville, Kentucky, was given while he and two other Texans were fund-raising throughout the East, seeking money to finance the Texas Revolution. The biographer describes the speech as a "classic expression . . . of . . . Manifest Destiny."[15] Austin's focus on liberty was nuanced with a Southern perspective. Cantrell cites in a block quotation a section of the speech that boldly emphasizes issues of Manifest Destiny, freedom of conscience, and rational liberty. Yet, the ongoing narrative reminds the reader of Austin's other agenda. Cantrell surmises that "Texas Independence was not just a fight for liberty, but it was necessary in order to protect the 'southwestern frontier— the weakest and most vulnerable in the nation'—from 'mistaken philanthropists, and wild fanatics' who 'might attempt a system of intervention in the domestic concerns of the South, which . . . might . . . at least jeopardize the tranquility of Louisiana and the neighboring States.'"[16]

The "southwestern frontier" of the United States was in fact the "northern frontier" of Mexico. The general westward movement of people was complicated by the crossing of international borders at the Sabine River between what is now Louisiana and Texas. The Mexican government initially encouraged immigration from the United States because the only significant population of Texas lived in San Antonio and the area of the Rio Grande. In 1819 a Missouri businessman named Moses Austin decided he could make a fortune by establishing a colony of settlers in what was to become Central and Southeast Texas. In 1820 he traveled to San Antonio and met with the provincial governor, Antonio Martínez. Although initially dismissed, Moses Austin approached the governor again, this time with the help of a self-invented baron named Philip Bögel. A previous *alcalde* of San Antonio, Bögel, also known as the Baron de Bastrop, was fluent in Spanish and had previously negotiated with Spain regarding colonization of a valley in Louisiana.[17] Bastrop's intervention was successful. Martínez had been working for some time to "develop the economy of the frontier province," believing the lack of settlers provided minimal defense against "American invasions or hostile Indians."[18] With Martínez's approval, Austin's application was forwarded to the provincial deputation in Monterrey, Nuevo León.

Moses Austin died in June 1821, shortly after returning home from San Antonio. His son Stephen continued the cumbersome and lengthy negotiations with the Spanish (and later Mexican) government. Stephen traveled to Mexico City and spent sixteen months working to promote his colonization bill through the evolving Mexican government. Mexico won its independence from Spain in 1821, two months after the death of Moses Austin. Even though small skirmishes had been erupting in Mexico for ten years, a weakened Spanish monarchy provided limited defense when the principal royalist general, Agustín de Iturbide, joined *los insurgentes* (the insurgents) and took over the capital.

In his lifetime, Moses Austin had established and lost several fortunes. Originally from New England, he had established a store in Philadelphia, another one in Richmond, Virginia, and a mine in southwestern Virginia. He eventually founded a mine in upper Louisiana, now the state of Missouri. With each new business he left behind the previous enterprise. The Panic of 1819 left Austin heavily in debt. It was at this point that he began to plan the idea of a colonization project in Texas.[19]

Stephen Austin was educated in a cultured and refined manner. Having been sent to school in New England, he also had an understanding for differences in culture. The younger Austin also attended Transylvania University, making him one of the more educated men in his colony. Yet, his background was varied. Moses Austin's mine in northern Louisiana was located in what was initially a French outpost frequented by traders, Native Americans, slaveholders, and their bondsmen. Stephen Austin traveled well among varied groups of people. Even so, he did not have a career when he assumed his father's venture. At the time, he was living with a prosperous family in New Orleans, supported by their generosity.

The grand plan of settling the Texas frontier came from a family that was acquainted with taking on new and risky ventures. Behind each movement, Austin is said to have been always considering the recuperation of the family's fortune. The reworked idea of Manifest Destiny, implanted beyond the boundaries of the United States, provided an opportunity not only to create fortunes, but to reinvent the personal history of those who pursued it.

At times Austin's trajectory is difficult to decipher. His passion for his colony was often overshadowed by his sense of cultured privilege, which was belied by his intense relationships with Mexican aristocrats and his disdain for his brutish Texas colonists.[20] With his refined bearing and education, Stephen Austin consorted with the leaders of Mexico. Between 1821 and 1833 he spent at least three years in Mexico City. He taught himself the cultured Spanish needed in communications with upper class Mexicans. Austin was the friend and confidant of presidents and cabinet members. He was more than an acquaintance to presidents Anastacio Bustamante and Valentín Gómez Farías, General Manuel de Mier y Terán, Lorenzo de Zavala, Cabinet Minister José Manuel de Herrera, and the brilliant and polemical Fray Servando Teresa de Mier, among others.[21]

Austin's alliance with Mier is noteworthy. In 1794 Mier, known as *la voz de plata* (the silver voice) for his outstanding oratorical ability, spoke openly against the cult of the Virgin of Guadalupe. After being banished to Europe, he traveled from country to country, presenting himself as a French priest, constantly being imprisoned and just as quickly escaping.[22] The Fray was a prolific author: among several books he published *La Historia de la Revolución de la Nueva España* in 1813. His experience in France made him an influential actor in Mexico's revolution against Spain.[23] In 1822 Mier was imprisoned by the Inquisition on charges of conspiracy against Emperor Agustín Iturbide. Austin's choice to visit Mier under these circumstances is curious since at the time, Austin was supporting Mier's opposition.

In the early eighteenth century, Mexico was (and continues to be) a nation supremely aware of its racial composition. Mier was born in the northern state of Nuevo León, which is known for its (assumed) "white" population.[24] The idea of racial mixing was so prominently on the minds of the elite of Mexico that a body of art known as *pintura de castas* (caste painting) was developed. "Casta painting represents the ordering of colonial society and in so doing partakes of the very construction of racial identity."[25] The paintings continued to be produced until the early nineteenth century. The new Mexican ruling class disapproved of the genre, however, because the paintings "highlighted Spanish rule and superiority."[26] In Mier's writings, he decried the paintings, claiming that "chimerical-colored distinctions" were detrimental to Mexico and that the Spanish "had purposefully spread the false notion in Europe that everyone in the colony was either black or mulatto."[27] Katzew infers from Mier's statements that the "*sistema de castas* promoted the false idea in Europe that everybody was a hybrid inferior."[28]

Austin's colonization of Texas with white Americans somewhat diminished the pressure facing the new Mexico regarding its darkened color. Mexico's needs joined with those of Austin. At the boundary with the United States, the population of Mexico would not be a hybrid inferior. Simultaneously, the new colony would serve the American South, while maintaining slavery and continuing the fundamental social division between whites and African Americans. Mexico's frontier, now populated with white "Anglos," would protect the whiteness of the frontier of the United States.

Paradoxically, Mier's outrage against the colored images in the casta paintings belies the reality of Mexico as a nation populated by the Other, a majority of indigenous people who could not be identified as white. Mier's denial was imbedded in Austin's reticence. Although Austin consorted with Mexicans for years, he kept silent about his own opinions. Only in his closest relationships with family members did he express what he really thought. Notwithstanding the inordinate attention and time he devoted to his relationships with Mier and other high-ranking Mexicans, Austin perceived the Mexicans as Others, so much so that he told his . . . brother that, "to be candid the majority of the people of the whole nation as far as I have seen them want nothing but tails to be more brutes than the Apes."[29]

One of Austin's biographers places the blame on the Catholic Church, relating Austin's disgust with the ideological and moral control the Church had over the people of Mexico.[30] This perception of the church was accurate. Yet, describing a group of people as needing only tails has a more dramatic and disturbing connotation than disapproval or disgust regarding a problematic religious institution. After the battle of the Alamo, Austin wrote a letter to Lewis F. Linn, U.S. Senator from Missouri. Subsequently published in numerous U.S. newspapers, the letter stated that "a war of extermination is raging in . . . Texas . . . a war of barbarism and of despotic principles." Most disturbing is Austin's description of Mexicans as a "mongrel Spanish-Indian and Negro race" that was fighting "the Anglo American[s]." A foreshadowing of post–Civil War conflicts enters his text when he mentions that the people are "all mixed together" and are "all the natural enemies of white men and civilization." Ultimately his concerns about the "horrors of negro [sic] insurrection" laid the foundation of a rigid Texas society where bondage was the acceptable solution to the potential risk of a war with savages.[31]

Again, Cantrell apologizes for Austin's having "turn[ed] his back . . . on México and his people."[32] Cantrell surmises that the statement was for the general public and did not reflect Austin's true feelings. Stephen F. Austin's ability to present a façade of acceptance and amiability as he entered the world of Mexico's political elite was essential to his success. An attractive young man of exceptional intelligence, he attached himself to men who had broad experience and knowledge not only of other nations and continents but also of other revolutions. His perception of Mexicans as mongrels did not impede his friendship with Lorenzo de Zavala. This relationship was pivotal in the creation of Texas.

The Mind behind the Republic

Roberto Blum, among numerous Mexican intellectuals, believes that Lorenzo de Zavala was responsible for the American acquisition of Mexico's territory north of the Rio Grande. In a article in Mexico City's *El Economista,* he writes that Zavala, *"Un mexicano excepcional . . . decepcionado de lo que veía que estabamos haciendo para destruir el país, se fue al Norte."* (An exceptional Mexican, Lorenzo de Zavala, disillusioned by what we [Mexicans] were doing to destroy the nation, left for the North). Zavala joined with the Texas insurgency. Blum believes that Zavala's defection was the cause of Mexico's loss of the northern territories.[33] In Texas, Zavala's participation is perceived as minor in comparison to iconic giants such as William Travis, David Crockett, and Stephen F. Austin. The push for diversity in the twentieth century brought Zavala some additional attention: Zavala's name has been given to a Texas county as well as the state archives building and a few public schools. In 1996, well-respected Texas historian Margaret Swett Henson published a biography on Zavala, after she met Rolando Romo, the founding director of Houston's Zavala Chapter of the Tejano Association for Historic Preservation. Her slim volume is easily read and accessible. It has even been published as an electronic book, making it possible for almost anyone to read about Zavala. She is respectful of his many accomplishments. Yet, there continues to be something undecipherable within her text. Traces of Zavala's genius are shown at certain moments, yet Henson does not grasp, nor is aware of the multiple layers of Zavala's knowledge and influence.

Evelia Trejo found what eluded Henson. Trejo is a historian of religion. In 2001 she published an analysis of Zavala's *Ensayo Historico de las Revoluciones de México* (Historical Essay on the Revolutions of Mexico) in *Los Limites de un Discurso* (The Limits of a Discourse). She appears to have been searching for a sensibility, rather than specific documentation of a particular event. She explains that Zavala's intention was to write *"de sucesos significativos ocurridos en su pasado reciente, pero a la ves con una visión que se remonta a un pasado mas lejano, que él pretende explicar más que describir* (significant happenings

that have recently occurred, but with a vision affected, or corrected by a remote past, in which he attempts to explain more than describe)."[34] *Ensayo*
Historico was first published in Paris and New York in 1831 and 1832. In his
introduction, Zavala explains that he is hoping to correct the inaccurate accounts regarding Mexico's separation from Spain. There so little is known
about the situation in Mexico that he believes it is urgent for him to proceed
with his *Ensayo Historico*.[35] He continues to explain in the polemical manner
for which he was known that authors who wrote previously on the revolutions of Mexico did not have the knowledge and understanding of the persons
and events, nor the coherence of relationships; they also lacked the objectivity
necessary for their writings to be given credibility.[36] This commentary by Zavala was an uncanny premonition. It is probable that in 2005, Zavala would
say the same about historians of the Texas Revolution.

Austin's determination and passion for the new colony and the Texas Republic was more intense than Zavala's.[37] However, Zavala's interests were far
larger than Austin's new colony and the Texian insurgents. Zavala was born
on the Mexican Peninsula of Yucatan, an isolated area far from the center of
Mexico, then called New Spain. He was fluent in English and French, freely
able to write and converse with Americans and Europeans. A son of *criollos*,
he, by the age of twenty became known for his revolutionary activities. He
was imprisoned for three years as one of the organizers of the 1813 Revolt of
San Juan de Ulloa (during which incarceration he studied medicine). In 1821,
when the political conflict settled, Zavala was sent as delegate to the Spanish
corte. He returned in the same year and took successive positions as Governor of the State of Mexico and Minister of Hacienda.[38] While he was never
elected president or vice-president of Mexico, for over eight years he was in
the middle circle of national power, often exerting significant influence on the
selection of national leaders and other major issues. Zavala left an astound-
ing mark on Mexico. During his years as state governor and congressional
leader he established the first university system (which became la Universidad
Autonoma de México), the first public library, and introduced the bill that
created the nation's *Districto Federál,* similar to the United States' District of
Columbia. Subsequently, the seat of national government moved to the city
of Toluca, away from the center of Mexico City.[39] His repatriation of agricultural land has led some scholars to consider him the father of Mexico's agrarian movement. He founded several newspapers in Yucatan and Mexico City,
and is one of the handful of men associated with Mexico's liberal movement.[40]
Zavala was a Freemason and is considered one of the founders of Mexico's first
chapter of the Masonic lodge of the York rite.[41]

These events and Zavala's writings are generally acknowledged by most scholars who have studied his life. In a sense, though, it has taken almost two centuries since the first publication of *Ensayo Histórico* for the phenomenon of his elegant discourse to be discovered. Zavala's *Ensayo* was republished in 1845, 1918, 1949 (twice in this year), 1950, 1969, 1981, and 1985.[42]

Even though Austin was not an integral part of Mexican politics, his biographer, Gregg Cantrell, emphasizes Austin's role in the development of the Mexican Constitution. Austin's interest in constitutional law and an abundance of free time allowed him to write three drafts of a working plan to reorganize the Mexican government. He states that the plan submitted by Zavala in 1822 "bore some similarities" to Austin's third proposal. Ultimately, Austin (according to Cantrell) wrote "A Plan of Federal Government" and shared it with Miguel Ramos Arizpe. In December 1823, Ramos Arizpe submitted the *acta constitutional,* the "blueprint" for the 1824 Mexican Constitution. Cantrell surmises that "some latter-day scholars . . . conclude that Ramos Arizpe used Austin's constitution as a guide when writing the *acta constitutional.*"[43]

In a curious reversal, after explaining Austin's influence on Ramos Arizpe's document, Cantrell states "Austin's plan probably had relatively little influence on . . . Ramos Arizpe." The Mexican statesman had already collaborated in the development of the Spanish Constitution of 1812.[44] While Cantrell's later observation produces the appearance of objectivity, his explanation of Austin's constitutional writings places his subject, with significant authority, as author of the 1824 Constitution. The biographer's statement that Austin did not influence the writing of the document is presented as an afterthought, with much less authorial positioning. The reader has already digested Austin's constitutional forays; what can be made of their immediate dismissal? While Cantrell states doubt in Austin's political influence, his clear and detailed explanations of how Austin's writings became the basis for the work of Zavala and Ramos Arizpe may likely stay in the mind of the reader.

Concerning his colonists, Austin's warnings to stay out of politics and "revolutionary activities" is also contradictory, since Austin himself was not able to stay out of Mexican politics "at the very highest levels of government."[45] Austin's own inability to present a sincere trajectory was projected onto his mentors. In a letter to his cousin he describes his attitude towards Mexicans. Being aware of the problems associated with this perspective, Austin had previously warned his brother not to let these opinions be known in Texas. He writes, "They are a strange people, and must be studied to be managed. They have high ideas of National dignity should it be openly attacked, but will sacrifice national dignity, and national interest too . . . so as not to arrest public attention. *Dios Castiga el escandalo mas que el crimen,* (God punishes the exposure more than the crime) is their motto."[46] Perhaps Austin underestimated Zavala's sagacity, not taking into account Zavala's varied relationships with national heads of state. Zavala's experience with intrigue and fantastic revolutionary plans made it very likely that he was aware of Austin's duplicity. Zavala, however, by the time he joined with the Texians, had few choices. He had been banished by the Mexican president. Much of the literature explains that he could have returned to Europe. However, he preferred to stay with Austin and the backwoods colonists to see if his revolutionary ideas could finally be put into place.[47]

Double Narrative

There are two stories that at moments overlap and contradict the history in varying moments. The first story is Austin's perspective on the colony: a combination of saving Texas by paradoxically allowing the (American) wild man to tame the wilderness. The second story is that of the settlers' descendants who have written histories that place them leagues from any semblance of wildness. The themes of purity and original nobility are enmeshed in their self-descriptions. The two narratives conflate into the common theme of redemption. Civilization is brought to the wilderness; darkness is obliterated.

Wild Man in the Wilderness

. . . It was the oppressed, exploited, alienated, or repressed part of humanity that kept on reappearing in the imagination of Western man—as the Wild Man . . . Sometimes . . . as a threat and a nightmare, at other times as a goal and a dream. . . (White 1978, 180).

Davy Crockett is the personifaction of White's "wild man." Crockett, already a national figure before he died at the Alamo, took over the American imagination. Before his mythic demise at the Alamo he was a three-term Tennessee legislator. His initial image of the "half-horse/half-alligator frontiersman," a wild man who had conquered the wilderness, was celebrated by two major theatrical works. "The Lion of the West" was the first that had Crockett using a "wildcat fur" cap. The second, "Davy Crockett; or, Be Sure You're Right Then Go Ahead" ran for twenty-four years (from 1872 to 1896). Historian Paul Hutton describes Crockett as "an American Hercules—wading the Mississippi, riding an alligator up Niagara Falls and wringing the tail off Halley's comet."[48] Hutton's description is uncanny in light of Hayden White's description of the medieval Wild Man: "In most accounts of the Wild Man in the Middle Ages, he is as strong as Hercules, fast as the wind, cunning as the wolf, and devious as the fox. In some stories this cunning is transmuted into a kind of natural wisdom. . . ."[49]

The half-wild hero held the public imagination after Walt Disney produced a television series in 1954–1955 on the adventures of Davy Crockett. The first words of the title song were "Davy, Davy Crockett, King of the Wild Frontier. . . ." Many American children under the age of ten at that time had a coonskin cap like Crockett's. He embodied the goal and dream of the frontiersman seeking to tame the wilderness. The summit was the conquering of nature and the American West, of which Texas was and remains a potent symbol. For the children in the 1950s who wore the caps and chased each other with facsimiles of Crockett's gun "Old Betsy," the hero represented their own imaginary transformation from a mere human (or faulty human) to a warrior of mythic proportions. In the story of Crockett, the Wild Man moving westward finds the frontier and both are transformed. The grand narrative of Texas origin is similarly epic.

Small Transgressions

Although the histories of early Texas are replete with honorable narratives about the "Old Three Hundred," the first group of Austin's settlers, the more common story is that of men who moved to Texas for more than an adventure. W. J. Cash's timeless book, *The Mind of the South,* explains: "Men of position and power, men who are adjusted to their environment . . . such men do not embark on frail ships for a dismal frontier where savages prowl and slay, and living is a grim and laborious ordeal."[50] Cash continues to explain that it is the starving laborer, the debtor leaving jail, the apprentice escaping his master, and the shopkeeper facing bankruptcy who leave for the frontier.

In 1822 the *Arkansas Gazette* and the *Missouri Republican* wrote of Texas and its many "murderers, horse-thieves, counterfeiters, and fugitives from justice."[51] Cantrell writes that it was standard practice to ask newcomers what their name had been before they left for Texas. This practice did not escape even Austin's circle. Samuel Williams, who became Austin's most trusted administrator, first presented himself as E. Eccleston. Austin, Williams, and the Baron de Bastrop all left significant outstanding debts when they immigrated to Texas.[52] There was a rhyme circulating about Austin's headquarters, the town of San Felipe (located forty miles from Fort Bend County):

> The United States, as we understand,
> Took sick and did vomit the dregs of the land.
> Her murderers, bankrupts and rogues you may see,
> All congregated in San Felipe.

W. J. Cash tells of a type of competition in the South, of "tooth and claw struggle, complicated by wildcat finance and speculation."[53] He mentions Joseph Glover's *The Flush Times,* published in New York in 1853, which explains business practices in Austin's colony. The "elaborate machinery of ingenious chicanery" produced "tricks of the trade" where coffins were sent out to graveyards, "with negroes inside, carried off by sudden spells of imaginary disease, to be 'resurrected' in due time, grinning, on the banks of the Brazos." Jared Groce, known to be the wealthiest man in the early years of Austin's colony, arrived in 1822 with over a hundred slaves. Austin's biographer notes that "evidence later surfaced indicating that Groce may not have actually owned a substantial number of the slaves he brought to Texas."[54] It was also discovered that Groce left behind a business debt of $10,000 in Georgia.

Yet in this environment, where the primary task was to establish and maintain the colony, a questionable past was overlooked. Groce provided supplies when needed, paid his fees promptly, occasionally lent Austin money, and leased slaves to him. Groce's usefulness to the colony led Austin to overlook "whatever misdeeds Groce might have committed in the United States and any small transgressions in Texas."[55] As the nineteenth century continued, so did local violence. Clarence Wharton's *History of Fort Bend County*[56] describes twenty-nine incidents of homicide (where one or more people were killed) and three attempted homicides. In all Wharton's narratives, only three people were actually tried: two were found guilty. The first was a white man who was hanged in 1834. Wharton noted that "this was probably the first and only legal execution" during the colonial period.[57] The second defendant, in 1837, was also white; he was acquitted on the grounds of "justifiable homicide" in the first murder trial in the District Court of Harrisburg County (Houston, Harris County).[58] The third trial occurred in 1888. An African American named William Caldwell was accused of shooting a local planter, J. M. Shamblin, who was reading the Bible at the time he was shot. In what seems like a prelude to the twenty-first-century criminal justice system in Texas, Caldwell was tried in the Criminal District Court of Harris County (Houston).[59] His case was escalated to the Court of Criminal Appeals and ultimately to the United States Supreme Court, which refused to hear the case. He was found guilty and was executed by hanging. Clarence Wharton, an attorney, noted that Caldwell's attorney for his first trial was A. C. Allen, son of one of the Allen brothers, Houston's founders. Wharton explains: "Few cases in the annals of our criminal jurisprudence afford a stronger record of guilt and few show a more painstaking trial or more competent defense. The defendant had every aid and guaranty which an accused could have."[60]

Three Hundred Settlers

As has been shown by the ongoing interest in the battle of the Alamo, the story of Texas continuously interests (and sometimes impassions) many Americans. The story of the initial three hundred settlers brought by Austin has blended into the story of the Alamo and its importance as an icon of American identity. In Wharton's *History of Fort Bend County*, the author titles the first chapter "The Texas Mayflower." The first white settlers came to be called "Old Three Hundred," so as to distinguish them from "other hundreds who came afterwards."[61] The three hundred and the thousands who came later eventually rebelled against the government of Mexico. From this conflict came the battle of the Alamo. Their success in separating from Mexico and their ability to form, at least temporarily, their own nation-state gave these settlers of the 1820s and 1830s an identity that encompassed a strong national persona. The Old Three Hundred were seen as the first, the beginning. History before their arrival was not modern history. The slaves that accompanied them were not considered of their number.

So much does history seem to begin at this one juncture with the Old Three Hundred, that S. A. McMillan describes Santa Ana's entry into Coahuila y Tejas in 1836 as "the Mexican invasion,"[62] forgetting that Texas was still Mexican territory at that time. Originally inhabited by the badly maligned Karankawa tribe who have been (perhaps inaccurately) described as cannibals, the region may have been explored briefly by the Spanish. Sowell describes the Spanish as "a strange race of people . . . marching up the Brazos Valley in glistening armor and gaudy colored banners flying, striking the natives with terror and astonishment."[63] It is said that the metal helmet of a Spanish officer was found (at the end of the twentieth century) on land owned by Sugar Land Industries.[64]

The territory was sparsely populated in 1821, with no significant settlements east of San Antonio. It was also the year that Mexico won its independence from Spain. Just as Mexico was becoming its own nation-state, its government was negotiating with Moses Austin regarding a new settlement. Austin's son, Stephen, finalized negotiations in 1823 and arranged for three hundred families to come to Texas. The actual dates given for the settlement vary. McMillan writes that William Andrus erected the first structure on the Bend in 1819.[65] A. J. Sowell proposes that Stephen Austin himself selected the location of the fort in 1821, leaving five young men behind to build a stronghold to protect incoming colonists.[66] According to Pauline Yelderman, William Little, one of the five men left to build the fort, brought the first slave into the area. Moses Austin brought a slave (named Richmond) with him as he traveled through Texas to Mexico City.[67] Mexico condoned slavery although there were laws against the slave trade.[68] Land allotments were increased for those who owned slaves. The land in the county was extremely fertile, which attracted many who wanted to establish plantations. As Pauline Yelderman explains: ". . . with an economic system based on slave labor, the way of life—the culture—of the county became purely Old South."[69]

Conflation of Colonizer and Colonized

Genealogy would at once become an obsession (Cash 1969, 66).

The history of the county is imbedded in its genealogy.[70] Wharton's reasoning for differentiation between the first three hundred settlers and "other hundreds who came afterwards" becomes a synecdoche for the larger issue of difference, or rather hierarchy. Hayden White writes of the synecdoche that indicates the "integration of all apparently particular phenomena into a whole . . . the possibility of understanding the particular as a microcosm of a macrocosmic totality."[71] Considering this possibility, distinguishing the "Old Three Hundred" from those that came afterwards is a concise way of one group of colonists receiving all that is valued and desired. This could be argued, however, since texts that refer to the Austin's first settlers often blend valued colonists "who came later" with the primary group. While anyone genealogically related to the three hundred is distinguished in textual narratives, subsequent white settlers are not devalued for having come later. The common denominator is their whiteness and their English or Scottish ancestry. Yet the redundancy of the term "Old Three Hundred," its proliferation in text after text, even to the schoolbooks of children in Texas public schools, is significant. The intensity of its presence belies the rhyme that tells the reader how the "dregs of the land" came to Austin's colony. Perhaps the three hundred were divided from the others so as to mark them as better than the desperate people who came later. Being marked as one of the three hundred transformed the former Wild Man into the Hercules who had a quixotic dream and achieved a superhuman goal. They were the first to go beyond the edge of the world, the "trackless wilderness of Texas" as described by A. J. Sowell in 1904.

The image of transformation is complete by the beginning of the Civil War. As W. J. Cash describes, the uneducated settler, perhaps a recently released indentured servant (or his son) finds land in the South and within five years makes a profit from his labors.[72] The next generation was provided for in an environment that is less frontier-like, with larger land holdings and a grander home site. The plantation grows as does the number of slaves. Each successive generation experiences more privilege. The uneducated settler who works the fields with his wife day and night is now the gentleman planter with more than one hundred slaves. He is marked as the master (of his family, his slaves, and his land), his delineation emanating from his membership in the "Old Three Hundred."[73] His power is founded on this taxonomy.

In a curious work of history, Austin's settlers were simultaneously colonizers and colonized. The lack of civilization that was ascribed to them made them constant subjects of ridicule and devaluation. They were the "dregs" of the nation. The only way they could have stayed behind in their native Kentucky and Tennessee (and not be maliciously labeled) was to incorporate the social rules and control provided by the new nation; to be controlled so to speak, so that their "wild" nature could be colonized into a "civilized" group of people. Instead, they moved outside of established civilization and colonized themselves (or at least presented themselves as such). As they transformed into "more civilized" men and women, they were themselves also the colonizers of Texas, eliminating and suppressing the Karankawas and the Spanish/Mexican history and identity of the territory. Thus the narrative about President Santa Ana's entry into Texas in 1836 to quell a rebellion mutated into a "Mexican invasion." The colonization was complete. It changed the story of history and made all other origins non-existent.

The idea of taxonomy and the Old Three Hundred is salient to Ann Stoler's discussion on colonialism and "being European." In *Race and the Educa-*

tion of Desire she explains: "Being 'European' was supposed to be self-evident but was also a quality that only the qualified were equipped to define."[74] The differentiation of the "Old Three Hundred" places authority and legitimacy into their descendants. It is this authority that resurrects their political world after Reconstruction. The image of this power was so intense that the reincarnated order of the Old South remained in place for another sixty years.

A Spy Named Maillard: Richmond, Texas, 1840

Sixty years later old Dr. Feris said of him [Maillard], "He certainly knew how to mix some good drinks" (Wharton 1939, 108).

Traveling from England in 1839, N. Doran Maillard arrived in downtown Richmond three years after the Texas Revolution with the purpose of writing "an unvarnished account of what Texas and the Texans really are."[75] Austin's Colony, considered the "first official" white settlement in Texas, had begun nineteen years before. His descriptions horrified county residents when his book was published three years later. Even though he addressed the Earl of Aberdeen in his text, it is unclear who specifically was Maillard's patron. His study included a history of the Texas Revolution, the "character" of Texans, the practice of slavery, the indigenous population, the landscape, wildlife, and the agricultural value of the state. Although he titles his work as being about "Texas" as a whole, most of his descriptions concerned southeast Texas and Fort Bend County. County residents described him as a British spy.

He was in ill health when he left England in November 1839. It took two months to cross the Atlantic and enter the Gulf of Mexico. He arrived in New Orleans before Galveston. New Orleans was a frequent contact point for the new Texas settlers. The ship named The *Lively,* which carried some of Texas' first white settlers, departed from New Orleans. Many county planters purchased their slaves in New Orleans, yet there is little (if any) documentation of their experiences buying slaves at the city's large slave market. While in New Orleans, Maillard saw a slave woman "with an iron collar around her neck." The spikes of the collar were inverted, so that every time she moved her head the points would tear her skin. She carried a nursing infant at her breast. Maillard believed the infant was "the child of a planter." Only a British writer could have easily published this type of information during that time period. Even though commonly practiced, sexual relationships between slaves and their owners (and the resulting miscegenation) was not addressed publicly, especially in publications dealing with Fort Bend.

From Galveston Maillard went on to Richmond, where he stayed at the boarding house of the widow Jane Long, called the "Mother of Texas." Her fame is related to the several months she was stranded on an island off the Texas coast with her infant daughter and a seven-year-old female slave. Maillard was not very pleased with the conditions of Long's rooms. In his general statement about Texas hotels and boarding-houses he writes their "charges are exorbitant" and they are ". . . conducted in the most miserable way, being extremely filthy, filled with vermin of every description, and wretchedly supplied with food."[76]

In what could be seen as imperialist ethnography or merely muckraking, Maillard wrote passionately about his disgust for most Texans. What outraged the county people most upon reading the book was the memory of his friendliness and cordiality with most of them while he was in Richmond. He was invited into their homes and provided what they saw as sincere hospitality.[77]

A Conflation of Narratives

From the genius of Zavala to the adaptable Austin and his frontier colonists, the people of the nineteenth-century Republic of Texas were perhaps the most diverse group of immigrants yet seen in North America. While history emphasizes the ingenuity of the Colonists and their "Father," it censored the numerous complexities that led to the formation of Texas. It is certainly correct that the colonists braved violent confrontations with Native Americans (who were quickly extinguished), and that they ran desperately from Santa Ana's impending "invasion" in 1836. The first small farms carved out of the leagues of land distributed by Austin grew into the grand plantations that were producing enormous cotton crops by 1860. Colonists who could not so much as spell their names became honorable ancestors.[78] The memory of Zavala's extraordinary intelligence and achievements was minimized or erased, along with that of settlers who came from places other than Kentucky, Virginia, and the rest of the Old South.

Roberto Blum, noted Mexican journalist, commemorated the 190th anniversary of his country's independence with an essay in *El Economista*. He notes that the "exceptional" Lorenzo de Zavala left Mexico to become the first Vice President of the Texas Republic. Mexico then "quickly" lost its "immense" northern territories. Blum implies that Zavala's intellectual and political prowess strongly influenced the outcomes of Texas Independence and the U.S.-Mexican War. If Blum is correct, Texas has permitted the "production of history" regarding Austin and his colonists. The history of Zavala's influence on Austin and the establishment of the Texas Republic was not authorized.

Chapter three

The Colonel

Jefferson Davis, Senator from Mississippi, defending slavery, said in the [U.S.] Senate that the South had solved its social problems so that the white population could become the leisure cultured class and the slaves would do all the drudgery. This was the ambition of our two thousand white people in . . . [Fort Bend] County in 1860 (Wharton 1939, 167).

They went to war to protect the sacred institution of the South (ibid., 171).

In the foyer of B. F. Terry High School once hung an oversized oil portrait of a Confederate officer, the handsome Colonel Benjamin Franklin ("Frank") Terry.[1] County people greatly admire his numerous exploits and acknowledge his importance to the successful economy of Fort Bend. The mythology of his background, his character, and his victories embodies the Southern ideals of the county. With a genealogy older than the Texas Republic, he became its idealized hero. As a planter and an entrepreneur, he enriched the county. Clarence Wharton, an early partner of James Baker's law firm, Baker and Botts, wrote the following in his often-cited history of Fort Bend: "He [Terry] looked like one of the Norsemen who came over with Leif Ericson. A man of great dynamic force, he was a tireless rider and unerring shot. His aggressive nature did not irritate but by common consent gave him a leadership which the county folks were ready to acknowledge."[2]

B. F. Terry High School, built in 1980, was the second high school constructed on the western side of Fort Bend County. Journalist and local historian Tim Cumings told me that, when the school was named, Terry was

considered a local hero and the school board was not hampered by any mis-
givings about his Confederate past. Indeed, in the 1980s B. F. Terry High
School conducted fund-raisers for the parent-teacher organization in which
their African American school principal dressed as a slave with chains on his
legs and was auctioned off to the highest bidder. Community protests ended
the mock slave auctions some years later. Several Terry alumni from the mid-
1980s have told me that they and many other former students did not find the
event offensive; in fact, many still consider the auction to be just another way
in which to generate monies.

For many years, the large image of the colonel in his gray uniform so
prominently displayed at the entrance made it impossible for anyone at the
school to forget the Confederacy. Yet, in an odd juxtaposition, the Confederacy is remembered, while the reality and terror of slavery have been forgotten. I wonder, though, how many who come through the doorways are aware
that the school buildings were constructed on land once worked by slaves.
After hearing that the "slave in chains" event is still not seen as problematic,
I imagine that the county's slave history stands in a similar place of neutral-
ity. It is as if the colonel's portrait and his slave labor have become "presences
of diverse absences."[3] The grandness of the hero and his massive numbers of
slaves working the county's plantation land create the metaphorical space of
Fort Bend. The spirits of the slave-owning hero and his laborers in bondage
are "like the gothic sculptures of kings and queens that once adorned Notre-
Dame and have been buried for two centuries in the basement of a building. . . . These 'spirits,' themselves broken into pieces in like manner, do not
speak any more than they see. This is a sort of knowledge that remains silent.
Only hints of what is known but unrevealed are passed on."[4] Thus, the slave
auction fund-raiser, with its resulting ambivalence, is a hint of the past. The
terror remains silent.

Frank Terry, a broad-shouldered man more than six feet tall, does not of-
fend with his "aggressive nature." The distinction of appearance, relegating
the colonel to a Nordic genealogy, augments his position as hero. Wharton's
reference to whether his subject offended others is significant. Throughout
the texts written by local authors the idea of whether men are polite, humble,
or proper is constant.[5] This is especially notable when the descriptions are of
African Americans. "Polite" equals "good." Yet the aggression of the white war
hero is considered valuable.

Wharton uses the word "conspicuous" in describing Frank Terry's arrival
in the county. His entire narrative about Terry is infused with continued ide-

alized descriptions of the colonel. Even though Terry was not one of the Old Three Hundred (except by marriage), his genealogy is impeccable. Both his grandfathers were officers in the Revolutionary War. He is an important figure in the county's nineteenth-century history. The Terry family came from Kentucky. In 1824 they moved to Mississippi and in 1833 traveled on to Texas without Frank's father. They first settled in Brazoria County (on the southeast boundary of Fort Bend) with Terry's maternal uncle, Benjamin Fort Smith, one of Austin's later settlers. Fort Smith was a slave trader who fought with Andrew Jackson in the War of 1812.[6]

Although Wharton does not mention Terry's connection to the California gold rush, other textual sources report that Terry and his business partner, William Kyle, left on a wagon train for California with a group of forty people in 1849. Robert Armstrong, in his book on Sugar Land, reports their return to Texas three years later with a great sum of money after striking "it rich in prospecting for gold."[7] Curiously, Armstrong indicates that the source of the money is not totally clear. He continues: "[A]nd this seems to have been borne out by the amount of money they spent in buying and enlarging the Oakland plantation."[8] The plantation was purchased in 1852 from the heirs of Sam Williams, Stephen F. Austin's personal secretary. Terry and Kyle then renamed it Sugar Land.[9]

The most significant business venture that Terry and Kyle undertook was to construct the first railroad in Texas. They were awarded the contract in 1851 and completed a thirty-mile line from Houston (then called Harrisburg) to Richmond in 1856. The line provided the beginnings of an infrastructure that significantly enhanced the economic success of the county. The planters could now transport their cotton to Houston. Property values increased dramatically, some as much as sixteen times the value assessed in 1850.[10] Between 1850 and 1860 the number of slaves increased from 1,559 to 4,127, more than double the white population of the county.[11] At the onset of the Civil War, Fort Bend was the wealthiest county in Texas.[12] In 1860 Terry and Kyle owned 150 slaves and had a combined worth of $300,000.[13] Even though Texas had been a state for only fifteen years, the county's socioeconomic structure was already strikingly similar to that of other Southern states with much longer histories of white settlements.

The state of Texas convened a "Secession Convention" in January 1861. Terry represented Fort Bend and belonged to a group of delegates who endorsed the reinstitution of slave importation that had been banned in the United States since 1808.[14] He joined the Confederate Army, served with General Longstreet, and "distinguished himself" at First Manassas, also known as the battle of Bull Run.[15]

The Farewell: Oyster Creek, August 1861

> History stopped for us in 1865,
> then started again as memory:
> the grey and gold
> of the good-smelling, broadcloth uniform,
> the new, beautiful, handsewn battle flag,
> the West Point strategists, the Ciceronian orations,
> the cavalry charges—
>
> (Richard Tillinghast, "Sewanee in Ruins," 1983)

Emotion, loss, and separation are intricately tied to departure. De Certeau writes that departure and debt blend together in the making of history.[16] The emotion of the departure does not leave with the departed. It stays behind in those who watch him leave. They remain with an obligation to continue not only the hero's (the colonel's) narrative, but the structure of life that he created on his plantation. After he is killed in battle, the ongoing repetition of his departure narrative keeps his last interaction alive.

1861: Sugar Land, Texas

Frank Terry died in December 1861, shortly after leaving Texas with his new regiment, Terry's Texas Rangers.[17] The story of Terry's last days has become local mythology. Clarence Wharton's 1939 history of the County describes a farewell scene rivaling that of *Gone With the Wind*, with the colonel's wife and children on the porch of the great house, his slaves lined up singing to him, and Terry himself atop his beautiful white horse, elegantly dressed in his Confederate officer's uniform, carrying his uncle's sword as he prepares to leave for war. The sword had seen Andrew Jackson and the War of 1812; it had seen the Creek Indian Wars and the battle of San Jacinto. It is richly nostalgic: the handsome officer wearing a "new and splendid uniform," mounted on a "superb horse." The plantation is at its zenith. The "thousand acres" of cotton are about to be harvested. The plantation slaves have a holiday. He asks them to sing "plantation melodies" as he stops briefly to "gaze across the beautiful valley of Oyster Creek." He rides over to see "some of the older negroes (sic) who were ill and unable to be out and see him off." He "bades" [sic] his slaves to be "obedient to their overseers," and to take care of his family. "With tears" they see him ride away.[18]

In documenting Terry's scene of departure, Wharton is also staging a farewell for the South. It is as if the colonel himself is the South; beautiful, tall, and strong. It is the moment when Terry relinquishes his position as master of the plantation. He reminds his family and bondsmen of their obligation upon his departure. Do not change things, he asks. The bondsmen are entreated to maintain the hierarchy between themselves and the Master's family. Take care of them, he says, thus solidifying their position as servants to the privileged once the central authority figure on the plantation is no longer present. As a general would review his troops before battle, Terry reviews "his people." It is an opulent sight. Wharton is clear in his description of an outstandingly successful agricultural operation, worked by slaves who are undoubtedly enamored of their colonel. The purity of Terry's intentions are displayed in his respectful visit to the older slaves who, because of infirmities or illness, cannot stand at attention for his last review of his property.

In rushing off to defend what would become the Lost Cause, he leaves his family and property vulnerable. Between June and December of 1861, Terry leaves Texas to join the Confederacy, fights at Bull Run, returns to Texas, organizes a company of 1,800 men, leaves for Kentucky, and dies in his company's first battle. His empire dissolves with his death. Wharton uses this early death to create a romantic narrative of the mythical warrior who died defending his right to be master. The colonel's departure stands, not only for Terry's upcoming death, but also for the end of antebellum Southeast Texas.

No-Name Woman: A Speculation

For years, as you drove southwest on U.S. Highway 59 from Houston, if you looked to your right after you passed Sugar Land, you could see men on horseback with guns. Nearby, prisoners in white uniforms were standing and working on the rows of cotton or corn. There are five prisons in the county. The prison land bordered the highway and the men with guns were "captains" supervising the men in white, who were prison workers. There are also signs along the freeway with red letters that say "Prison Area: Do Not Pick up

Hitchhikers." There are no visible signs of any type of plantation. The Terry mansion, located about a mile north of the refinery (and old U.S. Highway 90), burned down during Reconstruction. The fields worked by slaves, prisoners, or ethnic Mexican laborers are now mostly filled with new subdivisions.

These are the minimal remainders of what seems to have been an otherwise almost secret past. The remaining history, containing ninety percent of the narrative, is missing. I cannot find it. I recall de Certeau's words from "Walking in the City": These are the "deserted places of my memory,"[19] and the portrait of the colonel at the local high school represented "the Prince Charming who stays just long enough to awaken the Sleeping Beauty of . . . wordless stories."[20] There is an unnamed slave woman in the famous story of the colonel's departure. She appears just as the colonel is about to leave the plantation: "[A]s he [Terry] remounted his horse an old negro [*sic*] mammy came running from the house with his little five-year-old son, Kyle, in her arms, holding him high as he cried for his father. The warrior reached down and caught the little fellow in a last embrace, handed him back to his mammy and rode away."[21]

The same story is also told by Yelderman and Lovett.[22] Each repetition presents the emotion but does not identify the woman. I ask local historian, Tim Cumings about her, since I can't seem to find anything with a name or other description. Cumings tells me that the story is probably only a legend. But I remember de Certeau's insistence regarding the "repressed" and how it surfaces in "mystical expression" through folklore and legend.[23] The relationship between the woman, Terry, and the child has lost some of its narrative. The remainders stayed tied to the legend. I think she may be buried in the cemetery since it is located only about two miles from the "big house" of the Terry plantation. I try to look for her; she is not listed in the census records. The roster of Terry's slaves lists only fourteen individuals by age and gender, but no names. Should I try to find a bill of sale? Would these still be in the courthouse records?

The 1880 census records provide a clue. I find a Rachel Terry, born in 1835 in Mississippi. In 1860 she would have been twenty-six, not an old woman as described in the legendary narratives. She lived near the Colonel's plantation during the Reconstruction period. By the 1880 census, she had moved twenty miles farther southwest. She is listed with her son, John Terry, near the town of East Bernard, just outside the county. Could this be the same woman? There is no way of knowing. Most former slaves left their plantations after the war. Rachel Terry may have first traveled to the next large farm and then

gone farther southwest to the eastern edge of the next county. However, this
is only speculation.

The difference between the narratives about the colonel and his slave is
striking. In his overvalued eminence and beauty, his figure completely over-
shadows that of his female slave. Her presence is only liminal. There is an outline of a form—an old woman—who, still with significant energy, runs and
thrusts the colonel's child up so many feet toward his father. Her assistance
in the scene and ensuing disappearance create an interesting constellation.
Even as she disappears, she completes a narrative triangle: the colonel (the father), the five-year-old boy (the son), and a dark female being, not considered
a whole person, yet presenting some type of image that quickly disappears,
like a ghost. These three central figures are the story of the South; noticeably
lacking is the "pure" white woman whom idealism has paralyzed. The intimacy of the disappearing woman's (Rachel's?) relationship to the father and
the child belie other narratives as well. Was she the colonel's lover? How important was she in this household? What impelled her, with the child in her
arms, to run to the colonel? Why did the child's mother herself not run to the
father? In this gesture, regardless of who commanded her action, the woman
is indicating the importance of the relationship between the father and the
son. Her awareness of this places her within the emotional intimacy of these
male actors. In Sharon Holland's eloquent book, *Raising the Dead,* the author
proposes that the imaginary surrounding the supposed "silent dead" holds the
most information.[24] Rachel, as the black mammy, is the "silent dead"; she is
the embodiment of the black female body (i.e., the female slave) and is herself
the "terrain between the living and the dead, between the ancestral and the
living community."[25]

Remnants: Who Speaks?

*Perhaps the best way of encapsulating the gist of an epoch is to focus not
on the explicit features that define its social and ideological edifices, but
on the disavowed ghosts that haunt it, dwelling in a mysterious region of
nonexistent entities which none the less persist, continue to exert their ef-
ficacy (Zizek 2000, 3).*

*There is an abandoned cemetery on the banks of Oyster Creek, about a mile down-
stream from the center of Terry's plantation. It is known only as the "black cem-*

etery" or the "prisoner cemetery." It borders San Isidro Cemetery, separated from it by a tall chain link fence. Until recently, the overgrowth was too entangled for anyone to enter. In 2004 the San Isidro Cemetery Association began clearing most of the two and a half acres, but John de la Cruz still reminds me that rattlesnakes have remained. This has kept me from going farther. I have asked about the space, but no one can tell me its history. They just say that prisoners and probably slaves were buried there. People remind me that there are other black cemeteries in the Brazos Bottoms whose histories have not been lost. At the cemetery next to San Isidro, there continue to be no stories.

The silent narrative leads me to speculation. What stories could these graves tell? If their inhabitants were slaves, who were their masters? Who is buried there? Is it the "old Negro mammy" who carried five-year-old Kyle Terry the day his father left for the war? If she could speak, what would she tell me? What is the significance of her silenced knowledge?

Sharon Holland's analysis of Benedict Anderson's commentary on nationalism discusses silenced narratives: "If we were to interpret Anderson's formulations liberally, then we would obviously conclude that the nation exists precisely because the dead do not speak. . . . The ability of the emerging nation to speak hinges on its correct use of the 'dead' in the service of its creation."[26]

The silence of Kyle Terry's mammy in contrast to the overembellished narratives about Colonel Terry gives me pause. In reading about Frank Terry's family life, I learn that he married Mary Bingham, the daughter of Francis Bingham (Bigham/Biggam), who was not sure how to spell his name. He settled farther south on Oyster Creek, on the boundary between Fort Bend and Brazoria counties. In his 1991 history of the Imperial Sugar Company, Robert Armstrong presents Terry's father-in-law as "Sir Francis Bingham." I could find no indication that Bingham (or Bigham/Biggam) was ever officially given this aristocratic English title.[27]

Oyster Creek serves as the geographic connector between Terry, Bingham, and the unnamed old Negro mammy. They all lived on the banks of Oyster Creek. The two plantation owners and a female slave have been provided different trajectories. Some stories are enhanced and others are diminished or erased, at least from conscious history.

The colonel's body, accompanied by his son David, was returned to Houston by train. He was given a hero's funeral, attended by masses of people. Hobbs describes Terry's funeral as follows: "Terry's body was sent by train to Nashville, Tennessee, where the legislature adjourned and joined in a procession escorting the remains to be held in state at the Tennessee Capitol. The body lay in state in New Orleans and then Houston, where the funeral procession was described as 'the most imposing ever seen in this state.' Governor Lubbock lauded Terry in the state Senate: 'no braver man ever lived—no truer patriot ever died.'"[28]

The colonel's father-in-law, Francis Bingham (Bigham/Biggam), fought in the Texas Revolution but was not a war hero. His death is recorded, and the location of his grave is public information. He is buried in the Sandy Point Cemetery in Brazoria County, Texas. The cemetery has a website that announces its inhabitants.[29]

The edifices of history that include Terry and Bingham do not explain the "gist of an epoch." It is the "disavowed ghost" of Kyle Terry's nursemaid that cues the narrative of Oyster Creek and its plantations.[30] If her grave borders San Isidro, she is indeed a link between the living and the dead.

America's National Sin

Wharton[31] has described Kyle Terry's nursemaid as "old," yet there is no way of knowing her actual age. The colonel was forty years old when the described events occurred. As described by Wharton, "the warrior" was at the zenith of his power and virility. It is quite possible that the "old" female slave was the same age as her master. The difficulties of bondage, excessive physical labor, and repeated childbearing may have aged her prematurely. Margaret Walker notes in her autobiographical novel, *Jubilee,* that her great-great grandmother, a slave in Georgia, died a broken-down "old" woman at the age of twenty-seven.[32] Ultimately, Wharton decided whether the Negro mammy was an old woman. She may not have actually been old. Considering the perspective of the time, it would be natural to contrast the youthful appearance of the forty-year-old warrior colonel with the obvious aging on the face of the female slave.

There is no documentation about any other interactions between Colonel Terry and his female slaves. Even so, without the specific information, the idea of a relationship is eternally present in the narratives told by the descendants of slaves. Stories told in Fort Bend County recount that young female slaves were called to the beds of their masters, a Southern equivalent of the "right of the first night."[33] The intimacy between the master and his females slaves is frequently narrated in the history of the South.[34] The paradox of these relationships is what Eric Sundquist terms "America's national sin."[35]

Their complexity, ambivalence, and ambiguity are internal to different forms of conflict that have continued for well more than a century. It is the double bind that kept "slaves as beasts and lovers alike."[36]

Terry and Kyle owned more than 150 slaves, having paid for and obtained "title" to them; Terry then worked them as he did his oxen, horses, and mules. How could the unnamed woman also be his lover? Did he have any feelings toward her? In an essay on Thomas Jefferson's lover, Andrew Burstein suggests that Jefferson, because of issues of hierarchy and social class, could not have actually been in love with Sally Hemings, his slave. Yet, the possibility of a sexual relationship is a given, Burstein explains: "In Jefferson's time, wives—let alone slaves—had no right to deny sex to that man to whom they were legally bound."[37]

The written history of Fort Bend County detours around these uncomfortable narratives. They are not authorized. They are found either in the private stories of these women's descendants or in the context of fictional literature. In the instance of Fort Bend County, the repressed returns and explodes. A deadly feud erupted twenty-seven years after Terry's death. The planter's culture imploded in the center of the recreated Southern city of Richmond, Texas. Kyle Terry, now a young man, was at the center of the conflict. It is here that Eric Sundquist's suggestion appears salient. He proposes that both Harriet Beecher Stowe and William Faulkner focus (in their respective novels *Dred* and *Absalom, Absalom)* on "the sins of the fathers that led necessarily to the violence of the brothers."[38]

1888, Richmond, Texas: The Politics of the Jaybirds and the Woodpeckers

In 1888, Kyle Terry, the colonel's youngest son, is presented by the Jaybirds as his father's successor. In 1889 he becomes a Woodpecker. Kyle Terry was five years old when his father died. Their last interaction is when Kyle is thrust up to his father as the colonel sits on his horse, ready to leave the plantation for the Civil War. Twenty-seven years later, Kyle Terry plays a pivotal role in the changing (and violent) politics of the county. The story of the colonel's youngest son resonates with something told about the slaves at Monticello. In 1796 the Comte de Volney visited Thomas Jefferson and noted that the slaves were as white as he (Volney) was. They were "the same skin color as the legitimate Jefferson family."[39] In contrast, although Kyle was listed in the census as the son of Frank Terry and Mary Bingham, born in 1856, a close reading of county history indicates some doubts about his whiteness.

He was involved in the violence between the county political groups, the white Jaybirds and the black Woodpeckers. He was with a group of Jaybirds who rode to Kendleton (known as the slave colony) when they ran the black Woodpeckers out of the county in 1888. Yet when Kyle was thirty-two, he changed parties. He became a Woodpecker when he announced his campaign for county treasurer. In a county where good genealogy ranked supreme, the fate of Kyle Terry was determined by an indeterminate situation. Kyle Terry's identity became questionable when he became a Woodpecker, known as the scalawags of the county. His alliance with the scalawags and African Americans marked him as an undesirable: in the same category, according to Clarence Wharton, as an African American and purported cattle thief named Tom Taylor. Wharton indicates his disgust in the ways he describes Kyle and his actions: Kyle's large stature (a parallel to Wharton's description of the Taylor men), his lack of gentlemanly qualities, and a lack of control Wharton attributes to his fiery nature. For example, at a political rally Kyle is introduced as a "Southern gentlemen and the son of an illustrious sire."[40] Terry makes a speech that belittles another young planter, Ned Gibson, calling him a "paper-collared dude." Ned's brother, Volney, responds by saying: "Ned isn't here, but I'll represent him." Wharton reports that Terry becomes enraged and jumps from the platform with his gun in hand. A former slave from the Terry plantation throws "his arms around Terry" and says, "Marse Kyle, 'hav' yo'self."[41] As an added thought, Wharton notes that it was not the former slave who ultimately stopped Terry, but some Jaybirds who "interfered" and "induced" Kyle to put his gun away.[42]

Painting the Whole Town Black: The Death of Jolly Ned Gibson—Wharton, Texas, June 1889

On the other side were the Gibson boys . . . sons of Dr. Gibson who lived on a farm near Richmond and cultivated race horses . . . They were all blond and rather slight in build . . . In society the Gibson boys were jovial and well-mannered Southern gentlemen. . . (Sonnichsen 1962, 251).

Kyle Terry killed Ned Gibson with a double-barreled shotgun on the courthouse square in Wharton, Texas (thirty-three miles southwest of Richmond). Gibson was to be a witness in a trial concerning the illegal rebranding of a cow. The defendant was a friend of Kyle Terry. The case had attracted notoriety and a good number of Fort Bend people were present. Sonnichsen reports with specificity that Terry boarded the Southern Pacific train near Richmond at 3:56 A.M. on January 21, 1889.[43] Kyle was armed. His gun was "unjointed and wrapped in paper, under his arm."[44] He spoke briefly to a deputy sheriff who was standing at the rear platform, and entered the "water closet." He was not seen again until he stepped off the train when it arrived in East Bernard an hour later. He then borrowed a horse and rode into Wharton early the same morning.[45]

The confrontation occurred at 1 P.M. According to Wharton and Yelderman, Terry was waiting at the Malitz and Barbee saloon, hiding behind a screen door that provided a view across the square. Sonnichsen reports a more dramatic scenario. Kyle Terry and Mr. Barbee were sitting in the front gallery of the saloon when Gibson and his entourage left the Fort House Hotel for the courthouse. Barbee's "henchmen" had already warned Gibson, who "never hesitated, but came steadily on." Terry went inside the saloon to get his gun. When he returned, Bob Stafford, a county planter who was accompanying Gibson, yelled out to Terry, "My God, Kyle, are you going to kill your friends?" Terry responded, "No, I am only after those who have been waylaying me." The verbal confrontation did not deter Gibson's group from continuing their walk across the square. After answering Stafford, Terry "carefully leveled" his shotgun at Gibson. The buckshot injured Ned's shoulder, mouth, and arm; he died an hour later.[46] The obituary in the *Richmond Democrat* eulogized Gibson as a "brave generous soul," reminding readers that "the tear . . . we shed, shall long keep his memory green in our souls."[47]

After the confrontation in Wharton, Kyle was arrested and placed under a $25,000 bond. Judge Parker represented him in the examining trial, and the bond was reduced to $15,000. He was later seen in the saloons of Galveston, looking "threadbare and shabby."[48] Although he was acquitted of the murder, he was told it would be suicidal for him to return to the county, so he made plans to go to South America. A different form of emotional banishment was forced upon Kyle Terry. He had betrayed his community by joining the Woodpeckers and becoming a scalawag. He had spent what was left of his inheritance. He had lost what his community valued the most. He was dishonored, poor, and disloyal and would be shot if he returned home. There was nothing left to connect him with the colonel except the name Terry. In a society where former slaves often took the name of their master, even Kyle's surname was in question.

Gibson, the blond, slightly built young man whose father was a doctor, was an absolute contrast to the tall, "powerful and well proportioned" Kyle

Terry.[49] Kyle physically resembled his father, Frank Terry, a tall, robust man. An additional difference was that Kyle's illustrious father had died in the war when Kyle was only a youngster. The family's exorbitant wealth had already dissipated. Even though the colonel had thought of educating his children (he had brought in a teacher and established a school on the plantation), his absence kept Kyle from acquiring the "gentlemanly qualities" expected of Southern men. Wharton and Yelderman emphasize this deficiency.

Gibson's obituary narrative strikes at Terry: "Ned Gibson has gone to his eternal rest but I'd a thousand times be in his place than to stand for one moment in the shoes of the assassin, whose hands, reeking with the blood of an unsuspecting victim, are pressed against his feverish brow to rub away the brand of murderer!"[50] Nonetheless, it appears that Kyle Terry was already branded.

The legend surrounding Colonel Terry's wartime departure tells of five-year-old Kyle Terry being swept up into his father's arms for a last good-bye. It was not the child's mother that ran to his father, who is mounted on his great horse, dressed in his Confederate uniform. It was "an old negro mammy . . . running from the house" with the child in her arms, holding him high as he cried for his father. There is no mention of Kyle in Wharton's text for another twenty-seven years. Then, during the narrative of the bloody Jaybird-Woodpecker feud, his name reappears. As Wharton is describing the African Americans, the "undesirable politicians" who were being chased out of town by the Jaybirds, he briefly mentions Terry. His comment comes between a statement about a black restaurant owner who was read the proclamation of banishment "in a loud tone of voice" and a statement about "Tom Taylor, the other undesirable. . . . He and his brother were farmers and cattle thieves." The sequence of the narrative is strategic. Wharton places Terry in an ambiguous textual space:

> A negro [*sic*] restaurant keeper named Warren . . . was not in the resolution. . . . When the cavalcade reached his house he seized a gun and went to an upstairs window where he displayed it. He was at once covered with a hundred revolvers and came down to hear the resolution . . . in a loud tone of voice, after which he departed.
>
> Kyle Terry, who was with the marchers and an enthusiastic partisan of the Democratic Club movement, was in for doing violence to Warren, but was restrained.
>
> Tom Taylor, the other undesirable . . . was a County Commissioner and he and his brother were farmers and cattle thieves. (Wharton 1939, 202)

Wharton's sequencing is telling. Immediately after Wharton relates how Terry had to be restrained, his next comment concerns "Tom Taylor, the other undesirable." Taylor and Terry are conflated into one category. Tom Taylor and his brother, "big, black, burly fellows" who were "farmers and cattle thieves" were paired with Kyle Terry, a "big fellow."

Wharton creates a level of doubt about the man's origins, implying the question: How could a man sired by the colonel be so base? His descriptions of Kyle's violent nature remind me of Faulkner's writing. There is a moment in *Absalom, Absalom* when Thomas Sutpen's wife sees him fight his slaves in a performance he stages regularly for his friends. Sutpen and "his wild negroes" are "naked to the waist and gouging at one another's eyes." She imagines for a moment that Thomas himself is really black.[51] Faulkner reminds me that the boundary between white and black is much more fluid than is often assumed. It is not so much what people "really are," but more how they present themselves. Kyle's marking as a scalawag leads to other associations. A scalawag was a white person who sided politically with the freedmen after the Civil War. "Scalawag" can also mean scoundrel, or mongrel.[52] Kyle Terry's dilemma reads like Mark Twain's story of the false white master who betrays his "real" self. The most popular American writer at the time, Twain may have been voicing (or playing with) the concerns of worried white people in the novella *The Tragedy of Pudd'nhead Wilson*, where two babies, a wealthy planter's son and a white-looking slave infant, are switched. The proliferation of relationships between slave owners and their female slaves make *Pudd'nhead Wilson* a probable story anywhere in the South, making the issue of genealogy central to Southern white identity.

The plantocracy's denial of affiliation and identification with their African American slaves and workmen/women was often projected onto white people that were perceived to have broken the boundary of the caste system. The intimate relationships established (especially) on the more self-sufficient plantations such as Sugar Land significantly intertwined the lives of whites and blacks. The story/legend about the colonel's departure for the war places young Kyle with those plantation children who symbolically and emotionally had both black and white mothers.[53] The closeness of bathing, feeding, and constant care created intense emotional bonds, which ultimately became conflicted as the child grew older in a rigidly segregated society. The "full implications" of these relationships often caused "extreme discomfort" when these Southern white boys became men.[54] How black did a white child become when he was raised by a black mammy? Grace Hale writes of a woman named

Elisabeth Freeman, a "northern white woman" working in Texas in 1916. The editor of the *Waco Tribune* told Freeman that "only white southerners really understood African Americans. [Freeman explained,] 'He told me he was raised with them, had a colored mammy, nursed at her breast, etc.' 'Then,' I said, 'you are part colored.' At this he became very angry."[55]

Kyle Terry's behavior was not considered that of a Southern white gentleman. If race was judged by "appearance and behavior," the state of tension surrounding him could have easily fostered opinions that doubted his "whiteness."[56] Terry's identity would not have been the one to be scrutinized had the community been inclined to look elsewhere. In this moment, he had already been marked as the scapegoat and would receive the many projections of "unrecognized relationships" and possibly mislaid identities otherwise attributable to the rest of the county's whites.[57] Freeman proposed that, in the early twentieth century, three ghost stories haunted Southerners: white children and their black caretakers; white men and African American women; and, perhaps the most complicated, the resulting "mixed-race" children born to white men and black women. Faulkner's Southern planter, Thomas Sutpen, is caught in the condition of "slave production—that every master and every master's son is a black in white-face."[58] Sutpen sees his own face in his mixed-race son. With this recognition, Sutpen realizes that his grand design (plantation, home, social status, and other resources) could dematerialize as if it "had been built out of smoke."[59]

The racial boundary became dangerous after slavery ended. Whether biological, physical, or even political association, whites considered almost any contact or connection with African Americans to be socially or physically fatal. The only acceptable relations were those between employer and day laborer. The collapse of slave laws, which reduced the legal status of the master, left the whites vulnerable to contamination and even perhaps danger.

In the summer of 1888 the Jaybirds and Woodpeckers each held "elegant supper balls."[60] The Woodpeckers scheduled theirs first and decided to invite a number of Jaybirds. Highly affronted, the Jaybirds retaliated by redirecting the invitations. As a conscious insult, they were "readdressed and mailed to negro women prostitutes living north of the railroad track."[61] The neighborhood "north of the railroad track" was known as the county's red-light district, Mud Alley. It was public knowledge that mostly African American women and a few Mexican women prostitutes worked there. It was also commonly known that many white men used their services. Pauline Yelderman remarks in her book on the Jaybirds that Terry took the invitation incident "as a personal insult."[62] However, Yelderman, a college professor in a family of physicians, having lived all of her life in the county as a privileged white woman, knew that this type of affront to a white man, especially at the end of the nineteenth century, could easily have provoked murder. The Jaybirds who redirected the invitations were saying, in effect, that Kyle Terry had become a black man.

Terry confronted Volney Gibson at the railroad depot on the morning after the ball, telling Gibson, "The Jaybirds have been doing things I won't stand." Volney answered, "I would like to know what I am accused of doing." Terry "put his hand on his big nickel-plated pistol" as he responded, "Someone has sent out invitations to Negroes. If you did not send them, you know who did." Volney replied, "Anyone who accuses me of such things is a damned liar." This time Terry knocked him down and drew his gun again. Gibson was not armed. They walked a few steps as they talked, but then Terry slapped Gibson, knocking him down a second time. Volney was later arrested as he was leaving the Frost saloon on his way to the river bottom by the railroad bridge. He was carrying a Winchester. Terry was already at the river waiting for Gibson. The sheriff found him there and took away his gun.[63]

According to the planters' rules in Southeast Texas, Kyle Terry could have also become a hero. As did the other planters, he defended his honor by killing Ned Gibson. However, after Gibson's death, Kyle was informed that he would be killed if he returned to the county. For the next few months, it is said, he meandered about Galveston, drunken and slovenly, already having lost his father's inheritance. His wife and children had died some years before. His banishment from the county disallowed him from involvement in the Jaybird-Woodpecker feud. As previously noted, the feud was a battle between the all-white Jaybirds and the Woodpeckers (some of whom were black), and Kyle Terry was no longer considered white.

Thoroughbreds and Genealogy: The Descendants of Colonel Frank Terry

Great interest was manifest in fine horse stock and Churchill Fulshear had begun a racing stable which became famous. Dr. Mat Moore had bought 100 blooded mares and a great stallion that he called Frank Terry (Wharton 1939, 154).

Similar to Virginia plantation families, a number of planters in Fort Bend County "cultivated race horses,"[64] including Mat Moore, who in the early

1860s bought a stallion to breed with a hundred mares. The horse was named Frank Terry, after Col. Benjamin Franklin Terry, the county's Civil War hero. The possession of significant leisure and resources needed for the breeding of horses marked the planters as wealthy, aristocratic gentlemen. The raising of "fine horse stock" for racing was perfectly logical in a region where genealogy and "good breeding" were so vital.[65]

Fort Bend County has a certain resemblance to the island of Puerto Rico, where the more powerful families also gave critical importance to genealogy and "good breeding." The island at one time had many sugar plantations and vast numbers of slaves. For both places, this history continues to affect the present in many ways. Although no one in Fort Bend County would probably ever say (or maybe even think) this, in Puerto Rico it is common to hear people say that everybody on the island has at least a bit of African blood. Yet it is important to repeat that in 1890 there were nine thousand African Americans in Fort Bend County and only two thousand whites. There is no written narrative about any racial mixing in the area, yet stories of sexual relationships between white men and black women are thoroughly documented in literature on the South, both in scholarly texts and fiction.[66]

William Faulkner, whose novels are intensely immersed in the culture of the South, often focused on the South's internal conflict about race. Children from interracial relationships brought with them the ambiguity, conflict, and ambivalence initiated during their parents' sexual encounters. The tension surrounding these relationships created the ghosts that continue to haunt not only Puerto Rico but also Fort Bend County. In the latter, since the actual narratives are submerged or lost, a constant dialectic has surrounded whiteness and racial purity. Although far from resolved, Puerto Rico informally pays allegiance to its ghosts in its anecdotes on that bit of African blood in everyone on the island. I encountered remnants of this polemic at a provincial museum while on a visit to the island in October 2003. At the time I had not yet read about the "great stallion Frank Terry."

Attending an academic conference in San Juan, Puerto Rico, I was preoccupied at the time with a book proposal on racial mixing in Mexico that I was about to submit to a university press. I was already working on this present volume but had not yet connected Texas slavery with the pristine subdivisions that surrounded the focus of my project, an old Mexican cemetery. Two of us had ventured out from our Hilton Hotel in a rented car the day before and driven through the lush vegetation up and down the curving roads of the Puerto Rican countryside. Not very good with directions, I somehow missed a turn and ended up on the east side of the island, far from our intended desti-

nation to the south, the old city of Ponce. We arrived so late that we were able
to visit only El Centro de Cultura, where we bought some books and music.
When a young man at El Centro told us about a museum on a hill above the
city, we decided to return the following day.[67]

We arrived at the museum the next morning. It was a large estate with a
spectacular view overlooking the city of Ponce and had belonged at one time
to one of the "first families" of the city.[68] The walls of the mansion-turned-
museum were white stucco; the roof was Spanish tile. In the estate's elaborate
garden various colored flowers were blooming. We paid our three dollars each
at a small ticket booth at the end of the driveway. Our tour was scheduled at
ten. I was so struck with the landscaping that I entered the house after the
others. I couldn't find them initially, but heard their voices. I followed the
sounds through the hallways and up the steps made of dark red tile. The walls
were richly stained wood; the furnishings were from the early twentieth century. The family's lifestyle had obviously been elegant.

Many of the family's original furnishings and personal effects were exhibited in the museum, and a parlor and a large room served for entertaining. The dining table seated thirty people. Upstairs were many bedrooms.
The master bedroom had a small adjoining room that was specifically for the
seamstress who attended the mistress of the house. The house had a dumb-
waiter, and the servants' quarters were on the lower level. These rooms had
been converted into a small theater that showed a history of the plantation,
including its cultivation of sugar and the subsequent distillery that produced
Don Q Puerto Rican Rum. There was little mention of slavery. The Serrallés
family had constructed the estate during the Great Depression. I kept wondering why there was so much wealth here, when the rest of the world had
lost almost everything.

The gardens were outstanding; every imaginable flowering plant seemed
in evidence. Orchids grew in abundance in the large hothouse behind the
residence. They also grew in what seemed like appendages to many trees on
the property. Pathways with benches meandered throughout, giving the impression of a labyrinth. While sitting on one of the benches, I could see the
different levels of the garden and wondered who might have walked here during one of the presumably grand parties given by the family. Then I began to
notice the acorn-shaped shrubs. They were many, all large, perhaps as tall as
three or four feet. They gave the distinct impression of a penis, in the form of
a plant with many little green leaves. I mentioned this to my colleague, and
we laughed as we looked at the shrubs growing all around us.

The phallic "acorns" provided an introduction to the issues of sexuality, reproduction, and genealogy that confronted us as we entered the lower level of the museum. Visitors were provided an interesting conflation of family breeding and horse breeding. In the lower level of the house was a room with the family's genealogy meticulously detailed on a large wall. Nearby was a beautiful patio, full of flowers, with a fountain and small pool in the middle. Enclosed on all sides by the house, the patio was open to the second floor of the building, with skylights allowing the sun to shine through. In 2003 a wall of this patio contained the detailed genealogy of the family's most famous thoroughbred racehorse.

Breeding

Here is every encouragement to the breeding and rearing of slaves in the southern states of Virginia, Carolina, and Georgia, for sale, not only to the southern planters, but for export to Texas, a separate and independent republic (Maillaird 1842, 428).

The Old Three Hundred of Fort Bend County wanted to be like the Virginians. The idea of breeding racehorses would place them above the narratives of otherness. It was the only way they could redeem themselves. Perhaps if the Civil War had not intervened, Mat Major would have become an extremely wealthy planter in the county. His breeding of the stallion Frank Terry with a hundred mares would have produced numerous foals. If the stallion Frank Terry had possessed the qualities of the human Frank Terry, the next generation would have won every horse race in the South.

Well-bred people were produced by men and women who had "pure white" bloodlines. Even so, the trajectory of breeding human beings has additional meanings. The story of the great stallion Frank Terry and the hundred blooded mares could serve as a metaphor for all of the pure-bred white children produced by these fantastic unions. Male children would become model planters. Their father's genealogy would ensure their height, strength, leadership skills, and handsome features. The blooded mares would be certifiably pure, guaranteeing that no deplorable traits (especially excessive melatonin) would be visible in the offspring.

However, the problem with this idea is that white women were not supposed to have multiple partners, even if the sire were Colonel Frank Terry. Their chastity was as important as Terry's prowess. Since men were not as reliable when it came to their choice of reproductive partners, the white women of the county carried the responsibility of purity. It was up to them to produce well-bred white children.

The purity of the white women was most important. Were Mat Moore or Clarence Wharton unconsciously alluding to a harem? While it seems like an impossible thought, considering the dramatic excesses concerning references to the moral vicissitudes of the county's white women, it may have been the only way the men of the county could legitimately place any type of sexuality into their women. The idea of Frank Terry with one hundred pure, white, blooded women must have been very exciting. Since the idea was about horses, its intention—if about white human reproduction—could easily be denied.

There is another possibility as well. The story of the great stallion Frank Terry may have been a metaphor for the breeding of slaves. While written narratives about the county never mention miscegenation, stories of sex between white masters and female slaves are no longer speculation. These relationships have been documented from the beginning of slavery in the United States. In the late twentieth century, the nation's contorted acceptance of Thomas Jefferson's relationship with his slave Sally Hemings (and their resultant children) makes it no longer a subject to be avoided.[69] Slaves were bred like horses. While the offspring would not be "pure" in the sense of the stallion and the blooded mares, the infusion of white blood was also considered valuable. This did not make the children white, but some slave owners believed it made stronger "stock" and purposefully impregnated their female slaves for this reason.

New Orleans contained an entire society built on the concept of *mestizaje*. There, many elegant women, courtesans to the affluent white men of the city, maintained luxurious homes and raised "extra families" for these men. Faulkner, in his realistic novels of the South, describes this world of refinement. In *Absalom, Absalom!* we meet the quadroon wife of Charles Bon. Her beauty is almost beyond description, her skin is almond white, and her clothes are of the most recent fashion. Her manner is far more cultured than that of most white women in the South. She travels to Sutpen's Hundred, a Mississippi plantation where her husband lies buried. She arrives like a grand lady, in a carriage with her young son and a female servant. The boy is about five years old, dressed in silk and lace—a small boy-doll with dark, curly hair. Her maid is African American, a dark-skinned woman who comforts Mrs. Bon as she cries over her husband's grave.

Faulkner creates the ultimate Southern irony. Charles Bon, who as a wealthy, cultivated white man, attends the University of Mississippi, becomes the best friend of Henry Sutpen, visits Sutpen's Hundred, and is eventually betrothed to Henry Sutpen's sister, Judith. Shortly after the war ends, Henry murders Charles. The murder is provoked by the impossibility of Charles marrying Sutpen's daughter. Henry believes he is forced to kill Charles after Sutpen Senior informs him that Charles Bon is also his son.

Eulalia Bon, Charles's mother, is the dark-haired daughter of a French planter in Haiti. Her mother is said to have been Spanish. Sutpen migrates to the island with a grand plan to raise a fortune and create a proper family. After he rescues the planter's family and their plantation from ruin during the Haitian slave rebellion, he marries the daughter. After Eulalia has a child, Sutpen learns that she has African blood. He physically abandons his wife and child, while providing well for them financially. He returns to the United States and marries the daughter of a "fine Southern family."

Faulkner's motives focus on "the sins of the father." Sutpen's "sins" return to haunt him and ruin his new plan. Yet, I believe even more significant is the ambiguity of Charles Bon's racial identity. With money, education, and light skin, Charles Bon cannot be easily defined. How many others are there? How can white people know who they are? It is this ambiguity that produced terror in the South, ruptured the Confederacy after emancipation, and intensified throughout Reconstruction. A defining moment occurs when fear expands beyond the boundary of sanity. Desperation redefines the meaning of humanity, and the South turns itself back into an antebellum society without legal slavery. The definition of bondage is adapted to a new time. Instead, other words and phrases come alive. These include Jim Crow, lynching, sharecropping, prison labor, and the Ku Klux Klan. A need arises to clearly mark these ambiguous people so that the Charles Bons of the South will forcibly remain within the boundary of the new bondage. Freedom for them is dangerous. They must be eliminated, either physically or spiritually.

When All You Have Left Is Your Name

The white men of the county provided Kyle Terry repeated opportunities to prove himself a leader and a gentleman in the manner of his father, yet the young man was harshly judged for his indiscretions. The arrogance, impulsive behavior, and violence he exhibited were not significantly different from the conduct of other county white men.

The histories of the county describe large financial losses, with families selling off plantations after the Civil War. No skirmishes or battles took place in the area. The damage appears to have been financial and emotional. Kyle Terry's fortunes were strikingly altered by his father's death. The colonel's ingenuity might have kept the plantation together, had he lived. By the time Kyle was twenty-six, he had lost everything except his history.

After the colonel's death in 1861, William Kyle, Frank Terry's partner, managed the Sugar Land plantation. During the war, shortages of white men made it difficult to employ skilled laborers such as overseers and craftsmen. The blockade against the South diminished the market for cotton and made it almost impossible to obtain manufactured goods and equipment. Because the Sugar Land plantation was quite large, these problems made its continued operation almost impossible. Two months after Lee's surrender on April 9, 1865, federal troops disembarked in Galveston. The slaves were freed on June 19. The cotton crop that year was appropriated by the federal government, and many of the farms did not produce a crop in 1866. Robert Armstrong, in his history of the Imperial Sugar Company, writes of the Fort Bend plantations: "The fields which were once so productive were taken over by weeds; lack of maintenance and parts caused deterioration of buildings and machinery. Thousands of acres lay idle. Plantation values declined in some cases to 20 cents on the dollar. . . . Property evaluations had fallen from $2,600,000 in 1866 to $700,000 in 1870. The Fort Bend cattle population dropped from 100,000 in 1860 to 56,000 in 1870."[70]

Even with these considerable problems, the Sugar Land plantation continued functioning. Besides cotton, its main crop was sugar, which held at a high price after the war. In addition, the colonel's placement of a rail line to Sugar Land ensured a convenient connection to the sugar and cotton markets. The plantation had been developed into a functioning community before the colonel's death. This made it possible for the farm to sustain a significant group of day laborers and contract workers. Its large size and available housing for workers made the Sugar Land plantation one of the more successful sharecropping operations after the Civil War. The plantation also began to use prison labor after 1871.

Armstrong does not give a specific date but tells of a destructive grass fire that intensified when a great wind swept across the plantation. The Terry home burned down that day, along with the home of William Kyle. After this, the plantation could no longer function as a complete unit. It was subdivided among the heirs in 1875 and sold to Edward Cunningham after 1882.[71]

Misfortune continued to follow Terry. By 1888, his wife and one of his two children had died. There was a story that he was in love with the daughter of Judge Wesson Parker and had also declared himself a Woodpecker. Kyle had been on what was considered the "good" side of the feud until he joined ranks with the woman's father. Wharton denies that Parker would have considered Kyle for a son-in-law; it was only the influence of the Terry surname that convinced the Judge to allow Kyle into his political group.[72]

The position of Kyle Terry is pivotal in the history of the Jaybird-Woodpecker war. The tension between the Jaybirds and the Woodpeckers intensified after Gibson's death. At this point the people in Richmond believed that the situation was going to explode uncontrollably. If Terry so openly killed Gibson, there was no safety in allegiances. The Terrys were prone to violence, but their murderous rages had so far been directed to people outside their inner circle.

While never mentioned directly, the consistent criticism of Terry's behavior indicates at the least, disapproval and dissatisfaction in those who wrote about the feud. Clarence Wharton was the most vocal of critics. The author was a well-respected historian of Texas in the early twentieth century. He published eight books on Texas, in addition to a five-volume set titled *Texas Under Many Flags*. More importantly, he was partner at one of the most powerful and prestigious law firms in Texas: Baker and Botts. He was counsel for Houston Lighting and Power Company and the Houston Gas and Fuel Company.[73] These later became Reliant Energy and Enron Corporation. Wharton was within the circle of those men who were considered the founders of Texas industry. Wharton's voice endorses the official history of Texas. His implied disapproval of Kyle Terry's appearance and behavior explains how Wharton (and his contemporaries) perceived the origins and provocations of the Jaybird-Woodpecker feud. Wharton represents the power of Texas—then, as now, centered in the energy industry. In his narrative on the feud, Wharton implies that Kyle Terry, a poorly reared young man of possibly questionable origins, provoked the "good gentlemen" of the county into violence. No longer a legitimate heir, the colonel's youngest son became the scapegoat to be sacrificed in the service of purifying Fort Bend County.

Old and New Tragedies

. . . scalawags . . . [t]hese were, it is usually considered, the very lowest dregs of mankind; they were "southern white men . . . [who] sold themselves for office;" they were the veritable Esaus of the Caucasian race (Donald 1944, 447).

Pauline Yelderman describes the Woodpeckers as being "fused" with the blacks.[74] The term describes a loss of boundary, a melting down between two distinct entities, often in the blending of metals. Elise Lemire writes of a similar term, "amalgamation," used in the early nineteenth century. Technically considered as the process of joining together molten metals, it was used to describe the blending of "different race bloods."[75] Fusing and amalgamation are processes which melt down an object—a piece of metal—and attach it to another piece of metal.[76] In the late nineteenth century South the word "fuse" had a double entendre, indicating the duplicity surrounding sexual relations between white men and black women, which as a practice was quietly, yet clearly accepted. How strange and disturbing to use metallurgic terms for sex, the most intimate of behaviors. Is the employment of these terms an indication that sexual relationships between white men and black women were a mechanical process that excluded the human aspect? Then what is the nature of the children born of these relationships? The objectifying nature of their parents' relationship eliminates the white father's responsibility to the child, who in effect is just a product of a metallurgical process. Even though the colonel was not present to take responsibility for (and to legitimate) his son, the father's contemporaries could have stood in his place. Instead they denied the young man's legacy. Kyle became "fused" with nonpersons. Wharton's numerous disparaging comments show that the younger Terry was marked as a mistake of metallurgy, to be banished and humiliated.

Hubris

The problem originates in the fact that the father *(to whom one can be devoted)* no longer exists *(de Certeau 1988, 294).*

The coherence of the Southern way of life was shattered with the death of Frank Terry and the defeat of the Confederacy. In a sense, the South and the image of Frank Terry, the beautiful warrior, were one and the same. His mythological status (and disappearance) symbolized the South he fought for. By dreaming or reality, his descendants (cultural or biological) attempted to hold together the myth of that world long after his death. The reasoning that impelled his descendants to act is cloaked in excess. As de Certeau describes, a marriage between reason and "rubbish"—a narrative with a strong "element of grandeur"—blends with and overtakes the hubris of (in this case) the colonel, homogenizing the narrative into what seems almost like a hagi-ography.[77]

The colonel's (and his contemporaries') cavalier behavior creates a gen-eration of ambiguous, mulatto children who were seen by the planters as un-touchable "rubbish" that needed to be controlled or removed. After 1865 the Confederacy (as an official state) and the colonel were dead. An insatiable desire to continue a coherent Southern world led their descendants to con-struct narratives to cover their fathers' hubris with the death of what they had left behind, the "rubbish" of children who might question their rights to the fathers' symbolic inheritance. Narratives about white identity enhanced the colonel's reputation—while the hubris of his personal actions became increas-ingly nebular. Simultaneously, the death of the father/state created a hysteria of violence among his identifiably white descendants. Until a new father was designated, all of those who were seen as a threat to the dream and coherence of the Southern way of life were in danger of being eliminated.

The tragedy of Kyle Terry is related to the excessive presence of violence and desire. The individualism of nineteenth-century Texas allowed white men to construct a society that entitled them to the pleasure of transgression. Monetary debt was forgiven, murder was condoned, and concubinage with slave women and freedwomen was readily accepted.[78] This type of society was not considered "civil" and came to represent the slave-owning plantation re-gions of the Caribbean and the American South. As Joan Dayan points out, plantation regions—Southern colonial outposts—became known for their hedonistic societies. Saint Domingue gained such a reputation that the Mar-quis de Sade reportedly based his *One Hundred Twenty Days of Sodom* on life in the French colony there.[79] Southeast Texas was similar to de Sade's colonial slave society. It is also where the supposed gentrified colony met the uncon-trolled frontier of the Wild West.

The story of the outcast son in the plantation South has a mythologi-cal quality. The son, whether he is Kyle Terry the white son or Kyle Terry the black son of the planter, faces the consequences of his father's hubris. The tragedy for the privileged white sons was their loss of honor, as represented in their loss of agency and power over their political, social, and economic en-vironment. John Irwin's treatise on Faulkner and the South explains that "no one born in the South in this century and interested in literature can avoid . . . confronting the very personal significance of Faulkner's work to an under-standing of his own way of life."[80] That "way of life" is inexplicably tied to the South, where honor and a sense of privilege creates an "entitled" population. The sons of the slave and the planter are freed from bondage and then placed in the most precarious position imaginable. Kyle Terry was the mistreated, outcast son. His paternity was unacknowledged. Since he was no longer controlled by family ties, the planters and their families perceived him to be a vociferous animal, ready to kill, rape, and maim. Those with white skin can only be identified by their behavior. Whether white, yellow, or coffee brown, they have to be controlled or eliminated. Prophecies emanating from previous "slave rebellions" or "race wars" force the fathers to kill their unacknowledged sons.[81]

The son is not exactly sure who his father is. The father does not or cannot claim his son. In the colonel's situation, the father has died and is not able to give the son legitimacy. Still, there are clues to the young man's identity. He is large; he is violent; he is not successful. He failed his initiation to manhood. He has lost his property and his family. He has allied himself with questionable people. His father, the colonel, represents the South. The father has failed the son by rushing to his death in a useless effort to defend a decayed institution. In addition, the father has put his son's birthright in jeopardy by the excessive nature of his primal desires. Why else would Clarence Wharton write of the colonel as a pure bred stallion waiting to mate with one hundred mares? This overflow of carnality makes all of the colonel's children suspect. The remaining "fathers," local planters, have taken on the paternal role, especially the violent hero Henry Frost. Their obligation is to protect the myth of the father (therefore their own myth). Kyle Terry is defamed and banished as a generational incarnation of the colonel's primal desires. This probable son of the colonel and a slave, the son is destroying the county.

In the post-bellum South, and particularly in Fort Bend County, the unacknowledged son was condemned to tragedy. Before emancipation the child was born a slave, due to his mother's status. The control of the slaves and the extreme freedom of punishment exercised by the planters belied the possibility of disaster (at least in their minds), where slaves or freedmen would become so enraged at the planters they would kill all the whites in the county.[82] Similar to the attitudes of the white planters in San Domingue, the slave owners of the South (and the county) might have at certain moments wondered about the incongruity of fathering more slave children with their own slave women. The absolute control of the master provides a fantasy of safety; nothing can go wrong.[83]

The polemic intensifies after emancipation. There are no more bonds to control the behavior of the now-grown slave children. The new freedmen are armed with agency, voting rights, and political power. The ambivalent planter-fathers see only disaster in their sons. The county has a particular problem: in the post-Reconstruction era, thousands of former slaves migrate to Fort Bend. County planters believe they are in jeopardy. As previously noted, in 1890 there are over 9,000 African Americans, compared to less than 2,000 whites in Fort Bend.[84] Texts describe downtown Richmond as a "sea of darkness." According to numerous sources, the fertile Brazos Bottoms were bereft of white people because freedmen had taken over the area.[85]

The white planters fear the son not only for his supposed murderous inclinations but also for his mere presence. He is a reminder, the detritus of the father's illicit primal urges. He is the proven fact that the father is capable of polluting his own race/people. He is the actual evidence, therefore he must be eliminated. The son becomes the remainder, the outcast, the "spittle" that could "undermine" the father.[86] The mixed-raced son of the planter is consecutively displaced, first by his mother, who is taken away to perform her slave duties in the planter's home or the fields, and then by his half siblings, who are allowed to play with him as small children, but once they come of age are no longer allowed to associate as playmates for fear of contamination—especially if the white children are female.[87] After emancipation, the South has no place for the ambiguous son. His agency is feared the most.

Not all of the ambiguous sons were freedmen, and not all of them looked like black men. When I first considered the possibility that Kyle Terry was of mixed blood, the idea seemed almost ludicrous. In a conversation with literary historian Elizabeth DeLoughrey, I told her the story of Kyle Terry and his slave nursemaid. Elizabeth's first reaction was that the slave woman was his biological mother. *The Tragedy of Pudd'nhead Wilson* made the possibility sound even more plausible.

Published in 1894, four years after Kyle Terry's death, *The Tragedy of Pudd'nhead Wilson* is the tale of two blonde, blue-eyed boys who are switched at infancy. The slave child's mother, concerned that he would be sold sometime in the future, thought it would be safer to place him in the role of her white charge. But as Twain describes, the false white child, "Tom Driscoll . . . was a bad baby, from the very beginning. . . . [He] would claw anybody who came within reach of his nails, and pound anybody he could reach with his rattle. He would scream for water until he got it, and then throw cup and all on the floor and scream for more."[88] When Tom reaches adulthood, his mother admits to him that he is in reality a slave. Reacting to his violent nature, she tells him, "'It's de nigger in you, dat's what it is. Thirty-one parts o' you is white, en on'y one part nigger, en dat po' little one part is yo' soul.'"[89]

Liberal minded for his time, Twain, who decried lynching and the base nature of Southern culture, locates the wildness of the false Tom Driscoll inside his invisible African blood. Even Tom's biological mother believes this to be true. Is Twain asserting that the mark of the wild man remains even when his "bad blood" is indistinguishable? Described as having the "the widest public of any living American writer," Twain was mangled by a reviewer for overstepping the bounds of his genealogy (a man of respectable white genealogy should not write about miscegenation as if it were a common occurrence). In *Southern Magazine,* a reviewer asked, "Why it is that the Southern man who has an honest and decent pride in the fact that he comes of good stock fares so ill at the hands of certain literary gentlemen?"[90] Yet the reviewer's concerns relate to Kyle Terry's predicament when she notes that she has "more than once been asked by people who regarded themselves as very well informed if there were still in the South any pure blacks at all, or any pure-blooded whites." She blames the sentiment on Twain and other Southern writers who proliferated the assumption that "well-born gentlemen overstep the color line."[91]

Tore His Heart to Pieces: Cannibals and Polygamy

Galveston, Texas

A terrible tragedy was enacted in the courthouse here today [January 21, 1890, the day before the article's publication] in which Kyle Terry, nephew of Judge David Terry, was instantly killed. . . . The killing was the outcome of the Fort Bend troubles, which resulted some time ago in a battle between the citizens of Richmond. . . .

   A few minutes after . . . [10:00] Kyle Terry . . . and some others entered the front door of the Court House. Terry had turned toward the left towards the stairway, and had just reached the second step when the first shot was fired. It struck him under the right arm and came out under the left breast and literally tore his heart to pieces. There was a moment's lull and then four or five shots were fired from different directions. . . . Eyewitnesses say three men were shooting . . . all from Fort Bend County and all jaybirds [*sic*]. *New York Times,* January 22, 1890

Kyle Terry died in the Galveston courthouse five months after the Jaybird-Woodpecker confrontation. There were two murder trials from Fort Bend County that day. The first was for the murder of Robie Smith, an African American child who was shot during the violence in Richmond. The second was Terry's trial for his alleged murder of Ned Gibson. Terry was entering a stairway that led to a courtroom on the second floor. Volney Gibson was waiting for Terry "with both hands on his improved Colt-45 revolver." Kyle Terry was shot seven times, with the first bullet going through the heart. There is a story that Kyle had killed a Houston policeman some years before. In the confrontation, Terry drew his gun and the policeman attempted to draw his, but his gun became caught in the loop of his pants. Yelderman and other authors imply that Terry received justice because, when Gibson shot him, Terry's gun "caught in the loop of an undergarment."[92]

In the mythology of the México/Aztec Empire, narratives describe sacrifices in which the victim's heart is torn out of the body. As an act of barbarity, this practice often throws the multiplicity of Aztecan technological accomplishments into shadow.[93] In saying that Kyle Terry's heart was literally torn to pieces, the *New York Times* emphasizes the barbarity of Texas culture. Too far away to be involved in the subtleties of the demarcation of color, the *Times* was perhaps not aware of the battle over Kyle Terry's genealogy, or perhaps it was too easy to present a generalized conclusion that Texas was a barbaric state. And indeed, Texas convicted no one for the murder of Kyle Terry. Moreover, there is no known record of his burial place. His story is the "picture of savage society" as told by Southern gentlemen such as Clarence Wharton. The recorded narratives are "referential testimonies" to "identities formulated"[94] by discourse, releasing the observer (Wharton and other historians) from the stain of the primitive. Thus the assumptions of the *New York Times* and Fort Bend County historians are placed into the bodies of Kyle Terry and other ambiguous sons of the South.

The cannibalism of the highly developed México/Aztecs could in some ways resemble the savage behavior of the white planters of the county. The feud itself, which occurred in 1889, displayed a certain type of cannibalism. The planters turned on each other. Their violence devoured men from their own group. During the feud, a Texas Ranger (Ira Aten, who later became sheriff) reminded one Jaybird (Volney Gibson) that Volney would be shooting his own cousin. Gibson replied that his cousin "stopped being my kin when he became a Woodpecker-scalawag."[95]

The torture and maiming of slaves and later freedmen constituted an additional form of cannibalism. Burning, dismembering, and displaying the ears and fingers of the victims, as was common in the South (and probably in Fort Bend County), presented the victim's body as one to be cooked and consumed. Similar to when an animal eats its own offspring, many of the men who died were also family or children (whether acknowledged or not) of the "white caps" (KKK) who conducted these depraved spectacles.[96]

These familial relationships relate to Montaigne's idea of polygamy. The Southern gentleman's practice of having children by his slave women or (after emancipation) his domestic workers was considered the greatest trauma afflicted upon the marital relationship between the planter and his "legitimate," white wife. The practice of polygamy led to "extra" children, who then had to be "eaten alive" in order to protect the father and his white family.

The terror involved in all of this presses authors such as Clarence Wharton to seek out the savage and barbaric in those questionable citizens. The occulted cannibalism of the Southern gentleman is a foreignness (strange, barbaric, evil?) in the midst of what is ordinary (normal, near, quotidian, reliably the same?). The concept of projective identification lies heavily in the story of Fort Bend County. The heroes of the county projected their angst regarding their own barbarism and savagery onto Kyle Terry and the other black men.

Substituting the Father

Hereafter he must still give himself body and soul in order to receive the privilege of being a son *(de Certeau 1988, 300).*

According to local history, the social chaos that began with the death of the colonel and the loss of the Confederacy ended with the official birth of the Jaybird political party. Created with noble intentions and appearance, the organization based its bylaws on a centuries-old form of legal covenant. Yet, as de Certeau explains, the normal can hide the "persistence of the most uncanny things" when structures are established and "modeled according to law."[97] He proposes that the rules provided by patriarchy can produce the illusion of normalcy.

The hysterical violence of the feud occurring in front of the Richmond courthouse quickly transformed into an organized movement to establish a political brotherhood, a union of white men.[98] The change was sudden. In a matter of days there were rules and appointed officials: The Jaybirds created their own local government, based on the Magna Carta.[99] Association with this ancient English document added intensity to the pact signed by the group's members—increasing by tenfold the already powerful idea of a "pact" "that guarantees always (by an endlessly repeated lure) an assurance of existence to whomever 'applies' a law . . . [a] recourse against abandonment."[100] There was now a new structure to protect the white men of the county from danger, abandonment, and defilement. They had replaced the father.

They wrote a constitution giving only white men the vote in their political primaries, effectively disenfranchising all men of color in the county. The laws of the new party would run out of Fort Bend County any white man who refused to sign an agreement with the constitution. Those who signed became members of a brotherhood that officially sanctioned violence against those who had not (or could not) join the new family. Murder and other forms of violence against white men (by black men) were eliminated after the official inauguration of the Jaybird Party. Yet, the murders of black men (and the rape of black women) continued before and afterward in many different forms. All that had changed was the law. Again de Certeau reminds his readers that "the devil of yesterday is replaced by so many other successive nurturing laws, 'diabolical assurances drawn from a knowledge, a clientele, a confinement . . . thanks to the privilege of being a son'"—the right kind of son.[101]

Jim Crow officially began in Fort Bend County when the Jaybird constitution was signed. By 1890 the antebellum South had effectively been recreated.

Chapter four

River of the Demonic: The Brazos

This "displaced" ghost haunts the new dwelling. It remains the rightful heir in the spot that we occupy in his . . . place (de Certeau 1988, 345).

In 2005 the last Fort Bend County acreage available to developers was sold. The Texas Department of Corrections sold most of its county land. Master-planned suburban developments will soon be built, and the Brazos River bridge on U.S. Highway 59 is being expanded. The old Brazos Bottoms will decorate the new communities. The towering trees and dramatic drop down the steep banks of the river will be an exotic attraction to prospective homeowners. The vines and small trees provide a layer of green over the red dirt bordering the Brazos. Michel de Certeau explains that we may attempt to displace old ghosts with our new dwellings, but they never really go away.[1] The slaves, prisoners, and sharecroppers that worked the plantations bordering the Brazos are the historical heirs of this place.

Those who named the Brazos River *Brazos de Dios* may have been thinking that the powerful arms of God would bring prosperity to those who settled near its embankment. The fecundity of the land had no rivals.[2] It could be compared to the Fertile Crescent or the richness of the land bordering the Nile. The fertility of what came to be called the Brazos Bottoms created unlimited wealth for those fortunate enough to negotiate land titles. However, there is an unfortunate paradox created by this place of bounty. The fertility of the land spilled over into the fertility of the planters/slaveowners. They produced generations of the mixed-blood children that decades later faced unspeakable violence from their own blood-kin. The hopeful Arms of God reversed itself into a space of the demonic. The water of the river would be a dark red if it could show all the blood spilled on its banks these past two hundred years. During the antebellum era it was known to be the worst place to be a slave.[3] In the early twentieth century people called it the *hell hole of the Brazos*.[4] The incongruity continues in the idealistic mythology proliferated through local narratives of a wild Eden where hard-working migrants from the eastern United States fought with nature and built an empire.

Phantoms in the Water

Approaching the city of Kendleton on United States Highway 59 over a bridge about twelve miles southwest of Rosenberg in Fort Bend County, there is a white sign announcing Turkey Creek. In the spring of 2005, as I traveled past the sign on my way to a funeral in South Texas, I remembered a story told to me by a woman named Marjorie Adams. Driving seventy miles per hour on Hwy 59, a freeway between Houston and the city of Victoria, I looked quickly below the bridge, catching a glimpse of a gully; there was no water. Mrs. Adams had impressed upon me the importance of the site. However, the significance of her narrative did not become immediate until I actually saw the words "Turkey Creek" spelled out on the sign. I'm reminded that written words entering our field of vision imitate the presence of reality. The text that announces the location of Turkey Creek "neither preserves nor restores an initial content, as this is forever lost (forgotten)."[5] Yet, it provides a clue to the past. Since death is on my mind as I travel to the funeral of my relative, I think of the deaths associated with the creek. I wonder if I will ever know the real story. Regardless of my postmodern sensibilities, I am seduced by the need to prove that something really happened. Marjorie Adams described an event that involved at least a hundred individuals; numerous people were killed. It was a bloody confrontation between the blacks in Kendleton and the county sheriff's deputies. She gave me an approximate date, and I searched through old newspaper microfilms but found nothing about Turkey Creek. How could something so big just disappear?

Cognizant of the variability of narratives, I realize it is possible that the Turkey Creek event never happened. The necessity (and lack) of archival documents makes the tale a fantasy in my mind or that of Marjorie Adams. However, the mere existence of the narrative is significant.

Marjorie Adams is an impressive woman. She is tall and attractive, with snowy white hair and a dignified presence. Before I knew her well, I imagined her as a retired schoolteacher, and she is a teacher of sorts, a teacher of history. Her life is a narrative of legal and social histories. As a young woman, she was the secretary of the Fort Bend chapter of the National Association for the Advancement of Colored People. Her paternal uncle, Willie Melton, was a plaintiff in a 1953 U.S. Supreme Court Case known as *Terry vs. Adams,* also described as the "last of the white primary cases." These lawsuits were significant in that they brought down the exclusive right of private political parties consisting of only white voters (and candidates) to hold primaries that de facto elected their own members.[6] Adams's maternal grandfather was a Methodist minister with a church in Wallis (just outside the county). She was president of the Kendleton Heritage Society.

On a cool predawn morning in November 2004 I drive south on Highway 59 toward Kendleton. Marjorie Adams and I are traveling together to Austin. She will be attending a committee meeting of the Texas Historical Association. In an effort to have a several hours to speak with her, I had offered to drive her to the meeting. As I drive toward Kendleton, I remember how the city police were known for their strict enforcement of speed limits. Almost everyone I know has been given a speeding ticket in Kendleton. No other town between Houston and Victoria has the same reputation. There were many complaints in the last half of the twentieth century about the Kendleton police. Even a Catholic priest I knew had once been fined for going five miles over the speed limit. In the early 1980s I asked someone from Kendleton about the ticket situation. She told me the traffic that flew through Kendleton on Highway 59 was dangerous; there were numerous fatal accidents. She told me about a couple who were driving through town while the wife was eating a sandwich. They were involved in an accident, and the wife died with her hand still holding the sandwich. After that conversation I always put my car on cruise control (and set at the speed limit) when I drove through Kendleton.

By 2004, the freeway had bypassed most of Kendleton. I drive slowly through town at 5:30 A.M. and turn by the grocery store. I must drive an additional two miles and cross a railroad track before I pass Marjorie Adams's house. At first, I don't realize it is the right house, but then I see the figure of a tall woman standing in the front yard. As I drive toward Austin for the next two and a half hours, Adams begins to tell me about Kendleton. I know some of her story. Some people called the town "the slave colony." A Mr. Kendall sold the land to former slaves, who began a community whose political impact was felt far beyond the boundaries of the county.

She tells me the Brazos River holds many stories. There are stories of disappearances, murders, lynchings, bodies being thrown into the river, and houses being burned with whole families inside. I ask her why these things are not written anywhere.

She said it was the rule of the county; people had to keep secrets, or bad things would happen to them. She tells me of a woman named Arizona Fleming, a businesswoman who owned a funeral home in Richmond. Fleming was a strong, independent woman, respected in the community. Adams said Fleming spoke out too many times as a racial activist and she died impoverished. I knew about Fleming. One year, while I was in high school, I sat next to Ms. Fleming's granddaughter Mamie in speech class. When I told my father about my conversations with Mamie, he told me about Arizona, and described her as a woman to reckon with. My father had also been successful during the same decades that Fleming had her business. He was able to retain his wealth for a much longer period. Adams said this was because he was much more careful about how he related to the county power base. Perhaps Adams is correct. My father seemed to know how to straddle the boundary between civic activism and political cronyism, often telling me how in the 1950s and 1960s he would give the county attorney a bottle of scotch every few months so that when he asked for a favor, his request was often granted.

The county was and still is full of secrets. In the early 1990s, Leslie Lovett, a Rice University graduate student wrote a master's thesis about the Jaybird-Woodpecker Feud.[7] When I spoke with Lovett in 2004 she told me that during her entire research project she felt uneasy as she searched archives and interviewed county residents. She had a feeling of eminent danger should she ask too many questions or probe too deeply.

Two years before speaking to Lovett I encountered another curious narrative. I was sitting at a small table at a university reception for a Nobel Prize winner. Department faculty were expected to attend. Attempting to recover from the boredom of academic small talk, I sat at a small table with a fellow faculty member who had the same last name as one of the familiess involved in the Jaybird-Woodpecker Feud. We began talking about my research project in Fort Bend County. She then told me about a secret book, kept for over a century in the vault of one of the older churches in Richmond. The book is said to contain a list of all the crimes and murders that have occurred in the county, including those never prosecuted. Later that year I spoke with the county's district attorney. I asked him about the book. He did not give me any actual information confirming the book's existence, yet he did not indicate surprise at my question. The chronology of deaths located in the secret book (which may or may not exist) is a phantasmic record of the county's road to power. The bodies of those listed were laid down like stepping-stones to progress. The county has been consistently one of most prosperous in Texas.

There are stories about other murders among the planter class, and a few black men who were killed. Yet Marjorie Adams insists there were many more. Leon Litwack, in writing about racial violence in the South, explains that few murders were reported because of "the difficulty in obtaining evidence and testimony." White men avoided depositions because of "fear of personal violence;" freedmen would not report assaults against them because they would not be protected by local law enforcement.[8]

Many of the tensions in the county are said to have come from Reconstruction and the restrictions placed on Confederate sympathizers. The Civil War left its mark on the county. The fantastic wealth that preceded the conflict was gone. The response to the loss, combined with the emancipation of the slaves in 1865, destroyed the structure of that world, producing a complete inversion of the social order. Existing histories describe violence and chaos for the next twenty-three years; county government was in constant turmoil. After 1889, these histories report that legal order was restored for the Anglo/white population. They do not mention all the other types of terror that continued in the Brazos Bottoms.

Re-Construction and Destruction

After the war, the planters were enraged much of the time because of the restrictions brought in by the Reconstruction government. Freedmen were disappointed in the lack of true freedom after their official release from bondage. Having little or no resources after emancipation, Union offers of support, such as "forty acres and a mule," never materialized, even though they were temporarily considered after the end of the war. The planters used this against the African Americans, accusing the black men of making stories up in saying they were going to get free acreage and a mule. The perception of and resentment toward freedmen's expectations of Union recompense was still evident in 1979, when Fort Bend resident (and University of Houston faculty member) Pauline Yelderman published a history of the Jaybird-Woodpecker Feud. Yelderman states that county freedmen imagined the story of the forty acres, which is remarkable considering her academic background. How could she have missed the readily available documented evidence? The Reconstructionist government did have a plan of giving freedmen forty acres and a mule, but it was never implemented.[9]

Through the political aspirations of the national Republican Party who, as a group, believed that the additional votes brought in by freedmen would allow them to continue their control of the government, blacks were given suffrage.[10] The plan was successful; after the fifteenth amendment was ratified, county Republican voters outnumbered Democrats 20 to 1. Thus, a number of African American men were elected to county office. Reports say a few local planters paid the security bond (usually in the thousands of dollars) that was required of these politicians. The planters were consequently designated scalawags.[11] Ultimately, the division between the Republican scalawags and the Democrat planters transformed into open, violent conflict.

The Jaybird-Woodpecker Feud (discussed in Chapter 3) compelled the governor to call in the Texas Rangers and establish martial law. Once the flurry of public killings ceased, a veneer of controlled calm was established with the presence of Jim Crow. The white men of the county wrote their own constitution, as if they were creating their own countywide republic. In it, they delineated the rights and obligations of the county's white men. They reinvented their world, reworking and retrieving the surety of their antebellum social and political positions.

From the moment the local regiment (Terry's Texas Rangers), left their plantations to go to war in 1861, until the violent moment when the white men of the county began to kill each other in 1889, the question of Southern authority remained ambiguous and questionable. After two decades of uncertainty, the Jaybird Constitution of 1889 brought about something akin to a postbellum world that retained an antebellum way of life. It was so rigid and impermeable that only a United States Supreme Court ruling was able to dismantle the 1889 constitution. This finally occurred in 1953. Even so, the Supreme Court decision that made voting possible for African Americans remained in many ways a hollow pronouncement: the Jaybird political party that excluded non-whites from voting in its primaries no longer existed. Unfortunately, many other inequities remained—some larger, some smaller. As Avery Gordon reminds us, ". . . freedom is not secured when the state proclaims it thus. The pronouncement only inaugurates the lengthy walk in to the discriminating contradictions of the newly heralded modernity."[12]

Little Pieces of Rope: Walnut Bend Plantation, Oyster Creek—August 1888

Nineteenth-century newspapers and public records from Fort Bend County report continuous incidents of violence. Curiously missing are narratives about lynching. The only reference to a lynching is in the *Handbook of Texas Online*.[13] In 1869 an accused horse thief was taken from the jail in Richmond and hung from the Brazos River bridge.[14] No mention is made of his name or race. In addition, although not technically a lynching, the hanging of William Caldwell was a similarly public event. After the United States Supreme Court refused to review his case, he was returned to Texas for hanging. A few Fort Bend County men attended the event and returned home with pieces of the hanging rope pinned to their lapels.[15]

Marjorie Adams tells of many murders, lynchings, and disappearances. When I tell her I could find nothing on lynching in the county, she responds with stories about bodies floating down the Brazos River. It was the best place for disposal. Where are the stories? I asked her. People know, but don't say, she tells me. If someone were watching the river they would know many things. If the river could tell us what it knows, we would have the stories. There are, however, narratives about certain people, such as plantation owner J. M. Shamblin and the story of his death. The man executed for Shamblin's murder was given a most fair trial, as historian Clarence Wharton noted. The defendant had one of the region's best lawyers, A. C. Allen, son of one of Houston's founders.[16] The notation of fairness belies the more sinister face of men cutting an executioner's rope into souvenir pieces so that they could return home with the remnants of another man's death. The bit of rope adorning their clothing was like a badge, marking them as present when their friend's murder was avenged.

William Caldwell was executed for the murder of J. M. Shamblin. The deceased, a former justice of the peace, is described as an attractive and civilized man who was not afraid to use a whip on his black workers. Regardless of what he was really like, J. M. Shamblin was portrayed as a righteous man. C. L. Sonnichsen's manuscript, originally published in 1951, delineates the dead man's exemplary status: "handsome and aristocratic in appearance," within the fold of those "first families of the county."[17] In the same manner as Clarence Wharton, Sonnichsen overlays with nostalgia the righteous and valued quality of the hero. He gives Shamblin the biography of a pious man with family gathered near him. The exact date he was killed is repeated as the landmark for the beginning of the Jaybird-Woodpecker feud.

In a peaceful environment, surrounded by family as he read the words of God, Shamblin's life ended abruptly. As he was reading the Bible, someone fired a shot through the sitting room window. It was buckshot; Shamblin was hit, as was his Bible and the hallway of his house. His wife and sister had been sitting at a table while his "little daughter" Maude was "playing on the floor."[18] The family is sitting closely together on a summer's evening with the father reading the Bible; the father-in-law, W. D. Fields, lives in such close proximity that he not only hears the gunshot but is sensitive to the dangerous meaning of the sound. In his concern he rushes to his daughter's home. The shot that breaks through the glass of the Shamblin sitting room rudely interrupts the idyllic family portrait.

A doctor named Mayfield was called. He worked at the prison farm a short distance away. After examining the wounded man, Mayfield told the family that Shamblin would only live a few hours. Before dying Shamblin told Fields that a note found on the front porch had been written by one of his tenant farmers, William Caldwell.

The South's world of polite manners and deference allowed for occasional anomaly. The outspoken nature of Frank Terry was admired; so was that of J. M. Shamblin. As Clarence Wharton's 1939 text described Frank Terry in the most illustrious terms, C.L. Sonnichsen did for Shamblin his book, published twenty-three years later. Shamblin was "a man of strong personality" and "swung plenty of weight . . . the Jaybird Interest." Throughout the summer of he spoke at public gatherings and met privately with "negroes." "Some say he turned the scale against himself by running a bunch of electioneering darkies off his plantation with a cowhide whip."[19]

The power and admired arrogance ascribed to Terry and Shamblin was seen as inappropriate in less popular white men of the county and totally unacceptable in anyone else. The threat of the cowhide whip was significant in that it might have influenced Shamblin's assassin(s). The unquestioned acceptability of using the whip to eject people from his property indicates the incongruence of Sonnichsen's description. How could Shamblin present an aristocratic demeanor while simultaneously using a cowhide whip on human beings? The meaning of the term "aristocrat" in that space and time did not rule out violent behavior. In addition, violent behavior was even more acceptable if it were toward people who were not considered human beings. In this situation, Shamblin had attempted to subvert the voting power of local African Americans. The response to Shamblin's threats was delivered in a note found by Fields. It was placed on the gatepost during the night. From Wharton's *History:*

> . . . Mr. Shamblin: You have been Holding democratic meeting with the negroes [sic] and you have said that eny [sic] negro [sic]don't vote a democratic ticket on the election day is sticking a knife in your chiles [sic] side . . . the Republican parties is going to holdup their heads if they die hard we will have no democrate [sic] to mislead the ignent [sic] Negro Race astray. You are a man to lead them a stray and then cut their throats and suck their blud [sic]. I am a republican and have no use for a damn democrat this is a lesson to all damn cut throat democrats to hold noe [sic] more meetings with the ignorent [sic] negro [sic] race of people.[20]

Shamblin's threat of whipping black Republicans is minimized. The consensus was that someone wanted Shamblin dead because he was to be a witness in an upcoming trial involving the theft of a cotton bale. According to Sonnichsen, there were three African Americans involved in the theft. One was Hudson Caldwell, who may have been William Caldwell's brother (although this is not clarified by any of the authors). A second man who "turned state's evidence" was later poisoned by Hudson Caldwell's wife.[21] Wharton stated in one of his previous texts that the man's name was Ike Brown, describing him as "a negro witness against them [who] had died suddenly and it was thought Caldwell . . . poisoned him."[22]

As a response to the invisible presence of lynching in the county, the theme of restraint surfaces alongside William Caldwell's story. Sonnichsen writes that while Caldwell was in the Richmond jail, "some young Jaybirds had serious thoughts of lynching him."[23] The author notes that Sheriff Garvey was firm, and because of his "coolness . . . nothing regrettable happened. When the boys began to collect in front of the jail, he told them they couldn't have Caldwell without killing the sheriff and his deputy first." In addition, Caldwell "was not molested when he was brought back for his preliminary trial."[24] At the end of his narrative about Shamblin's death, Sonnichsen questions whether Caldwell acted alone, stating that "most people [were] wondering if the Negro had planned his own crime."[25] He continues: "The Jaybirds printed a proclamation in the Houston and Galveston papers resolving that 'the assassination of J. M. Shamblin is laid at the door of the Republicans of Fort Bend County.'" The Republicans denied the allegation, but Sonnichsen continued to imply that the reason for the murder was more political than personal. Caldwell's guilt was detailed in the texts written about the feud. Wharton specifically pronounced that the accused was given the best representation and a very fair trial. He informed the reader that this was the first criminal case heard in the Harris County Criminal Court, giving the names of the attorneys involved.[26]

Frost and the Brahma Bull and Red-Hot Saloon: Richmond Texas— September 3, 1888

The owner of the Brahma Bull and Red-Hot Saloon in downtown Richmond was named Henry H. Frost. The name of his saloon was an appropriate descriptor of his personality. In mid-August, Frost attended a social gathering in Pittsville. The town, which no longer exists, was located in the northern part

of the county. The occasion was a political gathering and barbeque, with numerous flowery political speeches, lots of drinking, and dancing. There is no
specific number of how many attended, but from the descriptions it sounds
like at least a hundred people or more were there. Sonnichsen writes, "By noon
there was a good crowd. As afternoon progressed, the buggies and hacks continued to accumulate until it seemed like the countryside from miles around
must be depopulated."[27] Along with the drinking and political oratory came
provocative behavior: Henry Frost physically and verbally intimidated three
different men that day. Frost told Clem Bassett (who later became sheriff)
to stand aside or his badge would be torn off. While a Judge Parker was speaking on the benefits of his political faction (the Cleveland and Thurman Party),
Frost demanded Parker explain how he could be a Democrat. Even though
Parker went for his gun and Frost grabbed his knife, they were merely postur-
ing, since neither one proceeded to attack the other. The third incident has
no real explanation. Frost's next target was his childhood friend, Jack Randal (who was white), the deputy tax assessor (assistant to African American
Henry Ferguson). Frost walked past Randal and called him Henry Ferguson.
Two weeks later, Frost was shot by an unknown assailant.

Parker, Bassett, and Randal were said to be undecided about joining the
Jaybirds, meaning they would still be considered scalawags. Yelderman, in the
most detailed text written on the feud explains that this "irritated" Frost.[28]
She blandly lists the affronts initiated by Frost, without any type of commentary on his behavior. Yelderman's positioning is curious because of her lack
of reserve in critiquing other people in the story, especially if they were African American. Frost had recently become the leader of the Jaybird Party, and
perhaps needed to take an aggressive position because of his newly acquired
authority. Even so, he would have been aware of the risk involved. The rules
of the day equated verbally confrontive behavior with threats of violence, especially if he called a white man by the name of an African American.

On the evening of September 3, Frost was shot as he closed up his saloon.
He was twenty feet from his front door. One bullet hit his arm and back,
another grazed his hat. His convalescence in a Galveston hospital took two
months. Sonnichsen adds to Frost's hyper-masculine persona by describing
his calm reaction to his attempted murder: "He neither fell nor wavered, but
marched on through his own door and coolly informed his family" of the
shooting.[29] Even though Frost did not know who attacked him, he indicated
that his friend Jack Randal had been involved in the shooting. The sheriff
promptly arrested Randal.

The Ellis plantation kept bloodhounds because they used convict labor.

Within three hours of the shooting, the dogs "were on the ground."[30] The dogs found a trail to the cabin of a black family. Fifty armed men were standing outside when a man came to the door with a gun. Three men were arrested, including a schoolteacher named John Donovan.

Four days before Frost was shot, an African American named Jim Bearfield from Sartatia (just west of Sugar Land) had been injured in the neck and hand by someone who shot through the door of his house. Sonnichsen describes the man as coming "to town in a panic with a small wound on his neck and a badly mangled hand."[31] Bearfield was convinced the attack was related to his knowing "the identity of the men who had whipped" two blacks in late August. Bearfield "swore out a warrant for H. H. Frost as one of his attackers"(ibid). Sonnichsen's relating of Bearfield's narrative as a preview to Frost's shooting indicates an association between the two events.[32] Bearfield was shot and responded with panic. One of his wounds was "small." Frost, in comparison, "calmly" walked into his house, even though his injury was so severe he was hospitalized for two months. Bearfield was less of a man since he exhibited panic, as did Frost's family (we can probably assume by "his family," Sonnichsen meant women and children although Sonnichsen is unclear about the family make-up). Bearfield's wound was small, but he panicked and sought "legal means" to respond to Frost. The idea that a black man would have the right to seek legal protection was absurd in the eyes of Frost and his cohorts. In narratives written about this era, men did not seek legal means for protection; they created their own "force," so to speak. This happened the day after Frost was shot.[33]

An Outraged People: Richmond, Texas—September 4, 1888

. . . feuds occur especially when law and order cannot be appealed to and a man has to right his own wrongs. "There are times when patience ceases to be a virtue . . ." (Sonnichsen 1962, 316).

By the mid-twentieth century the roads of Fort Bend County still made travel slow and cumbersome.[34] In rain it was almost impossible to travel between Richmond and most of the surrounding small towns. Yet, sixty years earlier, on September 4, 1888, hundreds of men were able to travel from all parts of the county to the Richmond courthouse within hours of the attack on Frost. By one P.M. the day after Frost was injured, four hundred white men arrived

at the courthouse from all over the county. What would propel so many men
to leave their work and travel for miles across bad roads on a moment's notice? How were they notified so quickly? The news of Frost's shooting must
have flown like a prairie fire from farm to farm. Many people had to stop their
work to inform their neighbors in time so all could arrive by one P.M. on September 4.[35] Gathering large groups of men was important. There had to be a
significant show of force.

According to historian Clarence Wharton, Richmond, the county seat of
Fort Bend, was named after Richmond, Virginia.[36] The allusions to Virginia's
aristocracy flavored the identity of the city. The white residents were mostly
descendants of Austin's Old Three Hundred. Within fifty years the group had
acquired an enviable pedigree. Numerous plantation-style homes surrounding downtown Richmond attested to the wealth of the county. Their white
walls and columns paralleled the whiteness of the settlers. Their identity was
worn like a badge of honor, allowing them to enter a space of power, privilege,
and entitlement. By 1951 Sonnichsen was writing that Austin's first settlers
could trace their ancestry "to the first families of Virginia, and even to William the Conqueror."[37] The mark of the three hundred protected them from
contamination and engendered any support, cooperation, or subservience
needed from anyone of a lesser position. In texts, newspapers, conversations,
and legal documents, the designation of Old Three Hundred provided a context for being above the rest of local society. It also nullified the constraints of
civil and criminal law.

The mark of privilege however, did not secure them from Reconstructionist policies. A man could not have served in the Confederate Army or
have voted for Secession to take the "ironclad oath." This eliminated most of
the county's white men. In 1867, registered voters numbered 152 white men
and 1,334 blacks. Aside from voting, county demographics became embroiled
in a giant migration. By 1888, the Old Three Hundred found themselves surrounded. Like a wagon train encircling for security, they found their numbers
smaller and smaller. Texas' geographic location, on the edge of the Southern
states and with such close proximity to Mexico, made it a natural destination
for many freed slaves. As stated in Chapter 3, the 1890 United States Census
found 8,981 African Americans to 1,605 whites.[38] Fort Bend County became
a precursor to twentieth century South Africa's demographic inversion. Sonnichsen's narrative is vivid: . . . From everywhere, particularly on Saturdays,
came a dark river of Negroes which overflowed the town. It flooded Railroad
Street so deep that trains had to hoot themselves hoarse in order to get a clear
track.[39] What concerned Sonnichsen even more was that "they could and did

vote and were the deciding force in local elections" because they "outnumbered the whites . . . four to one."[40]

The men that gathered at the courthouse after Frost was shot needed to form a group of many numbers. Although fear is never mentioned in any descriptions of Southern men, what other motive could garner such a response? Even four hundred men seemed minimal compared to a population of almost 9,000 African Americans. Rumors of black uprisings had circulated from time to time. There had been numerous slave uprisings in Texas the last few years before the Civil War.[41] Narratives about Nat Turner and the Haitian slave uprising were significant in Southern folklore long after slavery was abolished in the United States.[42] It had only been fifty years since the battle of the Alamo, where less than two hundred (mostly) white men died fighting, killed by five thousand Mexican soldiers. Other massacres, such as the 1842 Mier expedition (where two hundred Texans faced 2,000 Mexican soldiers) have been detailed in county history books, since there were county men among the soldiers. Described as a tragedy, where men who had surrendered drew beans to determine their fate, seventeen men that had chosen black beans were executed. A few that drew the white beans were released and eventually made it back to the county. The idea of being surrounded by a darker enemy foreshadows tragic consequences. Sowell's 1904 history of the county mentions in passing that the Mier expedition occurred after the Mexican army was defeated and driven back to Mexico. The men who formed the Mier expedition "were not satisfied" with the results "and were anxious to invade the Mexican country and fight them there also."[43] The issue of provocation is minimized; the aggressor is made the hero.

The day after Frost was shot, four hundred men, with Clem Bassett as presiding officer, agreed to a proclamation that placed responsibility for Shamblin's assassination and Frost's attempted murder on the leaders of the county's Republican party. They denied "hostility to, and have no fight to make with the laboring negroes [sic] of this county." Taking a paternalistic stance, the proclamation continues: ". . . we pledge to them to secure to them rights which we claim, safety in their homes and the right to live without fear of assassination."

Again the theme of restraint emerged. Yelderman reports talk of lynching, "but the more moderate view prevailed."[44] The group drew up a list of "undesirable" African Americans who "were ordered to leave the county."[45] This banishment was for "the public good"(ibid). The college-educated Charles Ferguson, three-term district clerk, was listed. Described as "a very aggressive person," he had been designated a delegate to the Republican National Convention. Along with Charles Ferguson were two schoolteachers, a restaurant owner, a barber, and the county commissioner, who was Ferguson's brother.[46] Peter Warren, the restaurant owner, was added later, after he stood at his second story window and pointed his gun at a group of Jaybirds approaching his home. Those on the list had ten hours to leave the county.[47] Charlie's brother, county tax assessor Henry Ferguson, was initially listed but later removed. Yet, after the feud, he sold his Fort Bend plantation and moved to Houston.[48]

After the meeting, in a scene that evokes more fiction than reality, the four hundred men rode as a "body in double file to the homes of the negroes living in Richmond."[49] They were heavily armed. Peter Warren had no choice but to give up or be shot; he resisted, but ". . . [i]mmediately hundreds of cocked guns were aimed at him."[50] By the next day, all the men listed had left Richmond.

The next task of the Jaybirds was to ride out to Kendleton, called the "Negro colony," on the San Bernard River, eighteen miles southwest of Richmond. A small group of men attended to this. Their main objective was to run Tom Taylor, the county commissioner, out of the county. Wharton and Sonnichsen describe him as a cattle thief.[51] The Taylors resisted, telling the Jaybirds, "We are not going to leave . . . until we are packed out in our coffins."[52] Wharton describes the scene:

> [The] . . . warning committee . . . reached the Taylor ranch at nightfall and did not make as impressive demonstration as the three hundred had done in the afternoon.
>
> Tom and his brother Jack, big, black, burly fellows, defied the committee. The visitors had been instructed not to use force and had promised to refrain from violence unless driven to it in self-defense. But for this the Taylors would have "gone out" that night. Tom told them that they were instigated by Mr. W. M. Darst (whose ranch was on the Bernard a few miles below and from whom they had been stealing cattle for years) and that he would get Mr. Darst. Darst was a member of this committee and heard the threat.
>
> Kyle Terry, who was with the committee visiting Kendleton, was in for doing violence to Tom and was restrained with much difficulty.[53]

The Santa Fe Railroad agent at Thompson (three miles east of Richmond) wired the Richmond agent, informing him that Henry Ferguson "was about to cross the Brazos with hundreds of armed negroes [sic] on his way to aid the Taylors in the Colony."[54] One-hundred-fifty men came to Richmond once they heard the news about the Taylors. Forty of them, armed with Winchesters, boarded the train for Kendleton the following morning. After they left, Wharton writes that the sheriff wired the governor of Texas and requested the Texas Rangers. That same week a military company was organized, with the governor placing a Colonel Pearson in command. The adjutant general ordered the Rutherford Guards from Houston. Sonnichsen reports that on September 6, "twenty-five men and two newspaper correspondents" arrived from Houston on a specially chartered train.

The rumors about Henry Ferguson gathering armed men was said to be false. The adjutant general came into town and met with a large group of Jaybirds. He was "forcefully" ordered to "advise the Governor against sending Rangers to the county."[55]

Dark Figures and Generous Violence

Running them out of the country was a generous act, for it gave them a chance for their lives (Sonnichsen 1962, 318).

The act of banishment was a popular form of punishment in eighteenth-century Europe. Yet banishment alone was often not enough. Foucault explains that oftentimes people were tortured or branded before they were banished.[56] Sonnichsen writes that banishment was a generous act because in this manner the person who had to leave did not lose his life.[57] Yelderman assures her readers that the banishment of the African American political leaders "must not be construed as animosity towards the negroes as a race. It was directed only against certain individual negroes who were parties to the manipulation of the negro vote, [and] by their arrogant behavior, had become objectionable to these whites."[58] Sonnichsen writes in tandem with Yelderman in his assessment of "the people involved." He explains that "nine times out of ten the descendants of the vigilantes and feudists of seventy-five or eighty years ago [late 1800s] are among the best people in Texas. I know because I know them."[59] These "good Christians" fell into "bad times working to pervert some of our best instincts."[60] His identification with the descendants of the feuding parties is manifested as he includes himself when writing the phrase "our best instincts."

There are multiple layers of punishment in the Jaybird-Woodpecker narrative. Violent actions directly correspond to the need for vengeance which in itself is a "mechanism of power."[61] The mangled hand of Jim Bearfield demonstrated how this power "exerted itself on bodies." The Jaybird's presence was "exalted and strengthened" by its visible manifestations of power. Rules and obligations between county residents were considered personal bonds; a breach, in the form of arrogance from an unauthorized person, could elicit vengeance. People had to obey the rules or be banished—sometimes killed. County blacks faced the spectacle of the verbal jockeying, the mass meetings, the large groups of armed white men facing the front door of an African American's cabin, relaying a sinister message to a man's wife who is alone with her children. For a time, the public spectacle of arrogance and verbal force was enough for the men of the county. Murders and attempted murders were carried out in the dark, through windows obscured by nighttime.

The possible fabulation of Henry Ferguson leading hundreds of armed African Americans in a ride across the Brazos River may have intensified the need to display a more menacing form of power. Hundreds of black men with guns and hundreds of white men with guns sounded like a war. At this point, Sonnichsen remarks, "all the ingredients for a first-class war seemed to be assembled."[62] It was no longer a Civil War between the North and South. It was now the war between the South and the South: the dark South and the white South, that is.

Turkey Creek: Southwest Fort Bend County—Sometime in the 1880s

The older people in Kendleton still know how it happened, even though the exact date is no longer remembered. Hattie Mae Green, the person who remembered the most, has died. Hattie was the daughter of Henry Green, the village constable.[63] Kendleton was already an established village when the event occurred. William Kendall had sold enough land to former slaves so that a solid community could be developed.

For an undetermined period of time after Reconstruction, the Fort Bend County sheriff's deputies made monthly raids on Kendleton. Marjorie Adams believes it occurred before 1889, but is not certain. The purpose of the raids was to rape the women of Kendleton. Eventually, the community decided to fight back. Henry Green was the organizer. The next time the deputies approached the village, residents waited with loaded rifles on the west bank of Turkey Creek. At the last minute the men abandoned their posts and the women took over. Grandmothers took up the arms and shot everyone they could when the deputies approached on horseback. Seventeen deputies were killed; their bodies remained in the creek until the next day. A temporary truce was called so the Anglo/white families could recover the victims' re-

Constable Henry Green, ca. 1890. Courtesy
Kendleton Historical Society.

mains. There were no reported deaths on the Kendleton side. After the confrontation, the raids stopped. It was called "the Feud at Turkey Creek."

Although I made notes when Adams told me, I could not get myself to
write about the feud in essay form for almost a year. What was my hesitation?
Was it the lack of documentation? Was it because the event fell somewhere
between folklore and history? Was I still obliged to the archival requirements
of the linear history often required by the academy? Or was it simply the
morbidity of recounting the incident? Initially, the "lack of evidence" was
seductive. Old Texas newspapers had to contain something about Turkey

Creek, I thought; Books on late nineteenth-century Texas history had to have something on the event. It was hard to believe there was absolutely nothing. I could not even find an event that described seventeen white men dying all at once.[64] The only thing I found came from Marjorie Adams herself. In a brochure on African Americans published by the Texas Historical Commission, there is brief note on Henry Green's house. "The house is associated with Reconstruction-era multiracial political activities in Fort Bend County because of the political career of its first resident."[65] A blurry photograph of two members from Green's family is posted above. The house existed, as did the photograph. Did the feud happen? Even the act of questioning is difficult, reminding me of someone being skeptical about Wounded Knee or the Holocaust. Is this text less academic if the author states that the Turkey Creek Feud "probably did" happen?

Michel-Rolph Trouillot proposes that academic historians are generally more conservative in their conclusions, especially regarding "blurry" facts.[66] If tenure is in question, can a scholar risk appearing less than academic? Yet logic continues to tell me that the Feud at Turkey Creek happened—though perhaps not the positivistic logic necessary to make an objective determination, but another type of approach to understanding "what could have" happened before. A few nights before this chapter was written I had a dream about an undetermined event that occurred in the county "a long time ago." It was something that continued to negatively affect its residents. In the dream it was suggested to me that I speak to a colleague who owns a bookstore (in real life she is a Jungian analyst) who is reported to understand all sorts of mystical and supernatural things. She has spoken many times to people who know about folkloric practices from the Caribbean. I am supposed to find out what happened so long ago that was so terrible and see if people will talk together about it. When I wake, I ponder the idea of Turkey Creek, or another location closer to the Brazos River, on the east side of the new bridge on U.S. Hwy 59. There is no event (that I know of) associated with the place near the river. However, as I often drive by, I look at the thick group of trees and wonder if something happened there, too.

A Prominent Slave-Mart: Houston, 1855

The existence of barbarous events is evidenced in numerous texts written in the nineteenth century. Just before the Civil War, Frederick Law Olmsted, whose most notable accomplishment was the design of New York's Central

Park, wrote a book on his travels to Texas. He describes an encounter he had in Houston in the mid-1850s:

> A tall, jet black negro [*sic*] came up, leading by a rope a downcast mulatto, whose hands were lashed by a cord to his waist, and whose face was horribly cut, and dripping with blood. The wounded man crouched and leaned for support against one of the columns of the gallery.
> "What's the matter with that boy?" asked a smoking lounger.
> "I run a fork into his face," answered the negro [*sic*].
> "What are his hands tied for?"
> "He's a runaway, sir."
> "Did you catch him?"
> "Yes, sir. He was hiding in the hay-loft, and when I went up to throw some hay to the horses, I pushed the fork down into the mow and it struck something hard. I didn't know what it was, and I pushed hard, and gave it a turn, then he hollered, and I took it out."
> "What do you bring him here for?"
> "Come for the key of the jail, sir, to lock him up."
> "What!" said another, "one darkey catch another darkey? Don't believe that story."
> "Oh yes, Mass'r, I tell for true. He was down in our hayloft, and so you see when I stab him, I *have* to catch him."
> "Why, he's hurt bad, isn't he?"
> "Yes, he says I pushed through the bones."
> "Whose nigger is he?"
> "He says he belong to Mass'r Frost sir, on the Brazos."
> The key was soon brought, and the negro [*sic*] led the mulatto away to jail. He seemed sick and faint, and walked away limping and crouching, as if he had received other injuries than those on his face. The bystanders remarked that the negro [*sic*] had not probably told the whole story.
> We afterwards happened to see a gentleman on horseback, and smoking, leading by a long rope through the deep mud, out into the country, the poor mulatto, still limping and crouching, his hands manacled, and his arms pinioned.
> There is a prominent slave-mart in town. . . .[67]

Turkey Creek occurred several decades later, when the lives of black people were even less valuable, since planters no longer had a monetary investment at stake. In a striking article in the March 1, 1888 issue of the *New York Times,* it was reported that a fire destroyed a home in Spanish Camp, not more than ten miles west of Kendleton:

> . . . Some unknown persons went to a house occupied by negroes and poured kerosene around the building and set it afire. As the inmates sprang from their

beds and ran to the windows to jump out, they were by fired on by assassins, who
were in ambush. Some of the negroes succeeded in getting out of the house, but
only to be killed in the yard. Two boys were shot down inside of the house and
left to burn with the building.

There is no note of who was charged with the crime. Mrs. Adams said this was
a common occurrence in those times. The logic is not necessarily of dreams
and their Jungian interpretation; it is of parallels. If a certain type of event
happened, why couldn't something similar happen nearby? If only a few decades before, people's ears were split open and their faces hacked with pitch-
forks, couldn't it be conceivable that a group of men gathered every month
and rode into a small black town and raped some women? If they were the law
of the county, there was no legal recourse.

Henry Green, Henry Ferguson, and the Jaybird-Woodpecker Feud: Mutilated Narratives

*. . . the scriptural operation which produces, preserves, and cultivates im-
perishable "truths" is connected to a rumor of words that vanish no sooner
than they are uttered, and which are lost forever (de Certeau 1988, 212).*

The ethnographer is the transmitter of information. Ethnography is about
documenting people. What happens when the story becomes a "work," as
described by Barthes? He explains that a "work" is akin to Lacan's idea of reality, while a "text" would be the *reél*—the discourse as it occurs.[68] The "text" is
held in language. The verbal construct of text/words/language is a phantasmic, slippery narrative that tells of the county sheriff and his deputies dying
in a creek outside of Kendleton, having been shot by a group of grandmothers, sometime in the 1880s. Without formal documentation, the Turkey Creek
story is similar to the slave rolls of the antebellum census, which give a slight
glimpse of something, but no definite outline or form that stratifies the story.
The identity of the slaves slipped away in the anonymity of the slave rolls,
being listed only by first name, gender, age, and whether they were mulatto.
The text can be easily erased because it is not authorized "by the father," as
Barthes explains. The "father," or authorizing historiographical entity, is not
part of the text, as it is not part of the story of Turkey Creek. The "fathers"
of the county created a work in the histories written by A. J. Sowell in 1904,

Clarence Wharton in 1939, and Pauline Yelderman in 1979. The work is given respect, as are the author's intentions.

In this particular situation, Barthes' description of a work authorized by the "father" is interesting in that the men killed in the feuds were most probably the literal (biological) fathers of many black children living in the county. A feud in which blacks, especially older women, killed a group of white men on horses was not only unthinkable, it was unspeakable.[69] There was no paternal authority involved in relating the narrative. In fact, the narrative was banished.

Barthes' "work" is the historiography surrounding the feud, where the county sheriff, a deputy and other white men were killed. A fragment of narrative is fixed to a particular space and time. Could I do a disservice to the people of Kendleton if I pursue the narrative of Turkey Creek? My less than perfect analysis and interpretation of the event could further press these descendants of slaves into an exotic *Other*world. Marjorie Adams believes the story should be told, even in its incomplete form.

A Reputation of Integrity and Stability: George Ranch Historical Park, Richmond, Texas—1998

These records bear witness to an era of much wickedness (Naomi Carrier Grundy, September 10, 2005).

Naomi Carrier Grundy is waiting for me at an upscale deli in Houston. We have never met in person. I found her name in a curious file posted on the Internet regarding a hearing about Texas school textbooks.[70] The file contained the only written information (or mention) of anything regarding the Feud at Turkey Creek that I have found in the ten months since Marjorie Adams told me about the incident. I tell her that it is urgent that we speak in person. I am close to completing my book on the county and am hoping that she can tell me something about Turkey Creek.

We both arrive at almost the same time at the deli, but do not see each other. She is at a table and I am sitting next to the entrance. After about fifteen minutes, I walk outside to make a phone call. As I am making the call I look through the glass door and see a woman coming towards me carrying a large manila envelope that reads NAOMI. We had forgotten to get information so that we could recognize one another. We quickly sit down to talk. There was so much to discuss I could hardly get myself to order any food. There were many things she told me about the county. Her most significant involvement with Fort Bend had been when she was a historical consultant to the George Ranch Historical Park.[71]

In 1995 Carrier Grundy received a phone call from the staff of the George Ranch. The organization had received a substantial grant from the National Endowment for the Humanities (NEH) and contracted with her for consultation regarding the ranch's African American history. Seeing an incredible opportunity, Carrier Grundy accepted. She was given full access to the museum's archives. For four years she studied the archives and found information regarding the plantation's slaves and the freedman that stayed at the plantation after emancipation. Carrier Grundy was commissioned to write plays for the Annual Texian Market Days celebration, including one play performed for the National ALFHAM (Association for Living History, Farm and Agricultural Museums) Conference in 1996, titled "Arcy Makes Room for Judith Martin: The Breakup of a Slave Family." Her NEH assignment yielded "Social Politics in Victorian Texas, 1890."[72] The play was performed at the George Ranch for the 1998 Juneteenth Celebration. After one performance, the play was cancelled and her consulting services were no longer needed.

The subtitle seems innocuous: "A Living Interpretation of African Americans and Their Responsibilities in the Home of J. H. P. Davis, Rancher/Farmer, Fort Bend County, Texas." It is a story about the household of an elderly woman named Polly Ryon. She was attended by her former slaves while living at her son-in-law's. There are a number of narrative threads, including Ryon's attempt to get a deed recorded to land her late husband gave two slaves (Robert Jones and his wife, Fenton) when he set them free in 1860, and the indifference shown by her son-in-law when she requests his assistance in recording the transaction. There is the mention of the Ku Klux Klan and a man named Jordan who had been lynched the month before in nearby Brazoria County, along with a "young Professor Mitchell" who "was run off" when the "Kluckers" burned down the school for the freedmen's children. Polly Ryon's domestic help were planning to attend a meeting that Saturday night at their church: the Klan would be discussed along with plans for a new school (and schoolteacher).[73]

While it is common knowledge that the Klan was active throughout the South, there is little mention of it in any texts published about the county. Polly Ryon, an important figure in county history, is presented as the kind slave owner who with her husband frees their slaves but does not formalize a gift of acreage that came with their manumission. Ryon tells her son-in-law, J. H. P. Davis: "Course, William didn't want 'em [sic] to abandon me, so he made me promise not to turn over the deed till after I had died, leaving instructions in my will."[74] Davis is shown as a preoccupied cattleman who does not seem to want to transfer the property title to the former slaves. The play ends without a resolution to the problem of the deed, although Jones shows that he does not need Polly's gift. His son already owns five hundred acres of Fort Bend County property. In the last scene, Bob Jones's daughter, who is now Polly Ryon's maid, is cleaning the bedroom. She tells herself "I longs [sic] to one day have me a bed dis [sic] fine."[75]

Perhaps the play countered the organization's mission of "integrity." J. H. P. Davis's reluctance to transfer the deed of property to Bob Jones was not an act of integrity, nor was the Klan's burning of the local colored school. In making their archives available, the George Ranch organization might have expected that these incidents would be exposed. Either the officials of the George Ranch Historical Park remained oblivious to the past or expected Carrier Grundy to whitewash (literally) her historical research. By banishing the play, they acquiesced to the county's continuing need to forget. Her entrance into the archives resonates with Michel de Certeau's archival study of another location with a history of the demonic, an Ursuline convent in Loudon, France known for a seventeenth-century epidemic of spirit possession. De Certeau explains: "the stocks of manuscripts and buried works, now conserved in national or municipal archives, allowed me to analyze initially how a diabolical 'place'—a diabolical scene—was organized through the play of social, political, religious, or epistemological tensions, and how this composition of place, this production of theatrical space, enabled a reclassification of social representation to function as shifts in frames of reference."[76] The parallel that is most disturbing between the archives of Loudon and those of the George Ranch Historical Park is displayed in de Certeau's next statement: the place (Loudon or the George Ranch) "is successfully a metonymy and a metaphor allowing us to apprehend how a 'state policy,' a new rationality"[77] replaces religious reason. The religious reason parallels two issues. One is that of conveying property already bequeathed and the humane treatment that would have been expected if this were not a relationship between former master and slave. Most striking is the hesitancy of Davis, who still makes no movement to register the transaction after he asks Bob how he is doing and Bob answers "Jest [sic] trying to stay 'above water Suh [sic]." Davis tells Jones: "I ain't one t'complain [sic]. What with over ten thousand head of cattle and hopes for a good cotton crop." The economic asymmetry of their situations does not move him to act. He leaves quickly without responding to his mother-in-law's request.

Dreaming the River

. . . water is the most faithful "mirror of voices."[78]

The conversation I had with Naomi Carrier Grundy went on for almost ninety minutes. I finished my salad and pushed myself to leave the table for a moment as I served myself more food from the buffet. I rushed back so that she could tell me more. I asked her about Turkey Creek. What she knew about Turkey Creek was told to her by Marjorie Adams. In all her research she had never found anything about the feud. We discussed the possibilities of other narratives that might have mutated from the Turkey Creek story. I told her that I had even considered the unlikely story that the Jaybird-Woodpecker feud might have been manufactured (or at least greatly enhanced) to cover a confrontation between the sheriff and Kendleton's black men (and women). How else could they explain the death of a sheriff and seventeen deputies? Why, for so many decades, would the white people of the county not discuss the events surrounding the Jaybird-Woodpecker feud? Notwithstanding that many other areas of the South were following similar patterns of banishing black politicians and restricting the vote to white male voters, it is still a worthy question to pose whether the Feud at Turkey Creek might have precipitated the completion of the Jaybird Constitution referred to as the Magna Carta of the county by historian Clarence Wharton. Once the constitution was in place, the entire social and economic fabric of the county reverted to an antebellum way of life. For the most part, this continued for another seventy years, although some of my informants argue that there are many aspects of the county that seem locked in the dark side of the nineteenth century.

The speculation about a narrated event that cannot be substantiated by the historical record is mitigated by the extreme violence and actual savagery emanating from the texts that are available. The George Ranch archives informed Carrier Grundy that a constant flow of violent events covered the county, from the establishment of Austin's Colony well into the twentieth century. The ranch's main house exhibits no trace of the plantation's complicated history. The Fort Bend Museum and the Museum of Southern History in Sugar Land make note of slavery, prison labor, and sharecropping, but they have eliminated the terror from their narratives.[79] What is missing in the museums and most of the published texts has left traces in old memoirs, early twentieth-century master's theses and dissertations, newspapers, and stories told by the elderly. The river has washed away much of the terror. Any bodies thrown in the water decomposed long ago. Yet Naomi Carrier Grundy and Marjorie Adams believe the feeling of terror remains in the landscape. The demonic quality of the place stays linked to a nineteenth-century description of the county's river bottoms. Fort Bend was called "the Hell-hole of the Brazos."[80]

Carrier Grundy argues that southeast Texas had so many violent narratives that a person could never stop finding things. I admitted that it had been difficult to finish the book I was working on. Every time I thought I was close to completion, I found something new that had to be discussed. I told her that the research had weighed upon me. Reading about the violence of slavery and post-Reconstruction in the county was a continuous journey into tragedy. Then she told me about her dream of the Brazos River. *She is running barefoot, north on Highway 59, trying to get across the Brazos. Behind her is a group of white caps, Ku Klux Klan members on horses. They want to kill her.*

Carrier Grundy had the dream while she was working at the George archives. She does not say if she survived in the dream. Yet it is clear that voices from the archives did not survive. The foundation has been successful in washing away the history of blood from the banks of the river. Carrier Grundy however, continues to write, conduct workshops, and perform theatrical productions with her company, Talking Back Living History Theatre. She also coordinates performing arts and teaches classes of school children about Texas history; and protests to public school textbook committees about the severe inconsistencies in the presentation of Texas history.

Chapter five

The Warrior

While Tizoc no longer exists in his old physical form, something of his ancestral power continues to act in the lives of his human relatives and heirs (Read 1994, 43).

During the 1950s and 1960s a dramatic image of an Aztec warrior holding his dying (or sleeping) lover circulated in thousands of calendars distributed in Texas. In the scene he looks noble, distinguished, and powerful. He is taking a moment to hold an irresistibly beautiful woman who lies in his arms with her eyes closed. Their image is elevated, as if they are on a mountain. Storm clouds are behind them. The woman looks at peace, her hands together almost as if she is praying. The warrior's strength is evidenced in his stance, which remains powerful as he holds the reclining woman who either has fainted, is dying, has already died, or is only waiting for a kiss. The 1954 painting is *Amor Indio,* by Jesús Helguera, produced during his lifetime contract with a cigar factory.[1] Paintings like *Amor Indio* were used to decorate calendars that advertised Mexican businesses. The calendars crossed the border with relatives or new immigrants. Texas Mexican businesses also began using the images for their calendars.

Thousands of families had these calendars hanging in their homes. With the development of the Chicano civil rights movement in the 1960s, the image of the warrior and the sleeping (or dead) maiden became a symbol of the powerful past (and potent future) of Mexicans in the United States. Art historian Tere Romo describes a similar calendar painting titled *La Noche Triste,* also by Jesús Helguera, in her grandparents' living room. In 1972 the Chicano rock group Malo appropriated Helguera's *Amor Indio* for a new album cover, which spiraled the painting's circulation beyond the Chicano movement.[2] As I read Romo's history of the painting I begin to recall the vivid colors of

Helguera's painting on the album cover I saw thirty years previously. It was a rock group that helped me remember *Amor Indio.*

Amor Indio: 1956

Two years after Helguera produced the painting, a second "Amor Indio" was released. This time it was a film titled *Tizoc: Amor Indio.* The director, Ismael Rodríguez, was internationally famous by the time he made *Tizoc.* Influenced by European and American directors, he must have been deeply enamored of either the historical Tizoc or the character Tizoc from the movie. He named one of his sons Tizoc.[3]

Pedro Infante, who continues to be the most popular Mexican singer/actor that has ever lived, portrayed the descendent of an Aztec (México) ruler who fell tragically in love with a white upper-class woman. When the film won Berlin's Silver Bear Award, the movie was described by the *New York Times* as a "drama about the color problem in Mexico."[4] The movie also won a Golden Globe Award for the best foreign film in 1957. It was considered the best of what was termed the "golden age of Mexican cinema."

In the movie, actor Pedro Infante plays the descendant of a sixteenth-century Aztec prince. In the twentieth century, Infante's Tizoc has dark skin (with the help of studio makeup). Four centuries after the conquest, Tizoc interacts meekly with his social superiors, with his head bowed as he talks. He is continuously guided by his parish priest. Ultimately (and tragically) he falls in love with a rich white woman. They both die in the end. Tizoc is portrayed as innocent and ignorant.

The image of Tizoc stayed in the minds of many Texas mexicanos. Mexican movies traveled to Texas, where they were viewed by people in run-down, segregated movie theaters. In Fort Bend County, the Spanish-language movies were shown at the State Theatre in Rosenberg. It was a block from the railroad station and had originally been the theater for the city until the newer and more modern Cole Theatre was built two blocks farther away from the railroad tracks. At the Cole, Texas Mexicans had to sit in the balcony, and blacks were required to sit in the back part of the balcony. Whites sat on the ground level. At the State, there was no segregated seating. People could sit anywhere. The carpet and seats were torn. The place had a musty smell, not so much of dirt but of age. The screen was much smaller than the one at the Cole. Movies were shown only on certain days of the week. It was here that the mexicanos of the county saw *Tizoc.* In his heritage at least, they found a productive connection.

After 1836, most immigrants from Mexico to Texas were strikingly different than the earlier heroes of the Texas Revolution. The two most significant immigrants were the aristocratic Lorenzo de Zavala and Juan Seguin. Zavala's education and experience as an international statesmen was something rarely seen in Mexico or the United States.[5] Seguin's position as a landed *ranchero,* military officer and congressional representative to the Republic of Texas allowed him much social and political latitude.[6] Land grants given to other, less influential Texas Mexicanos were sold or taken by force by incoming Anglos. Within a decade, the entire social structure in southeast Texas appeared to center on the division between two groups: those who labored (feeding and serving), and those who owned, supervised, and controlled (were fed and served). By 1842, Englishman Dorian Maillard reported that planters around Richmond did not consider it appropriate for a white man to do manual labor.[7] The hardworking frontiersmen who populated the Republic quickly turned into masters and patrons.

By the end of the Mexican War in 1849, most ethnic Mexicans remaining in Texas lived in poverty. The few who continued to immigrate to the state were generally escaping the peonage system of Mexico's large *haciendas.* After the Civil War, their numbers increased due to recruitment efforts caused by the planters' need to replace slave labor. The movement magnified after 1910 with the fall of dictator Porfirio Díaz and the subsequent Mexican Revolution. Recruitment efforts also intensified because prison contract labor was outlawed in 1913.[8] Texas farms and ranches needed labor. Farm workers were *mestizos* of predominantly indigenous origin and appearance. For those who retained some of the "whiteness" of their European ancestors, the sun burned their skin, marking them as a permanently dark labor force.[9]

The historical Tizoc, as implied in the painting and the movie, was the son of the México's (Aztecs') greatest ruler, Motecuhzoma Ilhuicamina. Tizoc ruled after his father's death, from 1481 to 1486.[10] He was not known to be an effective ruler, which brings in question Ismael Rodriguez' motivation for the movie and for naming his son after the main character. Kay Read's essay on México rulers explains that according to México tradition, Tizoc did not necessarily have to be a good ruler to be respected and to create some type of positive effect on his successor and future descendants.[11] In addition, Tizoc's legacy (akin to that of Egypt's Tutankhamon) was what he left behind. The year after Tizoc died by poisoning, his successor and brother Ahuitzotl dedicated the Templo Mayor in the México's capital city of Tenochtitlan. In a story documented by Diego Duran in the sixteenth century, ". . . All of the México's allies and those subjected to them attend the festival. Even their 'enemies' came; arriving in secret, they were sequestered in private rooms and lavishly treated. . . ."

We can see part of . . . this . . . fabled story about pre-conquest, pre-Spanish times depicted on the Dedication Stone, a plaque expertly carved out of greenstone in that same year. Dominating the plaque is the date glyph for the year 8-Reed (1487). Above this, Tizoc (on the left) and Ahuitzotl (on the right) stand facing a large woven grass ball with two bone piercers stuck into it."[12]

This material object that is still exhibited at a national museum six centuries later would have kept Tizoc alive without the painting or the film. Yet there is an additional aspect of the carved stone that resonates especially with those mexicanos who found themselves working as laborers and vaqueros on farms and ranches throughout Texas. The intricate carving on the stone presents a narrative of transcendence and provision.

Read continues: "These piercers were used to draw sacrificial blood from the fleshy parts of one's body, such as the earlobe or thighs. The ball collected the blood. Dressed as priests, these rulers (both dead and living) are piercing their ears with similar instruments. Their blood flows up over their heads, down to the grass ball and into an incense burner through which it enters the gaping mouth of the earth monster upon whose surface the brothers are standing. Blood flows from their legs as well."[13]

The narrative of two brothers "feeding the earth" with sacrificial blood is especially disquieting if the savage labor required of Texas Mexicans is considered in light of their duty to produce the crops and other food that nourished their world (and their *patrónes*). Read's passage on the sacrifice of feeding the cosmos is eerily reminiscent: "Méxica-Tenochca sacrifice in which human and nonhuman beings participated was regarded as the systematized manipulation of various life-giving powers via their feeding, which served to: (a) sustain, strengthen, and transform those powers; and (b) maintain an orderly and balanced cosmic eco-system consisting of many and diverse animated entities which were intimately, inherently, and reciprocally interrelated with each other. From within this tightly knit cosmic community, people have a moral duty, then, to feed the hands that feed them."[14,15]

Performance: San Antonio, 2005

This is a story within a story—so slippery at the edges that one wonders when and where it started and whether it will ever end (Trouillot 1995, 1).

The first chapter of Michel-Rolph Trouillot's *Silencing the Past* begins with a story about the Alamo, the pivotal 1836 battle between Santa Ana, Mexican president and general, and Texan insurgents.[16] An inversion occurs in the story. It is about a siege and a massacre that transforms into a battle cry of bravery, victory, and conquest.

In July 2005, on a hot Monday afternoon, Hector Aguilar, an attractive, articulate, young Latino in his late twenties, stands on a small stage in the back courtyard of the Alamo. Behind him are the Six Flags of Texas, symbolizing the six nations that claimed Texas as their territory (Spain, France, Mexico, the Republic of Texas, the United States, and the Confederate States of America). He gives an impassioned rendition of the battle of the Alamo and the Texas Revolution. A native of San Antonio, Aguilar tells an audience of over 100 people that the Battle of the Alamo was not about a fight between two countries, but between two groups of people that had different political interests. His oratory is striking. At moments, he closes his eyes as he speaks, or briefly touches one of the flags behind him. The audience appears mesmerized. He makes an effort to modify the polarization between the two warring groups. He minimizes the usual glorious descriptions of Davy Crockett, Jim Bowie, and William Travis, and emphasizes the involvement of the Texas Mexicans. He does not demonize Santa Ana. His narrative resonates with recent scholarship and critiques on early Texas history. His tone is convincing. I am sitting on a concrete bench in a tight spot between two Anglo families. My cell phone rings (I had forgotten to turn it off, not expecting to run into a lecture outside the Alamo) and I jump out of my seat and run out of the arena. After telling my caller I can't talk, I walk to the other side of the arena and find another seat. This time it is with a Latino couple, sitting slightly apart on a bench. The husband/boyfriend sits next to the empty spot. Before the interruption, I had observed this young couple from across the courtyard, noticing the empty seat and wondering why no one had taken it. I walked around the surrounding shrubs while Aguilar continued to talk about Texas heroism. Approaching the empty seat on the bench, with the young couple still there, I sat down and listened to the end of Aguilar's dramatic presentation. It was amazing. He had no props other than the flags. He wore the uniform of the Alamo employees: white shirt, black pants, and a red cotton vest. Now, seated more comfortably, perhaps with the fantasy of imagining myself *acompaniada* by someone who looked more like me, I was able to watch Aguilar more closely. It seemed as though he really believed what he was saying. For a very brief moment I felt as though I had absorbed the feelings his recitation evoked. The project of the Texas Revolution created a space of excitement inside me; yes, I thought, this was a wonderful thing "they" did.

After less than a minute I returned to reality, almost embarrassed at myself for letting Aguilar take me to that moment. The last words of his presentation abruptly dissipated my transient patriotism. I "woke up" when he said, "Remember the Alamo!"

As the crowd dispersed I ran after Aguilar. He was walking out of the courtyard with someone that appeared to be a friend or colleague. When I stopped them to ask Aguilar whether he could speak for a moment, his companion rolled his eyes. Aguilar, in his youth and attractive enthusiasm, probably had many people (perhaps women) seek him out after his entertaining performance. We spoke for about fifteen minutes. I quickly asked him as many questions as I could. People were beginning to stand near us, waiting for a chance to speak to him or ask a question.

I told him that his presentation was not as silent on Latinos as recent scholarship had argued.[17] Were the administrators at the Alamo taking a different approach? He said that he had the opportunity to meet many authors that came through the institution. He had been strongly influenced by the work of Steven Hardin and Gregg Dimmick.[18] Aguilar said he respected the work of Richard Flores (University of Texas anthropologist and historian) but disagreed with Flores's premise, which is that much of the Latino history of the Alamo has been silenced, minimized, and definitely politicized.[19] We exchanged e-mail addresses and information on sources of research. A few Anglos were eagerly waiting to speak to him. We were standing at the entrance of the courtyard near the place where a controversial plaque had previously been placed in honor of Adina de Zavala (Lorenzo Zavala's granddaughter), who was instrumental in making the Alamo a national monument. As I walked away I looked at his e-mail address: "The_man_from_the_Alamo@ . . ."

Aguilar spoke of Tejano war heroes battling Santa Ana's troops from inside the Alamo compound. During the last century the names of a number of them surfaced. Adina de Zavala was instrumental in placing them within the stream of narratives about early Texas history. Before her efforts, eighty years after the battle, their names were generally omitted from lists of Texas heroes. Zavala's own allegiance to or identification with Mexican Texans might have been ambivalent. Her Mexican grandfather had married an American. Her father, Agustín Zavala, had married an Irish woman.[20] It appears that her motivation might have been based on a desire to commemorate her grandfather Lorenzo Zavala, as well as his involvement in and support of the Texas Revolution. This removed Lorenzo Zavala (and Adina's heritage) from the image of Mexicans as passive and inept that evolved after 1836.[21]

The Transformation of Warriors

The illustrious histories of Lorenzo Zavala and Juan Seguín were significant to the beginnings of the Texas Republic. After their deaths, the history books focused on Stephen F. Austin, his three hundred colonists, and later Texan capitalists that developed million-acre ranches or found oil in the early twentieth century. According to circulating narratives, there were no more Zavalas and Seguíns. Specific names disappeared. What remained were vague descriptions of "Mexicans," many of whom were U.S. soldiers in the U.S.–Mexican War (1846–1848). The descriptions of Mexican life south of the Rio Grande conflated with those of Mexicans living in Texas (as often happened). Publications describing the Americans' heroics also detailed Mexican culture as barbaric, dirty, and without morals.[22]

In addition, there were descriptions like that of William Fairfax Gray in 1836: "Mexicans, or native . . . Texians . . . are a swarthy, dirty looking people, much resembling our mulattos, some of them nearly black, but having straight hair."[23] However, there was considerably more than the description offered by the erudite Gray. Resistance or outright insurrection by Mexican Texans continued into the early twentieth century.[24] What is compelling about these narratives of revolt is that, although occasional texts document these events, it appears that a type of amnesia has appeared within the confines of Texas history regarding the existence of the Mexican Texans.

Benjamin Heber Johnson describes this phenomenon in his excellent work on a 1915 Texas rebellion known as the Plan of San Diego: "The uprising was thus violent, large, and had important consequences. Then why had neither I nor my parents, all native Texans and products of the Texas school system, even heard of it?"[25] Almost no one has heard of the Plan. My own family, who lived north of the Rio Grande in the eighteenth century, did not know of the rebellion. My father, whose broad knowledge of Mexican and Texas history and who, in the 1950s and 1960s, took his children to the Alamo, Goliad, and San Jacinto, had never heard of the Plan of San Diego.

What people read or heard was inconsistent with the idea of a bloody rebellion. William Fairfax Gray portrays Texas Mexicans in his diary as "quiet, orderly, cheerful people, fond of dancing and gambling, unthrifty and unambitious."[26] Gray's description was (at some level) relevant a century later in Fort Bend County. José F. Hernández says that mexicanos were quiet, would not stand up for their rights in disputes with employers, and were exposed to many different depredations without complaint. This perceived passivity was attractive to ranch foremen. The Mexicans were known to be hard workers who tolerated harsh working conditions. In Neil Foley's book on the cotton culture of Texas, he describes the "personality" attributed to Mexican laborers in the early twentieth century. It was "believed that Mexicans were docile and nomadic by nature, [and] they made ideal seasonal laborers to harvest the cotton during peak season."[27] They were "easily domineered" and demanded only "the bare essentials in house furnishings."[28] Foley cites a 1925 article in which Edward Davis states in *Texas Outlook* that controlling Mexicans like Negroes was "what we in the South thought and still think."[29]

The Mexican Texans (immigrant or otherwise) recruited as workers on the large farms of Texas were narratively portrayed in a manner similar to the character Tizoc in Ismael Rodríguez's movie. He is innocent, easily led, and simple. The image endured. As late as 1968, a newsletter of the Basilian Catholic order of priests described the parishioners in the Basilian fathers' home and foreign missions in Southeast Texas and central . . . Mexico as follows: "Some of those [expressions of worship] found among the Mexican people seem strange—perhaps childish—to the sophisticated North American." The newsletter echoes Gray's narrative: "The poor Mexican is generous as well as grateful when help is offered him. He is patient almost to a fault. We must be patient with him. We are seldom criticized, even when language makes communication difficult."[30]

The words of the priest are troubling. The Basilian Order made significant inroads into the excessively difficult life of the Texas Mexican laborer in Southeast Texas. Its establishment in 1936 of what it termed the "Mexican missions" initiated a vigorous project of social justice (along with its desire to "bring the sacraments" to the people). Yet, the fair-minded fathers unknowingly established a church community that sought the betterment of the laborers' living conditions while adhering to an ideology based on Western values that could not relate to or respect the laborers' everyday activities and beliefs. All they could see was the striking differences between themselves and their parishioners.

These differences had drawn my attention since I was a child, when I attended first grade in a school at the Basilian mission while growing up amid the mexicano farm laborers in the county. Decades later, as an academic, I encountered multiple theories of oppression and racism. Arnoldo De León's work, in particular, detailed the depressing environment in which mexicanos lived in Texas.[31] I began teaching undergraduate anthropology classes in Mexican American culture in Houston in the mid-1990s, discussing the historical sequence of the lives of Texas mexicanos in the nineteenth and twentieth centuries. After weeks of readings and discussions, Latino students would often tell me of a despondency that overcame them as they learned about this history. In a conversation I had with De León in 1986, he spoke of his father, a farm laborer in South Texas. De León spoke with intensity as he explained that his father was a diligent worker and a responsible man who could never get ahead. De León believed that there was something wrong with Texas (or rather U.S.) society that kept his father from succeeding.

At first this did not make sense. How could people like Lorenzo Zavala, Juan Seguín, Antonio Navarro, and others involved in the revolution be replaced by men who had no agency and did not speak? Of course racism and oppression were present. Texas' designation as a slave state had determined some of the extreme circumstances required to create what John Bourke termed "An American Congo."[32] Mexico's social structure also contributed to the problem. Many immigrants left haciendas where they were treated as something between indentured servants and slaves.[33] Still, the whole idea was confusing. If the families that traveled across the Rio Grande past the Nueces River (which for decades was considered disputed territory full of Anglo and Mexican bandits) and found themselves able to adapt and survive in a world that saw them as less than human, they were not passive people, nor were they ignorant. There had to be more to the story—and there was.

The Road from East Texas: Wood County, 1844

Indeed, the contention that enslaved Africans and their descendents could not envision freedom—let alone formulate strategies for gaining and securing freedom—[and] was based not so much on empirical evidence as on an ontology, an implicit organization of the world and its inhabitants (Trouillot 1995, 73).

A man named Simón Gonzales, a former soldier of the Republic of Texas, died in Wood County in 1844. During an argument over a debt, he shot his neighbor, a man named Martin Varner, and Varner's son. The son died immediately. In return, Varner and his slave carried out a practice that in the Western world is considered barbaric; they skinned Simón alive.[34] The event was important to many Texans because the story circulated enough to be altered. Simón's name was lost in the transmission; the date was moved up to "soon after 1836"; and the location was moved three hundred miles to the south, to a county bordering Fort Bend.[35]

The Savage

Michel-Rolph Trouillot contends that, even when a pivotal event is located in accessible archives, if the information does not conform to the current world-view, the information stays where it is; it is neither noticed nor circulated. He describes this as the "uneven historical power in the inscription of traces."[36] He adds that not only the white plantation owners found it impossible to comprehend that African slaves were capable of rebelling; nonwhite plantation owners often agreed as well.[37]

The trace that remained visible appeared to me in a book on the history of Fort Bend County, published in 1904. I first saw it nearly five years before I wrote this chapter. I found it striking but did not investigate the circumstances. Perhaps I did not take note because the narrative did not mention the name of the dead man. He was presented as the silhouette of a human being, placed in a narrative that dismembered him further.

The curious life of narratives is at times incomprehensible. How an event could be moved six years earlier and several hundred miles to the southwest is an interesting phenomenon. I do not dispute the veracity of the event, and I admit that a positivist might discount the whole story because of its variance. Yet, this narrative, situated on page fifty-five of the first history published on Fort Bend County, is eminently significant for the mere fact of its appearance, regardless of the actual time and location.

Simply said, the author, A. J. Sowell, tells a story about a Mexican who was skinned alive. Sowell's unnamed Mexican shot Martin Varner, one of the Old Three Hundred colonists and a veteran of the War of Texas Independence from Mexico. Varner ultimately died from the gunshot wound but not before he used his own knife to scrape off all of the skin of his attacker. According to Sowell, the incident occurred a few years after 1836 in Brazoria County, on the southeast border of Fort Bend. Even though this was not specifically county history, Varner had come to Texas with another colonist named Henry Jones, who eventually settled in Fort Bend. Perhaps Sowell believed the details of Varner's last days would be significant to his readers.

Walter Benjamin would describe Sowell as a nineteenth-century raconteur who counseled his readers regarding the violence of his country's past.[38] He assumes the role of a counselor who is "inflicted by the Fates" to write the people's history. His positioning of the different characters aided the development of the area's historical myth, strengthened the heroic narratives, and intensified what "his people" believed to be immoral. In the following pas-

sage, Sowell details an incident of violence and terror In this vignette he indicates what a grown man is allowed . . . to do when seeking vengeance and
what he is permitted to do to another man's body: "Varner . . . had his league
of land located in Brazoria County, on what is now 'Varner's Creek.' He was
killed there some years later by a Mexican; after receiving the mortal wound,
he induced some of his friends to catch the Mexican and bring him within his
reach, and he then and there, with a sharp knife, cut him in pieces—actually
skinning him alive from head to foot."[39]

This story of the Mexican being skinned alive stayed on my mind for several years as I continued my research. I knew I would use the story at some
point but was not sure where I would insert it in the county's narrative. As
I came to a chapter where the history of mexicanos would be presented, it
seemed necessary to begin with Sowell's story of Varner and his flayed and
mangled assailant. If Sowell's practical narrative provided a behavioral guide
for county residents, how did this particular account influence the interaction
and relationships between whites/Anglos and mexicanos? Did this mean that
other types of torture were tolerated and encouraged? Sowell himself made
no comment about Varner's vengeance on the Mexican, moving from a vivid
description of the flaying to a new paragraph beginning with a matter-of-fact
statement about a marriage between two settlers who were friends of Varner's.[40] The everyday manner of Sowell's narrative may lead the reader to believe
that the flaying alive of Mexicans in the Texas Republic was a common occurrence, not seen as immoral or excessive. Varner's vengeance went beyond ending a life. When the Mexican was brought to him, Varner became the assailant,
seeking to demonstrate his power on the still living body. The narrative of the
torture may convolute the position of the hero (depending on who reads the
story), yet Sowell's 1904 text clearly displays the hierarchy of domination and
discipline in the early twentieth-century world of Southeast Texas.

The Real of Simón Gonzales

Simón Gonzales joined Martín De León's colony near Victoria sometime before 1835 and was a soldier in the Texas Army from April 18 to October 19
of 1836. Before his death he owned more than 760 acres of land in Brazoria
County and 2,100 acres in Wood County (East Texas), some of which had
been granted as part of a "bounty" distributed to military veterans by the
Republic of Texas. Martin Varner was his neighbor in Wood County. Simón

and Martin possibly had some contact before their last encounter in 1844, especially since they both owned land in Brazoria County before moving to East Texas. In the late 1830s Simón had been to Brazoria County, where Martin had his previous land patent. They were both in the Texas Army in April 1836.[41]

In 1844 the two men argued over a debt. Simón shot Martin. In an article written in October 2000, an East Texas historian explains that Martin's son came to help and that Simón shot and killed the boy. In retaliation, Varner, then seriously wounded, proceeded to "cut the tendons in Gonzales' . . . legs. . . . Gonzales pleaded with Varner to kill him quickly, but Varner refused, reasoning that a quick death would not be commensurate with the crime he had . . . committed. . . . Gonzales was thrown into a hog pen where the animals began to chew on his body. When he finally died the next morning, his remains were hauled to a remote part of his own farm and buried in a shallow grave."[42]

Varner died three days later. Sowell's account is the only one that locates the incident near Fort Bend. Two other descriptions state that it happened in Wood County, more than three hundred miles northeast of Brazoria County. The official Texas history Internet website states the following: "In a dispute with a neighbor, Simon Gonzales, Martin was shot in the back. When his only son, eighteen-year-old Stephen F., attempted to rescue his father, he was also shot and killed. Their loyal slave, Joe, subdued the killer, who later died from knife wounds inflicted by Varner. Martin Varner died three days later, on February 14, 1844. He was survived by his wife and six daughters. A marker has been placed by the Texas Historical Commission at the site of the home and cemetery of Wood County's first family."[43]

Information about Simón is available at the website of the Texas General Land Office.[44] The office welcomes requests for photocopies of its archival documents, at one dollar a page (as of this writing). In May 2005, I called the office and requested information on how to obtain the records of Simón Gonzales's land grants. I spoke to a staff member named John Molleston. Within a few days we had had two substantial conversations regarding Gonzales.

I explained that my search was regarding the possibility that a famous Texas settler named Martin Varner had skinned Gonzales alive. Molleston was helpful in suggesting sources and provided information regarding Gonzales's military record. However, he reminded me that it might not be the same Gonzales who confronted Varner. He suggested that further information might refute the story about Varner's behavior. When I mentioned that the incident actually occurred in Wood County, not Southeast Texas (as Sow-ell claims), Molleston said that Sowell was writing sloppy history. I also told him that the 1904 text had not identified Gonzales by name and that not until the end of the twentieth century was he given an identity. This was in contrast to Varner's biography, which was listed on the *Texas History Online* web page. Molleston responded that Varner was one of the Old Three Hundred, whose narrative was thoroughly documented. He also reminded me that Gonzales had shot Varner in the back, besides shooting his son. He did not add any ex-planation to this, but it appeared to me that he was implying that Varner had some justification for this type of severe vengeance. He also reminded me that Wood County was a long way from Southeast Texas, which led me to wonder what Simón's story had to do with my project on Fort Bend. I told Molleston that, even though some of Sowell's information was incorrect, the positioning of the Gonzales-Varner encounter in a history book on Fort Bend County was significant because of how the residents circulated the narrative about a white man skinning a Mexican alive. Sowell did not critique Varner's behavior. If Benjamin's theory is correct regarding the storyteller with a purpose, Sowell was giving the white people of Fort Bend instructions on how to deal with Mexicans. It was also an unequivocal categorizing of Simón and his people. As far as Sowell and Bowman were concerned, these people could be flayed, butchered, and thrown together with other animals. Men like Simón were ap-parently so low on the food chain that they could be fed to the hogs.[45]

Perhaps Sowell's attitude can be explained, considering his involvement in the Indian Wars, his own near capture by Indians as a child, and the general attitude of white Texas settlers and Texas Rangers in the early twentieth cen-tury. However, it is Bob Bowman's outlook that is unfathomable. Bowman is a former director of the Texas Institute for the Humanities and a member of the Texas Historical Commission.[46] His 2000 article is titled "A Tough East Texan." After mentioning that Varner and his slave cut Gonzales's tendons, Bowman explains that Varner "reasoned" that Gonzales's crime warranted torture. Bowman, as a respected member and leader of Texas historians (his biography states he has written thirty-one books), is a writer whose word is accepted as authoritative. Yet, his lack of critical reasoning regarding the in-cident gives me pause. Is there ever a "reason" to cut a man's leg tendons and allow animals to eat his body while he is still alive?

The search for Simón Gonzales brought still more surprises. On a web page for the DeWitt Colony near Gonzales, Texas, I found narratives about an incident called the Cordova Rebellion.

An Embodiment of Rights: Nacogdoches, 1838

. . . Early in August, 1838, it was found that a motley company of about
150 citizens, headed by Vicente Cordova, an early, intelligent and some-
what influential Mexican resident of the settlement, had secretly taken
up arms and encamped on the west bank of the Angelina [river]
(De Shields, Border Wars of Texas, *1912, p. 271).*

How far, I wonder, is Nacogdoches from Fort Bend? I look on a map and find
that both counties are connected by U.S. Highway 59, a little more than 170
miles apart, in a southwest-to-northeast line. Could a story that started on
an island in the Angelina River in far East Texas have affected people in the
Brazos Bottoms? If the two areas were connected by some type of trail, news
would have traveled easily. Cordova's Rebellion ended near San Antonio on
May 17, 1839. An uprising that moved across Texas and lasted for nine months
surely had to be noticed.

After a number of conversations with different individuals (who I believed
were fairly knowledgeable about Texas history), it became evident that very
few people know about Vicente Cordova and his rebellion. The *Handbook of
Texas History Online* provides an article about him, written by Robert B. Blake,
who died in 1955. The most Blake could say about Cordova's life before 1838
is that Cordova "was evidently well educated and was among the largest land-
holders in Nacogdoches in the late Mexican period. He served at various times
as *alcalde* [mayor of the city], primary judge, and *regidor* [rector].[47] He was for
several years captain of a militia . . . company."[48] After additional searching, I
found an essay titled simply "The Cordova Revolt," written by Paul Lack and
published in 1996 as part of an edited book on Tejano history. The author appears to have judiciously searched the archival records on Nacogdoches, yet he
mentions only that Cordova's family owned a stone house on the town square.
It is almost as if Cordova did not exist before August 1838.

In a detailed account of the conflict, Lack qualifies his findings by stating
that information on who initiated the revolt "remains a matter of perspective
and mystery." The need for documentary evidence causes further erasure of
Cordova's story. Lack continues: "This issue is complicated by the absence of
documents left by Tejanos; except for the proclamation of rebellion, all contemporary accounts come from Anglo Texas sources."[49]

John Milton Chance wrote of Cordova in his canonic volume on the Texas Republic, published in 1963 by the University of Texas Press. Chance devotes an entire chapter to the rebellion. Yet, there is an interesting aspect to the author's presentation. In the chapter, he uses footnotes to elaborate the background of two generals from the Mexican army, Vicente Filosofa and Valentín Canalizo. Even though the chapter deals with the "Cordova-Flores Incident" as Chance describes the rebellion, he does not give any biographical information on Cordova. Another work, James Michener's 1985 novel *Texas,* does not name Cordova or the rebellion specifically but mentions collaborator Manuel Flores. It appears that Michener combined Cordova's story with that of other Tejano rebels (perhaps Juan Cortina and Catarino Garza), naming his "outlaw" Benito Garza. The most recent reference is the web page of the Sons of Dewitt Colony, which presents excerpts from a number of texts that mention the Cordova Rebellion. One of these is written by the same author, A. J. Sowell, who wrote about Simón Gonzales, the Mexican who was skinned alive, in his history of Fort Bend County.[50] Sowell writes: "Cordova was on his way to Mexico from Nacogdoches, and had gathered followers as he went, stealing horses on the way, and committing other depredations. Most of the negroes [*sic*] were runaways from plantations in Eastern Texas."[51] He also mentions that Cordova was killed three years later at the battle of Salado, during which he was fighting on the Mexican side with General Woll.[52]

My discovery of Vicente Cordova's narrative occurred late in the writing of this book. There was no longer time to search out the story. That will remain a project for a subsequent volume on Texas history. In the meantime I continue to wonder about Cordova. Who was he? What rights were he and his companions losing? How severe were the "depredations" made against them (a term often used by authors when describing violence among Native Americans, Mexicans and Anglo settlers)? The tenacity of Cordova's group was amazing. They remained together for nine months, while being pursued for over 300 miles by the Republic of Texas Army, from Nacogdoches to Seguin. His collaborator, Manuel Flores, was killed, but Cordova escaped. Later, he formally joined the Mexican Army and was killed when Mexico attempted to retake San Antonio in 1842.

Perhaps there is more information in the Nacogdoches Archives, or those of the Republic of Texas. What does remain in circulation are two statements by Cordova. One is his response to Sam Houston's order to give up arms; and a second, handwritten in English, is to Manuel Flores about his intentions for the rebellion. Variations of this statement to Houston were published in

Chance's *After San Jacinto* and De Shield's memoirs. The following is from Lack's "The Cordova Revolt":

The citizens of Nacogdoches, tired of suffering injustices and the usurpation of their rights, cannot but state that having gathered together with their weapons in hand, they are determined to shed their last drop of blood in order to protect their individual rights and those of the Nation to which they belong. They confess, as they have in the past, that they have no knowledge of the current laws by which guarantees or their lives and property are offered. They ask only that their families not be molested, in return promising their good conduct toward yours.[53]

Lack's reference to the lack of documented evidence from the Tejano side of Cordova's revolt is inadvertently compromised in a later comment he placed in the essay's footnotes. He explains that "This proclamation exists in several printed formats . . . all with minor errors or inelegant translation. This version was . . . done by Jesus F. de la Teja from a copy of the original document, which is in the Cordova Rebellion Papers, 1838, Nacogdoches County Court Records, Civil Cases."[54] If the proclamation exists in "several printed formats," how can Cordova's proclamation be considered valid? Chance provides an alternate version that is shorter and with different phrasing, said to be in the Ashbel Smith Papers at the University of Texas.[55] If the words were said to be written by Cordova, yet were translated and copied numerous times and are now lying in different archives in Texas, there is no way to ascertain exactly what Cordova (or perhaps anyone involved in the revolt) could have said.

Tracing another document, Harriet Durst's "Early Days in Texas," Guillermo Cruz, an employee of the Durst family, explained why Cordova was fighting: "They were going to fight for their rights; they had been dogs long enough."[56] Chance and De Shields do not mention any loss of rights (for ethnic Mexicans) in their writing on Cordova's revolt. The decades between the work by Chance in 1963 and Lack's in 1996 allowed for somewhat of a more balanced explanation: "They [Cordova's group] were detained illegally by private citizens and punished by whippings and forced labor for minor infractions."

In a disturbing ending to the essay, Lack emphasizes that Cordova's group waited too long to respond to Anglo-Texan offenses, writing that "the Tejanos first fell into that form of passivity that comes from unpalatable alternatives." Theirs remained an agrarian culture, unlike, (as Lack explains) the Tejanos in San Antonio who collaborated with Anglo merchants. Forgetting that many Bexar Tejanos were also identified as traitors, he focuses on how the Nacogdoches Tejanos did not assist the Texas Republic during the revolution, which "set in motion a cycle of suspicion that only worsened their status." Lack believes that when Cordova launched "a rebellion of desperation," he "hastened the destiny of his people."[57]

Ethnic Mexicans in Texas have been allocated a destiny of passivity. The dearth of material evidence has allowed historians to project a less manly character on those who did not leave behind documents, which could prove things were different.

The Mask: Passivity as a Ruse

"You know," said Russell Means, "Indians have a long memory. They do not forget their fallen heroes and their land under occupation by 'foreigners'" (*Michel de Certeau 1986, 226*).

Vicente Cordova's history has blurred into the narratives of other defiant Texas Mexicans. As his name is lost, the significance of the name Gregorio Cortez has intensified. Americo Paredes published *With a Pistol in His Hand* in 1958. In that book, which is now considered a classic, Paredes tells of Cortez's ability to evade scores of Texas Rangers in the early twentieth century after being charged with the murder of a sheriff in a Central Texas county. More recently, Benjamin Johnson's work on the Plan of San Diego, a deadly revolt in South Texas that occurred in 1916, has brought to light information on the two men behind the plan, Luis de la Rosa and Aniceto Pizana.[58]

Michel de Certeau's essay "The Politics of Silence: The Long March of the Indians" resonates with the absent story of Cordova and Simón Gonzales. "Dominated, but not vanquished, they keep alive the memory of what the Europeans have 'forgotten,' a continuous series of uprisings and awakenings which have left hardly a trace in the occupiers' historiographical literature. This history of resistance punctuated by cruel repression is *marked on the Indian's body* as much as it is recorded in transmitted account or more so."[59]

In Fort Bend County, that punctuation is in the heart of the land and the sweat of the mexicano laborers' bodies. The permanence of this transmission, however, lies in the continued existence of San Isidro Cemetery. The body does not go away. The people who keep the cemetery alive—those who clean, organize, raise funds, and continue to bury their family members—have become their own historians. De Certeau . . . continues: "A unity born of hardship and resistance to hardship is the historical locus, the collective memory of the social body where a will that neither confirms nor denies this writing of history originates. It deciphers the scars on the body . . . proper . . . or the fallen 'heroes' and 'martyrs' who correspond to them in narrative—as the index of a history yet to be made. 'Today, at the hour of our awakening, we must be our own historians.'"[60]

The cemetery has become a text of sorts. The walls surrounding San Isidro protect the narratives of the people who worked for the Sugar Land plantations. The inscriptions on the headstones and the verbal narratives that circulate throughout the community about those buried inside the walls "metaphorized the dominant order: they made it function in another register."[61] Vicente Cordova, Simón Gonzales, Gregorio Cortez, and Luis de la Rosa continue to be represented by the actual existence of the cemetery. They also remain alive in the stylized image of the Aztec prince holding the sleeping princess.

The Battle at Home: War Hero Macario García

". . . in those days . . . Things were not good at all and that area between Fort Bend County really has a very poor track record as it related to Hispanics" (U.S. District Judge James DeAnda, November 2004).[62]

The day Macario García died was Christmas Eve 1972. I was in my room at my parents,' opening a Christmas gift from a friend, when I found out that my parents were going to have to work through Christmas. It happened often: We would be at a relative's wedding or some other family event; there would be a phone call; and my father would have to return home. It was part of the responsibility of owning a small funeral home. While home from college for the holidays, I would help at the office as I always did when in Rosenberg. García's funeral brought out many people I knew well. His older brother Carlos was married to Tomasita Martínez, the daughter of a prominent mexicano farmer in the county, Don Atanacio Martínez. The entire Martínez family was at the wake and the funeral. I had known Macario's brother Lupe, as well as Carlos, whom my father called *compadre* all my life. Compadre Carlos seemed to come by every few days; there was always lots of conversation. Our families had been close since the early 1950s, when Don Atanacio hired my father to work his cotton picker when the funeral home did not make enough money to support our family. Don A, as he was called, would always invite us to his home. There was always lots of food and company. His house, "la casa del cono" (the house with one peak), was out in the country amid fields of cotton, with rose bushes providing a boundary between the house and the farm.

In the past few years I had seen Lupe García at the cemetery and other events. Even though my father had told me about Macario García, I had not associated Lupe and Compadre Carlos with Macario's story. I never knew Macario (or at least did not remember him) because he lived outside the county and had a busy professional life working for the Veterans Administration. Thirty years after his death, my father told me they were frequent drinking buddies in the early 1950s.

You Can Have My Medal, Mr. President: Hürtgen Forest, Grosshau, Germany—November 20, 1944

According to a War Department Citation, [Macario] García
    . . . single handedly assaulted two enemy machine gun emplacements. Attacking prepared positions on a wooded hill, which could be approached only through meager cover, his company was pinned down by intense machine gun fire and subjected to a concentrated artillery and mortar . . . barrage. . . . On his own initiative [García] crawled forward along until he reach [*sic*] a position near an enemy emplacement. Hurling grenades . . . he . . . assaulted the position, destroyed the gun, and with his rifle, killed three of the enemy who attempted to escape. When he rejoined his company, a second machine gun opened fire and . . . again . . . [García] went . . . forward . . . disregarding his own safety. He stormed the position and destroyed the gun, killed three more Germans and captured four prisoners.[63]

Macario García had already experienced combat by the time he arrived at Hürtgen Forest.[64] He was with his group, the 4th Infantry Division, when the army reached the Normandy beachhead on June 6. He was involved in the capture of Cherbourg, relieving the 82nd Airborne, which had been trapped for thirty-six hours. He also took part in the capture of Paris in September and was one of first to cross the German border that same month. Just inside the German lines on September 16 (Mexican Independence Day, as Morin notes), García "captured a machine gun and the German gunner," for which he was awarded the Bronze Star.[65] For this accomplishment he became known as the "fearless Mexican."[66]

Two months later, at Hürtgen Forest, García's capture and destruction of an enemy emplacement saved his unit and won him the Congressional

San Isidro Cemetery: the gravestone of Pablo Moreno Ortiz, who was killed in Vietnam in 1968. Latino soldiers (along with African American soldiers) experienced a high casualty rate in Vietnam (2004).

Medal of Honor. Morín's narrative provides a nostalgic idealism: "By mid-November, with some of the worst winter weather hitting Europe, Macario and the men of the Fourth found themselves doing battles with the enemy in the dark thickets of the . . . Hürtgen Forest. . . . García went through the Hürtgen mud and splintered paths, and roadblocks interdicted with deadly machine gun fire. He well remembers the bitter cold, the heavy-mined and booby-trapped paths, and the smell of death that lingered on for many days . . . afterwards."[67]

Garcia was noted for his heroism and awarded the Congressional Medal of Honor by President Harry Truman in the East Room of the White House on August 23, 1945. The *New York Times* reported that "nearly a hundred relatives and friends of the recipients held equal rank with high army and navy officials."[68] A few days later . . . García was back home in Texas.

The Hero of the County

Fort Bend had a hero in the nineteenth century. The county honored Colonel Frank Terry, Civil War hero (and martyr) by naming a city street and a public high school after him. There is a middle school named after Macario García, the county's twentieth-century hero. He is the only person in the history of the county to be awarded the Congressional Medal of Honor.[69]

Macario García was born in northern Mexico in 1920, ninety-nine years after the birth of Frank Terry (in Kentucky, 1821).[70] They both moved to Texas as children (García at age three; Terry at about age twelve), and both lived and worked on cotton plantations. As a young adult, García was living with both parents when he was drafted to serve in WWII. Terry's parents died early. He was raised by his uncle, Benjamin Fort Smith, and moved to the county in his early thirties, after he found a fortune in the gold mines of California. Terry joined the Confederacy when he was thirty-nine years of age.

García grew up half a century later on what had been the western edge of Terry's plantation. The García family members were sharecroppers who worked for the Paul Schumann farm near Sugar Land. Macario was drafted into the U.S. Army in November 1942. He was twenty-one. He survived intense combat, and at the age of twenty-four he returned home after being awarded the Medal of Honor. García's return was not glorious (although he returned alive).

On September 6 the *Houston Chronicle* posted a small notice on page twelve of its front section: "Sugar Land Hero to Be Honored in City Tonight."[71] The article describes García as a "Sugar Land farm boy" who had recently returned from an awards ceremony in Washington, D.C. "Garcia, born in Mexico, but a naturalized American citizen" was "honored . . . by citizens of Fort Bend County and Harris County." In Houston, the League of United Latin American Citizens and the Mexican consul, along with a number of other Mexican American community leaders, greeted him with a reception in his honor. Also attending was Robert E. Smith, who was the unofficial "boss" of Houston.[72] At the time, Smith was the director of civil defense for Harris County and chair of the Good Neighbor Commission.[73] He also owned a large ranch just north of Rosenberg. García arrived late to the reception. His image as an inept Mexican farm boy was emphasized the following day when a local newspaper disparaged him for getting lost on the way to the reception in downtown Houston. The article appeared on the front page of the *Houston Press*. Titled "Honor Medal Winner Gets Lost in City," again using the description of "farm boy," the reporter explained how García arrived at the reception more than two hours late:

> Garcia . . . got lost while en route to . . . Houston. . . .
>
> The slight, Mexican-born youth really knew his way around the battlefields of France and Germany but Thursday he had one heck of a time trying to find the Second National Bank building. . . .
>
> At 2:30 P.M. the young hero arrived, out of breath and soaking wet.
>
> Sgt. Garcia grinned sheepishly.
>
> "Forgive me for being late," he said. "I got lost and couldn't find the building. I'm a country boy, you know."
>
> The swarthy young . . . sergeant . . . admitted he had to hitchhike from Sugar Land to Houston because he couldn't find anyone with the time to drive him here for the reception.
>
> Sgt. Garcia was one of 28 heroes awarded the Medal of Honor last week by President Truman.
>
> "The President was very nice," Sgt. Garcia said. "He shook my hand and gave me the award. Then he said. 'Son, I certainly wish I had one of those.' I told him he could have mine but he laughed and shook his . . . head."
>
> He is afraid of only one thing—women. "I'm 25 years old and suppose I ought to get married," he said. "But you know, women scare hell out of me."
>
> He never had a fistfight in his life, thinks fighting is foolish.
>
> But he wasn't that way at 10:30 A.M., Nov. 27, . . . 1944.[74]

Documented records do not list any type of welcome in García's own county. His presence was not significant enough for anyone to even provide him transportation to the only official reception given for him on his return from Washington, D.C.

The Fearless Mexican: The Oasis Café and the Richmond Drive-In, Richmond, Texas—September 10, 1945

The Richmond Drive-In was a low, squat building on the west side of the Brazos River, next to the U.S. Highway 59 bridge. From the 1950s to the 1970s it displayed a large sign that announced it had the "world's best enchiladas." In the age of the carhop, women would attend their customers, who sat in their cars in rows outside. The drive-in was two blocks from the county courthouse, the site of the Jaybird-Woodpecker feud. By the 1970s it was a worn building with some loyal customers, presenting a stark contrast to the nearby stately mansions owned by the descendants of the Old Three Hundred, who populated Richmond.

The story of Macario García and the Richmond Drive-In came up in conversations with my father, José F. Hernández.[75] I had not yet entered adolescence. As we traveled around the county together, he often told me stories as we passed by people's houses or businesses. He would tell me of different incidents, some successful and some tragic. When he told me the story of the Richmond Drive-In, I was not aware that he and Macario García had been close friends in the early 1950s. The most significant story (for my father) happened in 1945. Telling me that radio newscaster Walter Winchell started one particular program by saying "Sugar Land, Texas, is the sorriest place in the United States," he always added that Winchell should have said Richmond, Texas, where the incident actually occurred.

Macario was in uniform when he entered the café a few days after returning from Washington, D.C. He was probably aware of the potential for a violent confrontation since Jim Crow laws in the county and the rest of Southeast Texas banned people of color from restaurants and other public places. In Rosenberg, three miles to the west, Schaeffer's Pharmacy[76] had a separate window. African American and ethnic Mexicans stood outside to purchase refreshments from the store's soda fountain. They were not allowed inside to sit at the counter with white residents, even though they were able to make purchases.

The story I heard initially was that García entered the place and was immediately told that Mexicans were not allowed in the restaurant. He became angry and turned over tables and chairs. There is little detail as to the incident inside the drive-in. What is more sensational is how the story circulated. A speech given by . . . federal Judge James DeAnda in 2004 gives further explanation: "Garcia . . . [c]ame back from serving in the war and went to a restaurant over there in Sugar Land, as I remember, or Richmond—I don't know the name of the . . . place . . . They wouldn't serve him because he . . . was . . . Hispanic, even though he was wearing his Congressional Medal at the time. And somebody said, 'You're going to have to leave.' And as he did, he tipped a glass of water over on the table and there were two deputy sheriffs sitting in the restaurant at the time, and they took him outside and just beat the hell out of him and filed on him for assaulting an officer."[77]

Harold J. Alford discussed the incident in *The Proud Peoples*.[78] Alford does not cite his source of information, although he mentions consulting with George I. Sánchez. His version provides more detail:

Garcia dropped into the Oasis Café for a cup of coffee and was greeted by "We don't serve no Mexies in . . . here."

"You'll serve me," Garcia said. "If I'm good enough to fight your war for you, I'm good enough for you to serve a cup of coffee to."

"Listen, you dirty greaser," the proprietor said, coming around the end of the counter toward Garcia, "you disgrace that uniform just by wearing it. Now get out of here before I throw you out."

At a table by the window, two sailors were finishing their roast beef hot plates. "Hey, come on, give the sarge a cup of coffee," one sailor called.

"You keep out of this, sailor boy," the proprietor said. "This punk thinks just because he's got some stripes on his arms and ribbons on his chest he's as good as a white man."

He grabbed Sergeant Garcia by the collar and by the seat of the pants and was trying to swing him from the counter stool and lead him toward the door.

The two sailors were on their feet and coming over to try to stop the action. Three other customers were on their feet, too, coming from various directions toward the spot where the proprietor was still trying to unseat Sergeant Garcia.

But before any of them could get there, the sergeant's combat-trained re-flexes took over, and his left elbow dug into the proprietor's stomach. As Garcia spun on the stool, the side of his right hand caught the proprietor on the point of the chin as he doubled forward from the punch to his stomach. A split second sooner, and Garcia's hand would have smashed into the proprietor's throat, above the Adam's apple; as it was, the force of the chop sent the proprietor sprawling back into the arms of the two sailors.

By that time, the other customers had arrived where the action was, and Garcia found himself struggling against the pinioning arms of the two of them. Still another customer had grabbed the phone at the end of the counter and was . . . dialing. . . . The door burst open and a deputy sheriff charged in.

"Cut it out or I'll arrest the lot of . . . you!" he shouted. . . .

"Look at that ribbon," one of the sailors told him. "It's the Congressional Medal of . . . Honor. . . . Anybody who's wearing it ought to be able to eat any-where."

The deputy shook his head. "I don't know nothing about that," he said, "but I do know this place is a mess. I'm closing it up for the . . . night. . . . The best thing to do is for everybody to forget the whole . . . thing . . ."

Everybody . . . talked about it, and diplomatic channels from Mexico City to Washington, D.C., burned hot over the issue.

Then Walter . . . Winchell . . . told the national radio audience about the . . . insult. . . . As a result the sheriff, in order to "uphold the honor of the county," . . . arrested . . . Garcia and charged him with "aggravated assault."[79]

García's confrontation at the Richmond Drive-In became an integral part of ethnic Mexican folklore. The story has been repeated continuously in newspapers, web pages, and published essays. In 2002 Enrique Castillo of Los Angeles produced a play titled *Los Veteranos: Legacy of Valor,* which presents the story of García's being refused service at the Richmond Drive-In.[80] When García's name comes up in conversation in the Latino community, the incident at the Richmond Drive-In is often mentioned.[81]

I had thought that such a popular story would have been reported at least in local newspapers. I searched the Houston and Dallas papers' archives for most of September 1945 but found nothing on the incident. Other related articles (that did not mention García) appeared in the *New York Times* and the *Dallas Morning News.* They told of a sergeant from Arkansas, named James Hendrix, who had been refused service at an exclusive Washington hotel dining room.[82]

It seems odd that the Houston newspapers did not report García's problems in Richmond. The story of Winchell telling his audience about García has been retold numerous times. I began looking for audio recordings of his programs. Most libraries have only a handful of them, and none that I contacted had September 1945. His writings, however, are at the New York Public Library for the Performing Arts (Billy Rose Theatre Collection). I decided to make a personal visit to the library.

Macario García, a Mexican: New York City—September 23, 1945

The program during which Winchell discussed Macario García was broadcast from New York City. It was easy to find the microfilm containing the script for September 23, 1945. It contained Winchell's actual scripts with first and second drafts. He (or his writers) began writing the program in July. They completed a second draft on September 17, 1945. The date is significant because I have not found the exact date of García's arrest. The span of time, however, is limited to the days between the article in the *Houston Press* about his getting lost in downtown Houston (September 7, 1945) and Winchell's second draft (September 17, 1945). His script did not begin the show as José F. Hernández described. Since I have not been able to locate the audiotape, I cannot check to see whether Winchell decided to ad-lib at the last moment. The version he aired on the program differed from other accounts:

Attention, Mrs. and Mrs. United States

An American soldier, recently decorated with the Congressional Medal of Honor by the president of the United States, was terribly beaten with a baseball bat in Sugar Land, Texas.

This hero, who fought for our country and won the highest award our country can give to any man, is named Sergeant Marcio [sic] Garcia, a Mexican. The alleged attack took place at a soft drink parlor where Sergeant Garcia tried to buy a soft drink. He was refused service, although he was wearing the United States uniform at the time. When Sergeant Garcia protested, the beating with the baseball bat followed. Two American sailors, also in uniform, attempted to go to his rescue, and were also badly beaten—so much that all three needed hospital attention. The persons responsible for this disgraceful assault could hardly be Texans. Texans do not fight with baseball bats, and no matter what they fight with—from bullets to bayonets—they fight like men. Mexico City, Mexico, can afford to be calm. Lone Star justice is traditionally swift. Never has any Texan asked or needed assistance to defend the honor of Texas, and Texas has too many sons wearing the Congressional Medal of Honor to permit any home-grown Fascist to spatter it with any hero's blood.

Have a little irony—There is more peace in Berlin, Germany, and Tokyo, Japan, than there is tonight in Toledo and Detroit, USA.[83]

Walter Winchell most probably read the article about Sergeant Hendrix, also denied service in Washington, D.C. Information for weekly radio programs and newspaper columns was gathered from national news sources such as the *New York Times*. Why did he choose García over Hendrix to discuss treatment toward returning U.S. war heroes? Was it because García's story was more dramatic, with baseball bats involved? Or was it because the confrontation happened in Texas, a place geographically and psychologically distant from New York?

Hendrix was also from a region considered socially backward. The difference was that the event at the hotel occurred in Winchell's own territory. The prominent radio personality had probably been a guest at the opulent Willard Hotel[84] (and its dining room) numerous times. It is also curious that Winchell wrote about the Texans fighting like men with bullets and bayonets. Had he not heard about the continued violence in Texas toward people of color? The omission of Hendrix's problem in Washington may have been an indication that Winchell preferred to avoid the polemic about the mistreatment of white working-class military heroes. While it was beneficial that Garcia's story be disseminated, Winchell's choice to focus on a Mexican hero in Texas also told the world that this type of treatment toward people of color was still readily expected.

Regardless of Winchell's intentions, his discussion of García's experience at the Richmond Drive-In circulated around the world. The silence of the newspapers (and Winchell's mispronunciation of García's first name) did not keep people from hearing about Macario García. The broad circulation of Garcia's story speaks not only to the significance of the media (to ethnic Mexicans) in the mid-twentieth century; it is also a testament to one of those rare instances demonstrating when the spoken narrative is strategically placed and distributed, it can be more powerful than a written text.

Speaking in Code: Some White Country People from Arkansas— Washington, D.C., August 23, 1945

From its inception in 1850 to this day, the Willard InterContinental Washington has been a favorite choice of U.S. and international travelers. Known as the "Crown Jewel of Pennsylvania Avenue" or the "Grand Dame of American Hotels," the hotel ". . . enjoys its place as a major force in the social and political life of Washington DC."

García and twenty-seven other military men received the Medal of Honor from President Truman on August 23, 1945. The night before the awards ceremony, another Medal of Honor recipient, Staff Sergeant James Hendrix, accompanied by his parents, walked into the very elegant Crystal Dining Room of the Willard Hotel and were refused service. They were from Lepanto, Arkansas. The hotel is one of the most stylish in the nation's capital. The hotel's manager told the *New York Times* that the maître d'hôtel "refused to permit the Hendrix family in the Crystal Room because Sergeant Hendrix's father wore a sports shirt and was without a coat or necktie." Sergeant Hendrix disagreed, saying the elder Hendrix "wore 'trousers, coat, tie, shirt and even shoes.'" The statement following the "shoes" commentary is telling. The article continues: "He [Hendrix] emphasized there was no disturbance; that he and his family left quietly and had dinner at a downtown restaurant."[85]

The report of Hendrix being turned away at the Willard was informative—ethnic Mexican American military heroes were not the only ones receiving ambivalent responses upon returning to the States. Texas newspapers were silent about García's arrest at the Richmond Drive-In. On September 10, however, the *Dallas Morning News* decided to comment on the Hendrix incident. Journalist Robert Quillen,[86] a nationally syndicated columnist writing from South Carolina, reflected on Hendrix's experience in a tone reminiscent of antebellum Texas. Without mentioning Macario García, Quillen's narrative addresses a number of issues related to the Richmond Drive-In incident:

Not the Tyrant Himself but Slave Who Cracks the Whip

By Robert Quillen

Doubtless you have heard or read about the Medal-of-Honor [*sic*] sergeant and the arrogant brush-off given his parents and a lady cousin in Washington.

The sergeant [Hendrix] was there, along with twenty-seven others, to receive this highest of military decorations from the President, for heroism "above and beyond the call of duty." His people had been officially invited to witness the ceremony, and the government had assigned them to a certain swank hotel.

They were not city people, and the weather was hot, so the old gentleman entered the hotel dining room in his shirt sleeves.

A waiter asked them to leave and they left, shamed, humiliated and angry.

Not the Only Instance

I know how they felt, for I had a similar experience some years ago.

Near a North Carolina resort city there is a hotel surrounded by mountains, greenery and the rich aroma of solvency. The rates kept out the scum, but many tourists drove out to see the place, as tourists everywhere visit the local shrines and wonders.

One blistering July day I drove out there with my wife and daughter and two lady friends. Being a countryman in a hot place, I had discarded my coat.

Verboten

As we crossed the big lobby which was furnished with fat chairs occupied by fatter customers, a uniformed mulatto about 20 years old hurried to meet us. He circled around the ladies and said to me in a low but cold and arrogant voice: "The rules don't allow anybody in the hotel without a coat."

Well, I was an intruder and I hate a scene, so there was nothing to do but get out. The young mulatto kept a poker face, but his eyes revealed his enjoyment.

The strange thing about such incidents, which are frequent all over America, is that the arrogant ones who do the insulting are not the rich or aristocratic or powerful, but hired hands—menials who serve as tools. They are only obeying orders, but they do it with relish. Insulting people, with the authority of a big shot behind them, seems the next best thing to being a big shot.

Others to Swing the Whip

> No colonial gentleman ever struck a commoner with a bull whip. He could always find another commoner to do it for him—and lay it on hard. No tyrant or dictator ever overcame and cowed the little people by himself. Other little people were glad to do it for him at a price.
>
> The worse [sic] of snobs are in the "lower class." They have kept themselves down for thousands of years by selling out and betraying their own kind.[87]

Quillen, a folksy writer and journalist known as being sensitive to the white American working class, most probably responded to Hendrix's experience at the Willard Hotel because of the soldier's rural Arkansas background. The allusion to "country people" indicated that they were white and poor, or at least unsophisticated.[88] Quillen's reference to being from the country connected him with Hendrix. By also noting that he "hated a scene," he paired himself with Hendrix who avoided "a scene" by not creating a "disturbance" and leaving the Willard Hotel "quietly."

In a curious bit of timing, Quillen's article appeared the same day that García is reported to have tried to enter the Richmond Drive-In. Either the date of García's confrontation is incorrect as later published in the *Houston Chronicle,* or Quillen uncannily chose to publish the piece on Hendrix without knowing that a major event regarding another Medal of Honor awardee was simultaneously occurring.

Regardless of the article's publication date, the example of the young mulatto in a uniform ordering Quillen and his family out of the hotel provokes the image of the young García in uniform, ordering the Richmond Drive-In employees to serve him. The boisterous and violent García was the antithesis of the humble Hendrix/Quillen. García's background as the son of a sharecropper, relegated to the lowest social status in Texas society, next to the descendants of black slaves, whose purpose (as mentioned by Clarence Wharton) was to serve the white planters of Fort Bend County[89] could be identified as the villain, whom the journalist describes as one of those "arrogant ones who do the insulting . . . hired hands—menials who serve as tools." In being awarded the Medal of Honor by President Truman, García had become a tool of the president, he now had "the authority of a big shot" behind him. His actions exemplified that "[t]he wors[t] of snobs are in the 'lower class.'"

If the Richmond incident had already occurred and Quillen knew about it, it is possible that the Dallas article was meant as camouflaged criticism of Garcia's behavior. If not, Quillen was setting out the rules regarding the behavior of any undesirables toward the nation's war heroes. The title "Not the Tyrant Himself but Slave Who Cracks Whip," harshly criticized Hendrix's treatment at the Willard. The focus, however, was not the administration of the Willard, it was the character of the waiter who expelled the family. The reporter likened the waiter to a slave, the lowest in the chain of command, who nevertheless humiliates others.

If Garcia's confrontation occurred before September 10, Quillen may have been reacting to a Mexican-born soldier responding violently to the long-established Jim Crow laws commonly found in most parts of Texas. Jim Crow was more powerful than the honorable military service, even more powerful than extraordinary heroism and a Congressional Medal of Honor. Quillen's article intimates that the waiter at the Willard Hotel still carried the identification of being a slave. He had exhibited inappropriate behavior, which was overly aggressive and insensitive to the unsophisticated Hendrix family. Similarly, a number of narratives of García's Richmond Drive-In confrontation describe an out-of-control García "tearing the place up." The former sharecropper who became a national hero and was decorated by the president expected to be immune from Jim Crow. The county's rules of social conduct, however, prescribed that men of color did not act in impertinent or aggressive ways.[90]

Tradition: Fort Bend County Courthouse—November 2002

John Healey, the very handsome district attorney of Fort Bend County, organized a memorial reception for García in the rotunda of the courthouse. The DA, other local officials, and a retired army general gave speeches that day. As Healey spoke, he voiced respect for the county's war heroes and expressed concern that their memory be kept alive in the county. He helped initiate an effort to move a portrait of García to the center of the courthouse. Before 2002 it had been hidden in the alcove of the rarely used front entrance. After the speech he congratulated García's family and friends. They took many photographs. I took photos of the DA and García's widow as they stood in front of the portrait. After the reception, I asked Healey for an appointment to discuss local history.

We met a few days later. He is very cordial and forthcoming, even though he said he knows little about Fort Bend County history. Our conversation went on for more than ninety minutes. Healey is not originally from Texas. He is from New England; yet he seems to have learned the multiple idiosyncrasies of the local culture. He said he was glad to speak with me. He told me of his great respect for my father and, because of this, was glad to be of help.

Among a number of issues, we talked about Macario García. Healey had another version of the Richmond Drive-In story. He related the information without intensity, using a tone of objectivity. *García was very intoxicated when he arrived at the café. He was accompanied by a prostitute (or two) that he had brought from Mud Alley (Richmond's red-light district).* Healey did not question what he had heard. He did not say that there could have been variations of the story. His reference to my father carried an unspoken request: his respect for my father would equal mine for Healey. He knew that the information would be used for a book on local history. There had to be some concern about what I would say, considering the entangled racial history of the county.

Before the conversation ended, he also told me that García died in an auto accident while driving intoxicated. Two elderly women from Sugar Land also died in the collision. It was the first time I had heard the details of García's death from any source other than my father, José F. Hernández. This was something I knew because my father had buried Macario García. The day of the funeral I drove a station wagon full of floral arrangements to García's burial site at the Houston National Cemetery. I was present when the soldiers from Fort Sam Houston fired a twenty-one-gun salute.

Did the cordial Healey want me to have a balanced picture of Macario García? If so, in some respects, this is much more realistic. Macario García was a real person with foibles and weaknesses. Recent psychological studies of World War II veterans show that significant emotional trauma continues to affect them, decades after combat. It seems plausible that these effects could include a problem with alcohol.[91] Did being a larger-than-life hero who came from a place where his family replaced the work of slaves create an untenable dichotomy for Macario García? He was already drinking quite a bit in the early 1950s, when he and my father visited the bars in Houston.

The "unspoken" aspects of Macario García's narrative resonate with Michel de Certeau's commentary that a "historiographical research is articulated over a socioeconomic, political, and cultural place of production."[92] The occlusion of the incident at the Richmond Drive-In was demanded by tradition. The county is a place of historical production, and politics prevented the dissemination of a narrative about a Mexican sharecropper who was refused service at a white restaurant. The culture of the county refused to admit that such a person could be a hero, recognized not just nationally but globally. Even the silence surrounding García's death reveals a complexity not easily recognized. For ethnic Mexicans, it may be necessary to value the hero/warrior as blameless. The death of two elderly white women provides a facile explanation of a troubled individual who drank too much. There could be fear that the circulation of this story could easily slip García back into the space of the unhero.

The accident of his death, however, does not minimize what he did in his youth. His superhuman responses during the war were nothing short of remarkable, especially when compared to the military situation in the early twenty-first century (since most of our nation's leaders and their children have avoided military service altogether). García's stance at the Richmond Drive-In was the strongest counter to the myth of the passive mexicano. There have always been warriors. The problem has been that their stories were silenced in the historiographical projects of our national and state history. Their narratives have continued to be represented in the occasional reminiscence about what happened to Macario García at the Richmond Drive-In. In a more nostalgic and stylistic way, the image of Macario symbolically appears on all of those calendars inside the homes and neighborhood stores of ethnic Mexicans that show the Aztec warrior as the conqueror.

A Final Report

The *Houston Chronicle* finally published an account of the incident at the Richmond Drive-In—at least ten days after it occurred.[93] Robert E. ("Bob") Smith conducted an investigation in his role as chair of the Texas Good Neighbor Commission. It is likely that the *Chronicle* decided to release the information on García after Smith made the decision to investigate.[94] Almost fifty years later, on July 20, 2002, the Houston newspaper posted what it called a verbatim reproduction of the original article:

> *Houston Chronicle,* September 20, 1945
>
> The Texas Good Neighbor Commission is investigating the circumstances surrounding the refusal of a café in Richmond to serve Sgt. Macario Garcia, of Sugar Land, Congressional Medal of Honor winner, R. E. (Bob) Smith, Chairman of the commission, said Thursday.
>
> "I have been fighting for people like you and then you mistreat me," the sergeant was quoted as saying.
>
> He holds in addition to the nation's highest award for heroism, the Bronze Star Medal for gallantry and the Purple Heart for wounds received in action.

A search through the newspaper's microfilm archives resulted in something different. On the front page of the September 20, 1945, issue of the *Houston Chronicle,* to the lower left of an article on Shirley Temple's wedding and sev-

eral inches below the main headline of "Men in Army 2 Years to Get Out," is
a posting titled "Hero Refused Service in Café."

Houston Chronicle, September 20, 1945

A Texas Good Neighbor Commission is investigating the circumstances surrounding the refusal of a café in Richmond to serve Sgt. Macario Garcia, of
Sugar Land, Congressional Medal of Honor winner, R. E. (Bob) Smith, Chair-
man of the commission, said Thursday.

According to sworn statements taken by Richmond officers, Sergeant Garcia entered the café between 11 P.M. and midnight, on September 10 and was refused service.

A Mexican girl who preceded him into the café had also been refused service, a statement made by a waitress at the café said.

"I have been fighting for people like you and then you mistreat me," the
sergeant was quoted as saying.

Sergeant Garcia is in Washington awaiting discharge. The son of a farm
family who live near Sugar Land, he holds in addition to the nation's highest
award for heroism, the Bronze Star Medal for gallantry and the Purple Heart for
wounds received in action.

The Mexican consulate here had no statement to make on the incident.

Perhaps the *Houston Chronicle* was attempting to save column space when
it reprinted a condensed version of the article. Whatever the reason for the
omission, the inclusion of "sworn statements taken by Richmond officers"
would have provided a sense of legality to the text. The remaining text stated
that the Good Neighbor Commission was "investigating the circumstances
surrounding the refusal of a café in Richmond to serve" the army hero. "Investigating the circumstances surrounding the refusal" suggests the possibility
of a mistake or misunderstanding, providing viability to the District Attorney's account of the incident and diminishing the connotation of culpability
on the part of the restaurant's employees.

After reading all of Winchell's script and the newspaper accounts of García's problem at Richmond Drive-In, I asked my father for his reaction to all
of the different information. He said *he knew* that Macario García tore up the
Richmond Drive-In after they refused to serve him.

Ancestral Power

A life controlled by Jim Crow and the ensuing rigid control against assertive
behavior placed the desire for agency in the images of its warriors. The Aztec

prince that graced the living rooms of many Mexican American homes contained the myth of other possibilities. While Simón Gonzales and Vicente Cordova were silenced, Macario García's voice is still heard every time his story is repeated.

Playwright Enrique Castillo situates a fantastic Aztec warrior in *Los Veteranos*. In one scene the handsome ancient warrior is placing the Congressional Medal of Honor on a present-day mexicano soldier.

Chapter six

Litigation

The San Isidro Cemetery Corp. filed a lawsuit against the [Sugar Creek] homeowners earlier this month seeking permanent access to their cemetery through a gate on Sugar Creek . . . Boulevard. . . (Houston Chronicle, August 21, 1993).

Twenty years after Garcia broke up the Richmond Drive-In, two developers bought land from Sugar Land Industries with plans to build the Sugar Creek subdivision, an exclusive area for residents with six-figure incomes. By 1970 the land had more value as lots for new homes than it did producing cotton and sugar cane. The families living in Gran Centro and Bodame did not have much time to prepare;[1] they had to quickly find new homes. John de la Cruz explained that it was a great loss for them The housing was old and not really adequate, yet the families had been there so many decades. It all disappeared in a matter of a few days. A few years before, in the mid-1950s, the owners of Sugar Land Industries, the Kempner family from Galveston, had provided funds (assisted by monies from the Federal Housing Authority) to offer mortgages to what one historian termed "non-white" buyers.[2] Some families from the villages moved into new houses built in "the quarters" using loans offered by the company. Others moved to the "Fifth Street Neighborhood," an unincorporated area nearby.[3]

The new construction left a small city of opulent houses and gardens, many bordering Oyster Creek. Other homes sat on the boundary of the subdivision's golf course. The houses and the creek surrounded the cemetery. During the initial phase of construction, realtors told buyers that the cemetery was no longer being used. Others were told there were only ten to twelve funerals per year. Eunice Collier, whose family purchased a home bordering the cemetery in 1984, had "absolutely no idea" the cemetery was active when the contract to her new home was signed.[4]

Sugar Creek construction bounded San Isidro on two sides by large homes; a third side was bordered by Sugar Creek Boulevard, leaving Oyster Creek as the fourth boundary. The wooden bridge connected the cemetery to what had been Gran Centro but was now First Colony. The cemetery continued to be used.

I. H. Kempner met with me at the Sugar Land Industries corporate office in 1998. He remembered visiting San Isidro in 1972 with Robert Armstrong, president of the company. The five acres were already surrounded by new development. Gran Centro was gone. Sugar Land Industries had divested itself of most of its additional acreage and real estate. He wondered what the company was doing with a cemetery. Kempner recalled that the graveyard had a section that was overgrown; he thought it was the Mexican section. After we discussed the positioning of the graves, he realized he was speaking of what he called "the prison cemetery." After the 1972 visit, he wrote out a quit claim deed, giving the property to the Catholic Diocese of Galveston-Houston. Two years later it was turned over to the new San Isidro Cemetery Association, a coalition of descendents of ethnic Mexican employees of Imperial Sugar.[5]

There were no significant problems for more than ten years—until the bridge began to deteriorate. The trucks carrying construction materials for the new homes in Sugar Creek had overburdened the structure. In researching what action to take, the cemetery association found that the bridge belonged to "no one." The city of Sugar Land did not claim it, the county did not claim it, and neither Sugar Creek nor First Colony claimed it. In 1993 the bridge was condemned by the Army Corps of Engineers. Wanting to avoid a conflict, the San Isidro group contracted with an engineer for an estimate of expenses. A new bridge would cost more than $150,000 plus ongoing maintenance. Sugar Creek homeowners offered San Isidro $25,000; the Kempners offered $5,000. The priest supporting San Isidro encouraged the cemetery group to consider a less expensive option, which was to create an entrance through Sugar Creek Boulevard.

Since the cemetery was (and still is) being used for new burials, funeral processions periodically drive through the new Sugar Land neighborhoods. It is not unusual for several hundred people to attend the funerals. This means that every few weeks a hearse, followed by a limousine and scores of automobiles snake their way through the new streets toward San Isidro. Before the bridge was demolished, the processions took an awkward route across the creek through another subdivision called Settler's Way. While solidly middle class, these residents did not object to the funeral cars passing in front of their houses and community tennis courts. The Sugar Creek subdivision that directly bordered the cemetery had uncomfortably tolerated the funerals as long as the procession used the bridge to access San Isidro. The tall fence surrounding the cemetery kept the mourners out of the more affluent subdivision. For a number of Sugar Creek residents, however, the idea of a funeral procession driving through their neighborhood was untenable. Glen Clover, the attorney representing the homeowners association, told me he was horrified at seeing cars parked along the curb of the boulevard next to the cemetery; he "never knew what was going on" inside the parked cars. They were "unknown vehicles" to him. When the processions first started traveling down Sugar Creek, the cars often double-parked outside the cemetery; he saw this as a security hazard, limiting residents' access. He used the term *detritus* for the cemetery; it was left over from another time and had no value in its current context. I wonder whether he believed that the people buried there (in addition to their living descendants) were also filth that needed to be thrown away. During our interview, six years after the litigation, he was still incensed. He monitored the cemetery on a daily basis, watching any comings and goings from his upstairs study. If he saw cars parked by the curb, he reported them to the police. The neighborhood passed an ordinance that restricted parking on Sugar Creek Boulevard. In response to this, the cemetery built a large driveway leading to the cemetery parking lot. When there were funerals, someone from the association would guide the cars from the boulevard into the driveway. In the past, a number of association members received parking tickets from Sugar Land police.

Our interview was held in Clover's study, overlooking San Isidro. A telescope by a window faced the cemetery across the street. When the interview ended, as I walked out of the room, I glanced at the telescope but did not say anything. He then said, "I never use the telescope to look at the cemetery." I did not respond to him but thought about all of the visits I had made to the place and the times I had gotten down on my hands and knees to gather pecans that had fallen from the trees.

Within a few days of my meeting with Glen Clover I visited San Isidro to help with a general cleanup that was scheduled twice a year. The cleanups usually last two days. The organization often provides hot dogs and soft drinks for volunteers. Because there is so much movement in and out of the cemetery, the front driveway is left open. One day two groups of people not associ-

Grave with wind chime in San Isidro Cemetery (2005).

ated with the cemetery wandered into San Isidro. One was a family who lived in the neighborhood. A nun who was visiting from another part of the United States accompanied them. They asked permission to look around and seemed to be aware that it was not a place that was generally open to the public. A few minutes later two men came through the gates. They appeared to be in their sixties and were wearing polo-type shirts. One of them, named Williams, told me he was the developer that built Sugar Creek. He said he often wondered what had happened to the cemetery and was glad that it was so well tended. He knew the space because he and his construction trucks passed by repeatedly during the time he worked at Sugar Creek. I mentioned the problems with the bridge and subsequent gate facing Sugar Creek Boulevard. Williams told me that the trucks did not ruin the bridge. He said that it was already very old and would probably have needed to be demolished anyway.

The Fence around the Cemetery

Gates and fences around our neighborhoods represent more than simple physical barriers. Gated communities manifest a number of tensions: between exclusionary aspirations rooted in fear and the protection of privileges . . . and . . . ideals of the public good and general . . . welfare (Blakely and Snyder 1997, 3).

In *Borderlands/La Frontera,* the late Gloria Anzaldúa tells about the family cemetery:

> My mother tells me . . . *Mi papa se murió de un* heart attack . . . a smart *gabacho* lawyer took the land away; Mama hadn't paid taxes. *No hablaba ingles;* she didn't know how to ask for time to raise the money. My father's mother Mama Locha also lost her *terreno.* For a while we got $12.50 a year for the "mineral rights" of six acres of cemetery, all that was left of the ancestral lands. Mama Locha had asked that we bury her there beside her husband. *El cementerio estaba cercado.* But there was a fence around the cemetery, chained and padlocked by the ranch owners of the surrounding land. We couldn't get in to visit the graves, much less bury her there. Today, it is still padlocked. The sign reads "Keep Out Trespassers Will Be Shot."[6]

Anzaldúa describes the family cemetery that she cannot reach. The last six acres of land still belong to the family, but it does no good to own the mineral rights if Anzaldúa and her grandmother cannot get past the locked gate. Her narrative travels beyond those six acres in South Texas that were left after the smart lawyer took the land for back taxes. Her poetics seem to reach back to another century. Her story encompasses more than her family; it seems to be about people pulled in many directions. They became landless after other smart lawyers took Texas away from Mexico.[7]

Anzaldúa's people, as did the mexicanos employed by the Imperial Sugar company, worked the land but owned none but the few acres where their family is buried. In Sugar Land, once the construction trucks ruined the bridge that crossed Oyster Creek, people lost access to the family cemetery. At least the residents in Settler's Way did not object to the long lines of cars that wove through the streets when someone needed to be buried.

Those in Sugar Creek had a different conception of the boundary around their neighborhood. After the bridge was gone, the only way to reach the cemetery was to travel down the main street of the affluent subdivision, that is, if an officer from the Sugar Land Police Department did not stop the visitor.[8] The similarity to Anzaldúa's cemetery lies in the padlocked gate. Even though San Isidro could be reached from another direction, via Sugar Creek Boulevard, there was no way to enter the space. As in the story about Mama Locha, "there was a fence around the cemetery"; it was made inaccessible by the "owners of the surrounding land." The bridge was ruined by the trucks used to build the big, new houses. Once the houses were built, the homeowners' association also constructed a very tall fence without a gate. Without the bridge there was no way to get inside.

The Sugar Creek homeowners were strongly against the new gate. During the initial construction of the subdivision, developers placed a three-foot "green belt" between the western edge of the cemetery and the boulevard. Creating a gate across the green belt without the permission of Sugar Creek would, in effect, make trespassers of the cemetery association. Gary Stanford, spokesman for the homeowners association, said the decision to build a gate opening San Isidro to the center of Sugar Creek felt like a betrayal. Residents always assumed people would enter by means of the bridge, which approached the neighborhood from the west. The bridge was the "back door" of Sugar Creek. As I write this, I think of the servants' entrance to a building or, from Jim Crow days, the "colored" entrance. With the bridge gone, the funeral processions of Mexican mourners needed to enter through the main entrance of Sugar Creek, which was unthinkable.

In August 1993 the two groups entered litigation. The San Isidro group filed a restraining order against Sugar Creek, so that the association could build the gate. Terri Rodríguez, a member of the cemetery association and secretary of Saint Theresa's Church, had just been told that the diocese could not assist the San Isidro group because of a conflict of interest. The group had only one day to find an attorney to represent it.

Rodríguez heard about attorney John Burchfield and that his specialty was real estate. She contacted him. When he heard the story, he was so moved that he offered to represent San Isidro for free. The case never actually went to court. A series of depositions in 1994 led to the use of a mediator, an associate of a Sugar Creek resident who lived next to the cemetery. San Isidro won the right to a gate opening to Sugar Creek Boulevard, allowing traffic through the subdivision and into the cemetery. The gate to the boulevard was constructed in 1995. The bridge was never rebuilt.

Four years after the hearing I attempted to interview Burchfield. He refused to meet with me but agreed to a telephone conversation. Even though San Isidro was successful in obtaining the gate, Burchfield was bitter. He told

Grave with Virgin Mary, whirligigs, artificial flowers, and other small statues. San Isidro Cemetery does not prohibit families from placing personal objects on gravesites (2004).

me that everyone abandoned the cemetery association: the Kempners, the homeowners, the city, the county. Burchfield was caustic during our telephone conversation and said he was really too busy to talk, yet he spoke for more than thirty minutes and seemed eager to give me information, except for the location of the deposition transcripts, about which he was evasive. While listening to Burchfield and his complaints, I wondered what side he was really on. John de la Cruz, president of the cemetery association, described Burchfield as a great lawyer who was totally committed to San Isidro. Wanting to respect John's opinion of the attorney, I decided not to pursue the basis of Burchfield's intentions and attitude.

Initially, the attorney representing the subdivision was Glen Clover. Dur-

Virgin Mary and plastic beetle at a grave in San Isidro Cemetery (2005).

ing the same period, I was exhibiting some of my photographs at the 1994 Houston Fotofest. I met Glen Clover for the first time at the opening reception of the exhibition. He had learned of the exhibit from my father, telling me that he and his wife thought it was a good thing to do (to go to the opening). I felt violated when I learned that he was the attorney for Sugar Creek. What was he trying to do, make some kind of psychological assessment of the daughter of his witness by looking at her photographs? Of all the things to do in metropolitan Houston on a weekend evening, why would he attend the opening of my exhibit? He had subpoenaed my father, who would have been a hostile witness. Clover was later replaced as Sugar Creek's attorney, I wondered if his own hostility made him less effective in their case against San Isidro.

In 2000, when I interviewed Clover at his home, he told me that San Isidro won the case because "the judge was seeking re-election and wanted the Hispanic vote." My father had suggested the same. Even so, it seemed odd that in a county as seriously conservative as Fort Bend, people who were considered the "old money" of Sugar Land would lose a case to a group of Mexican laborers and their descendants. It didn't fit with the history of the county (or the state, for that matter).

The settlement allowed the cemetery association to create two gates, one for a driveway and a second for pedestrians to enter San Isidro. In 1994 the funeral processions of Mexican mourners were finally able to travel through Sugar Creek—to reach the gate of San Isidro—without needing a restraining order.

A Question of Waste

Three years after the case was settled, a different conflict arose. It was about the detritus of the detritus; the problem concerned the building of a restroom on cemetery grounds. In early 1997 during a funeral service, a handicapped person (a relative of the deceased) needed to use a restroom. Because of this, the service was delayed thirty minutes while family members took the person to a nearby gasoline station. Considering future instances of this need, in addition to the long hours association members spend at the cemetery during "clean up days," the group decided the building of a restroom was a necessity.

The problems began when the plumbing lines were dug to connect the restroom to the city sewer line. According to John de la Cruz, the person digging the line was accosted by a Sugar Creek resident. The worker was threatened with a shotgun. Gary Stanford said the problem may have been that de la Cruz did not remind the homeowner of the impending construction. Burchfield said the homeowner's violent reaction was because the lines had to be dug inside her yard, in what is termed "city easement." Shrubs she had planted in her back yard had to be removed. She supposedly was not aware in advance of this pending work and was surprised to find a man in her back yard taking out her shrubs. Burchfield termed the restroom "an outhouse," claiming it was an attempt by the San Isidro people to punish the Sugar Creek homeowners for their reaction to the cemetery's request for a different entrance. He indicated that it was an angry and unreasonable response to previous conflicts. His own anger during our conversation was in direct con-

Two graves with virgins, crosses, and whirligigs in San Isidro Cemetery (2004).

tradiction to (what I had been told of) his earlier enthusiasm for the cause of San Isidro.

When I spoke with the woman who lived behind the restroom, she did not mention the conflict about its construction. She was more concerned about the teenagers who crossed over the fence at night. There was an inconsistency between her description of the problem and the story of a plumber being threatened with a shotgun. Guns are usually displayed (at least in Texas) because someone's property is at risk. The plumber had stepped over the property line to set up the restroom. Yet, ultimately, everything was placed in its original order, even though the sewer lines from the cemetery were now connected with that of the residents. It is this idea that resonates with Mary

Black and white geese on the grounds of San Isidro Cemetery (2005).

Douglas' work in *Purity and Danger,*[9] concerning contamination by association. After the restroom was constructed and the plumbing lines were
connected to the main Sugar Land sewer system, the cemetery and the subdivision were tangibly connected. Even though the link occurred after the waste
of the residents and the waste of the cemetery had already flowed down the
sewer, there seemed to be a fear of the "presence of waste," as if it would ruin
something the residents had.

Even though Burchfield continued to be angry, the construction was ultimately completed and the plumbing lines were connected without further

conflict through another resident's property . The restroom is now used regularly by San Isidro association members. It has a composition roof and is a small, neat building inside the space of the cemetery.

The conflict was settled without any physical injuries, but the event itself is telling. The use of the shotgun could be said to be a stereotypical Southern (or Texan) practice. The gun shoots, kills, and eliminates a bothersome being, whether it is a person, an alligator in Oyster Creek, or an escaped convict. In Patricia Yeager's book on Southern women writers, the need to eliminate (or throw away) is exemplified as part of the Southern world.[10] For Yeager, African Americans, as slaves or freedmen, were seen as disposable. During slavery they were easily sold; after emancipation, they were killed if they became troublesome.[11] Ethnic Mexican laborers, seen as extensions of the black laborers, were generally not killed because they were often seen as good, docile workers. Yet, they were easily sent away, banished from the plantation or the mill. In the towns they were perceived as peripheral objects, meant only to serve and labor.

Clover sees the cemetery as detritus because the graves (as he sees them) are filled with individuals no longer necessary to the existence of the county (at least not in the fields). Their history carries no significance, making their grave spaces meaningless to those seeking the importance of living in the grand Sugar Creek community.

Transforming the Space of Death

At the cemetery the experience of alterity is not tamed by figuration—by the appearance, even threatening, of a face (Pandolfo, 1997: 238, 239).

There are photographic portraits on many gravestones at San Isidro. In recent years, families have begun purchasing monuments for graves that date back to the 1940s. The photographs are imprinted on ceramic, in the manner of nineteenth-century European cemeteries. A few are already broken, but most are still intact. The unaccustomed visitor is gifted with images of people that never age. There are also a number of wrought iron park benches, although vandals have stolen a few. Some of the tall trees have wind chimes, and a number of the graves have colorful whirligigs. Throughout San Isidro there are numerous statues of the Virgin Mary, all different sizes. Some are of the Virgin of Guadalupe. There is one Guadalupe whose cloak is painted a very bright green. Her aura is fluorescent orange. A number of the graves look as if the families created their own altar for the dead. They have small figurines of angels, saints, and porcelain animals, often shaded by colorful artificial flowers. Not knowing the individual narrative behind each grave, I wonder if each object is part of a life story that is kept alive by its presence.

One of the association members built a barbecue grill with "San Isidro" on the cover. It is permanently placed under a large tree, available for gatherings where food is provided. There is now a pavilion at the center of the cemetery that seats at least a hundred people. It has a broad aluminum canopy with a concrete foundation. It stretches out from *el descanso,* the original spot where the caskets were placed during the graveside rituals before the 1950s. Association members gather there for meetings several times per year. In the fall and in the spring they organize a "clean up day" where members come to help keep the landscape in order. They also have fundraisers: raffles, golf tournaments, barbeques, and dances. Expenses are usually related to tree trimming, plumbing, electrical work, or building materials. Association members often provide the labor for needed maintenance.

A wrought iron fence that creates a boundary between the cemetery and Oyster Creek was constructed in 2003. Below is a wooden embankment, made necessary by erosion. Every year the cemetery lost several feet of ground. A number of older graves were washed away into the water the last three years, before the embankment was constructed. The gravestones were salvaged and moved to higher ground.

Day of the Dead: November 1998

As a child, the only *Dia de los Muertos* that I remember was comprised of a few dozen people walking through a cemetery at dusk. This occurred in the 1950s. I was spending the day at the home of Chana Salinas. I was about five years old. Her daughters helped take care of me while my parents worked. It happened to be November 2. We walked about half a mile just before dark and went single file by the graves. Everyone carried a lit candle. The idea of home altars and skeleton cookies was not as common in Southeast Texas before the great migration at the end of the twentieth century.

In 1998, I attended the *Dia de los Muertos* at San Isidro. It was raining that morning: not a heavy rain, more like a drizzle. The light was gray. There was a large crowd of people at the cemetery. The priest was late. When he arrived he moved from grave to grave, giving his blessing. Most of the time there were family members standing next to the graves. Sometimes there was no one.

People brought new flowers, making the place more colorful than usual. It was not a celebration. The blessing seemed to be a gift from the living to the dead. It did not have the flavor of the *Dia de los Muertos* celebrations that have in recent years become so common at art galleries and other public spaces.

Lori Rodríguez, a *Houston Chronicle* reporter, had contacted me a few days before and arranged to have a newspaper photographer take pictures at the event. It felt awkward seeing him move around, standing by trees and tall shrubs. John de la Cruz has always been careful about who is invited into the space. He says that publicity sometimes creates more tension with subdivision residents and makes things worse. A long article was written with a few nice color photographs. The title, "Homes versus Heritage" indicates how the opulent homes of the upwardly mobile residents reduced the ethnic Mexican past to detritus. John de la Cruz told the reporter, "Some of the homeowners who live out here have no respect for us. Some of them almost run over us. Some even speed up faster and honk. They're decent grown-ups with Mercedes and they'll still stick their heads out the window and yell, 'Get the hell out of the way.'"[12]

In response to the Rodríguez article, Sugar Land City Council Member Brian Gaston published an essay in the *Houston Chronicle* editorial section: "Sugar Land a Growing City that Embraces Its Diversity." The piece was a public relations attempt to counter Rodríguez' report of the tensions surrounding the cemetery's placement inside of Sugar Creek. Gaston explains that "Sugar Creek is a community of up-scale homes occupied by educated, middle-class citizens who respect cultural differences . . . the primary reason for the rude behavior is that the processions wind through neighborhood streets and traffic can be problematic, regardless of the cause."[13] At the time he wrote the piece, Gaston was in his second term on the city council. He denied the problems that de la Cruz discussed and promoted the city as a place where everyone was welcome. Gaston's promotion of diversity was an effort to clear himself (and his subdivision) of appearing racist.[14] Glen Clover made the same attempt in our conversation. He told me about his undergraduate degree (that he earned while on scholarship) at Harvard University. He had also been a member of a prestigious law firm that included a former Texas governor. Were Gaston and Clover indicating that if people are cultured and highly educated, they are beyond having prejudices and exhibiting poor behavior? This appears to have been their intention. They both condoned the harassment of cemetery visitors, with excuses of traffic problems and security issues from not knowing who was inside the cars. Yet the definition of being cultured and educated is usually associated with not "losing one's cool" under stress. Making people be-

Angel holding Easter eggs in San Isidro Cemetery (2005).

lieve they might be run over is really not acceptable under any circumstances. When it does occur it is usually related to the behavior of rebellious adolescents, not affluent, college-educated subdivision residents.

The cemetery has had the opportunity to request being designated a Texas Historic Site. The association decided against submitting the application because of concerns that the state would attempt to control how the cemetery is maintained. The association decided to place a sign with "San Isidro Cemetery" at the entrance on Sugar Creek. Yet because the cemetery is located inside of Sugar Creek, the homeowners association had to be consulted. The rules of the Sugar Creek homeowners association require the subdivision to authorize the placement of any signs. San Isidro's request was denied. In

2005, the cemetery remains anonymous to any unknowing travelers driving through Sugar Creek Boulevard. The tall fence that runs alongside both San Isidro and the black cemetery still looks like it borders the large back yard of one of the subdivision's mansions. If the gates are closed there is no way of knowing what is inside.

Narratives, Stories, *Cuentos:* The Song

Mira como ando, mujer, por tu querer
Borracho y apasionado nomas por tu amor
Mira como ando mi bien, muy dado a la borrachera y la perdición

Look at how I am, woman, because of your loving me
Drunken and impassioned because of your love
Look how I am, so given to drunkenness and destruction

("Tú, sólo tú" [lyrics by Felipe Valdés Leal])

Three months after the Latina singer Selena was murdered, Selena's distributor released an album that contained a fifty-year-old song titled "Tú, solo tú." The song became wildly popular, partly because of the tragic and passionate aspect of her death. She was shot after meeting a former employee in a Corpus Christi motel room. Speculation made a media circus event of the subsequent murder trial that was held in Houston. Gossip columns alleged a lesbian affair between Selena and the employee; others described a frustrated affair with a plastic surgeon from Monterrey, Mexico.

Selena's rendition of the song was released the year after San Isidro and Sugar Creek settled their legal entanglements. Years later it was still played regularly on local Spanish language radio stations. Whenever I am driving and happen to hear the song, I am reminded of Hilario Semersky singing "Tú, solo tú" when he died.

Murders do not often call my attention, but the circumstances surrounding the death of Semersky seems almost uncanny to me. My father has told me the story many times. There is something compelling about the act of singing such a passionate song at the moment of death. I know the song from a Cuco Sanchez album my mother used to play; Sanchez was a Mexican singer from the mid-twentieth century. His gravelly voice made him sound like he was crying as he sang. Even though Semersky died in 1950, two years before I was born, his death seems very immediate to me because I was always hearing "Tú, solo tú."

Gran Centro—Sugar Land, Texas: 1950

Hilario Semersky and his family lived in Gran Centro, across the creek from San Isidro, in a building that had once been a prison barrack. A few months before, he had allowed a young man to come live in his home. Without notice, the young man left one day with Semersky's wife, leaving behind the children. Afterwards the community looked at Semersky with some suspicion. He no longer had a wife to care for the children. He was a man alone. There was some concern that he might want to take someone else's wife.

There are a number of versions of his murder. The first one I heard in the 1970s: Semersky was working in the fields and returned home; he built a bonfire outside the barracks and started to sing. Aniceto Sanchez, who lived with his family in the other half of the barrack building, returned after Semersky. When Sanchez saw and heard Semersky singing, Sanchez went inside his home, got a shotgun, and killed Semersky. Sanchez readily admitted this to the judge.

When I began working on the cemetery project, I went to the George Memorial Library in Richmond (the county seat) and found the court records in a folder, sitting on the shelf of the special collections section on the second floor of the library. It was only my second year of graduate school and I was still very excited every time I found new information. Old textual sources seemed particularly interesting, especially if they were from Fort Bend County. Having grown up there, I always felt that the past was buried in some inaccessible place. Finding a reference to something that happened to a *mexicano* in the county fifty years before felt to me like a whole layer of history had been uncovered.

The opinion written by the presiding judge, which refused the appeal, was slightly different than the version of events I had heard. It placed the murder around midnight, instead of early evening. The document was brief, only two legal-size pages, yet the few words it contained said much about the history of the county:

> The evidence discloses that appellant, a Mexican, was a farm worker and lived on a large plantation in a cottage within a few feet of that occupied by the deceased. On the night of the tragedy, shortly after twelve o'clock, the deceased came up to the residence of appellant where he was engaged with others in drinking beer. He was singing a song in Mexican which, interpreted, is entitled "You, Only You" and is said to be a Mexican love song. Apparently this incensed appellant who, without any words, went into his house, got his gun, came out and shot, killing the deceased a short distance from his front door steps. About this there is no controversy.[15]

The word "plantation" startled me. I had never thought of the land owned by Imperial Sugar as a plantation. I knew the word was popular in the county. In the 1980s a master-planned community had been built just outside of Richmond, named Pecan Grove Plantation. Yet, perhaps I was in denial of the real history of the place. I had not yet digested the idea of slaves and plantations existing where I had grown up. The statement that Aniceto Sanchez lived on a "large plantation" was the beginning of a new and at times terrifying awareness for me, of a consciousness that now recognized a history even worse than the demeaning and controlling world often described in the lives of ethnic Mexicans and African Americans in twentieth-century Texas. The nineteenth century had begun to spill into my project. It reminded me of a comment by Patricia Yeager in *Dirt and Desire* as she discusses the work of novelist Ellen Douglas: "The question that Douglas unearths . . . is frighteningly simple. How do you write a story everyone knows but nobody hears?"(2000: 10). I cannot say I was really oblivious to the plantation world of nineteenth-century Fort Bend County. Yet I have to admit I had never really heard the stories as they were told; they did not reach me, did not get integrated into the space of my mind that made them real. I believe they were too close and too ominous. Growing up in a space that saw people as cattle, where people were casually tortured and murdered (as I came to find as I waded through old texts) would have created too much anxiety in the mind of a child or a young person. I defensively created a selective type of vision. I knew Jim Crow existed, but I didn't let myself remember that slavery and its varying forms of continuation existed into my lifetime. The moment I saw the document noting that Aniceto Sanchez lived on a large plantation was when I finally let myself walk into the history that most people in the county (and perhaps in many other places) have defiantly avoided.

The Lawyers from Houston: Some Good Works for the Folks— Richmond, Texas, 1952

My mother, Millie Carroll Parrot, and my father, Frederick Douglas Parrott, Senior, were the first in each of their families to obtain advanced college degrees. They were professionals. My mother was an elementary school teacher, my father a dentist. Both their fathers were dirt-poor farmers; my mother's parents were born slaves. Knowingly, my parents dismissed the consequences of their humble origins. Their raw energy to achieve was their main capital. They turned that into hard work and determination. Then both courageous and foolish bids to become part of this country's middle class. (Blue, 2003: 51)

It is extremely difficult to look at differences within a group that has been considered subaltern, especially if it concerns the writer's own family. Yet, I begin
this section with an excerpt from Carroll Blue's *Dawn at My Back* to bring
attention to class issues among people of color. Similarly, in Aniceto Sanchez'
subsequent trial, social class was a central, if unspoken, component.

Sanchez' attorneys, James de Anda and John J. Herrera, were from Houston. De Anda attended Jefferson Davis High School and was in the military
during World War II, eventually being named a federal judge. Herrera was
known as a scrappy civil rights lawyer, greatly respected by the Latino community in Houston. He was called "*el abogado garras*" (the lawyer in rags).[16]
Some narratives explain that it was because early in his career he did not have
enough money to dress well. Others relate it to his job at the City of Houston
Sewer Department during law school. Herrera was also well known for his genealogy. His great-great grandfather was Jose Francisco Ruiz, one of the sign-
ers of the Texas Declaration of Independence. His other great-grandfather,
Blas Maria Herrera, was known as the Paul Revere of the Texas Revolution.[17]
Even though John Herrera was known as the lawyer for the people and suf-
fered financial hardships while in law school, he was from a historically notable family. His father was a sheriff in a Louisiana parish, which placed him
in a significantly different position than Aniceto Sanchez.

De Anda had recently passed the Texas Bar Examination but had not
been able to find a job. He called at least half of the attorneys in Houston
and had been turned away. Eventually he was hired by Herrera. De Anda's
first assignment was to do legal research for the Aniceto Sanchez case. Herrera worked on other cases in Fort Bend and had never seen a Latino on a
jury. After de Anda found documentation to support Herrera's observation
they decided to make it a test case to challenge Jim Crow laws regarding jury
participation in Texas. Ultimately, their client was sentenced to ten years. In
a speech that mentioned their appeal, de Anda remarked, "Mr. Sanchez was
a somewhat reluctant guinea pig, because he didn't think ten years was a bad
deal."[18] A social science brief written by his attorneys in hopes of softening the
severity of the sentence, states: ". . . the Defendant herein who is uneducated
and speaks little English."[19]

John J. Herrera was a founding member and pivotal figure in the development of the League of Latin American Citizens. Benjamin Marquez, in his
essay on LULAC, critiques the organization, explaining that while it brought
closure to some of the worst Jim Crow moments in the lives of ethnic Mexicans, it was dominated by a middle class trajectory that set out to educate,
"socialize," and "refine" their people.[20] Marquez cites early LULAC leader

Alonso Perales, who wrote ". . . many Mexican-Americans were docile people, content with their 'primitive lives.'"[21] de Anda's comment on Sanchez being "a reluctant guinea pig" because he thought a ten-year sentence was reasonable belies a troubling polemic. Even though de Anda had not been able to find a job as a young lawyer and Herrera was given the title of "the poor lawyer," their lives were a complete opposite of Sanchez,' who worked for subsistence pay as a farmer for the conglomerate Sugar Land Industries, had no education, did not speak English, and lived with his wife and ten children in what had once been a prison barrack.

Herrera and de Anda had never lived in those types of conditions. While not minimizing their best intentions and actual assistance in dismantling Jim Crow, they still represented the accomplished (well-bred) professionals defending an illiterate man who lived in an old prison barrack. Their perception of Sanchez was evident in a conversation they had one day during a trial break at the infamous Richmond Drive-In (where Macario García was refused service in 1945). While having lunch they discussed the case, and wondered if indeed Mrs. Sanchez was involved with Semersky. Herrera jokingly responded by saying that she was too ugly, and anyway, how could she be attractive after having ten children? The judge's opinion stated that Semersky had been found under the Sanchez' bed, but did not indicate when this occurred. The attorneys had proposed this event as having precipitated the murder, hoping that it would release Sanchez from culpability because in the State of Texas, if a man found his wife in a compromising position with another man, he had the right to kill him. Yet, since Semersky was only under the bed, and not actually in *flagrante delicto* with Mrs. Sanchez, this avenue was not valid.[22] They continued the conversation about the Sanchez family and decided to stage an event that sounded as if it came from a 1940s film. The ten Sanchez children were brought to court, with hopes the judge would develop some sympathy. The ploy was successful. Sanchez was only given ten years. It could have been a sentence of twenty years of more.

The narrative explaining how the Sanchez children ended up in the court room was discussed by James de Anda.[23] Yet, I also know about the story because my father was present during the conversation on the subject of Mrs. Sanchez' beauty (or lack thereof). He had been hired as a translator for the trial. In his memory, Sanchez was never sent to prison.

In 1974, shortly after I returned home from college, my father took me to visit John J. Herrera at his Houston office. He explained to me that Herrera had been a significant force in the dismantling of Jim Crow for *mexicanos* in Houston. I don't believe he knew about Herrera's illustrious genealogy, for if he did, I'm sure he would have told me. He used to say Herrera was interested in helping "the little people." At the time I was sensitive to my father's empathy, having seen him do many things to make life easier for ethnic Mexicans in the county. A few decades later, I better understand the complexities of this idealized relationship between the professional man and "the little people."

Even though it was always important to have a purpose and make a difference for the lives of other *mexicanos,* the issue of difference was significant. My father told me once that it was an important thing to be a professional person. A professional person had more education, dressed better, and had higher standing in the community. This resonates with Marquez' comments on the nature of LULAC's position regarding social class and public behavior. It is a conflicting narrative that evokes inequalities and the desire to maintain a certain status. John Herrera told my father in the 1950s, that he (Hernández) was the only one in Fort Bend County that knew anything. My father took it as a compliment and did not see it as an indictment of the "primitive lives" (as Perales described them) of all the other ethnic Mexicans in the county. In categorizing the rest of the Mexican population as "not knowing anything," the people were left with the label of ignorance, which paradoxically ignored the oppressive nature of their political and social world.

In the fall of 1997, I took my students to San Isidro. One of them found Semersky's grave. The letters engraved in the headstone had recently been painted with gold. Semersky had not felt as real until I saw the small curved gravestone with the gold letters. Every time I go back to visit the cemetery, I look for his grave. There are usually a few colorful flowers next to the stone. Someone changes them regularly. This past year someone has placed rocks in an outline around the grave. Richard Covarrubias, a member of the cemetery association, told me that Semersky's children went to live with his brother in San Antonio after his death. He also said that Aniceto Sanchez was his (Covarrubias's) cousin, and that he was a good man, explaining that Sanchez killed Semersky because he thought the song "Tú, solo tú" was being sung to Mrs. Sanchez.

Chapter seven

Re-Membering in the Land of Oz

"The road to the City of Emeralds is paved with yellow brick," said the Witch, "so you cannot miss it" (Baum 1900, 7).

The Sugar Land Town Square, built in the new millennium, evokes an eerie resemblance to the yellow brick road in Frank Baum's *Wizard of Oz*. It has a path of bricks about four feet wide that meanders from the fountain in the middle to the front steps of city hall. The trail along Baum's yellow brick road is full of adventure and tragedy. His wizard sends the protagonist on an almost impossible quest. She returns triumphantly, finding her way back to the Emerald City by way of the special brick road. Yet, once she enters the city and sees the wizard for who he really is, "the little man [says] meekly, 'I have been making believe.' 'Making believe!' cried Dorothy. 'Are you not a Great Wizard?' 'Hush, my dear,' he said. 'Don't speak so loud, or you will be overheard—and I should be ruined. I'm supposed to be a Great Wizard.' 'And aren't you?' she asked. 'Not a bit of it, my dear; I'm just a common man.'"[1]

Fiction and Reality

In *The Wizard of Oz,* "Baum created a children's story with a symbolic allegory implicit within its story line and . . . characterizations. . . . In the form of a subtle parable, Baum delineated a Midwesterner's vibrant and ironic portrait of this country as it entered the twentieth century."[2]

The story of *The Wizard of Oz* is an icon of American culture. Millions of children and adults have seen the movie based on Baum's book. Since the advent of television, it has been broadcast frequently, entertaining many people in the United States since the 1960s. The plot is fantastic and simple. During a tornado, an orphaned girl in Kansas is blown away (in her house) to a faraway land, "a country of marvelous beauty."[3] In an effort to return home to Kansas, the girl seeks out the "Wizard of Oz," the powerful leader of the "Emerald City."

On her way there she meets three characters: a tin man with no heart, a scarecrow with no brain, and a lion with no courage. They all decide the wizard can help them obtain what they lack. Together the four of them follow the yellow brick road that leads them to the wizard. Upon consultation with the wizard, they find he plans to test them before granting their requests. According to his directive, they have to kill the "Wicked Witch of the West." To find her, they must travel through wild country, where there are no roads or farms.

After being imprisoned and escaping from the witch, they douse her with water and she melts away. They return to the Emerald City, expecting the wizard to grant their requests but find that he is a fraud. He has kept his secret for a long time, duping even the evil witches. In an effort to appease Dorothy's companions, he gives the tin man a red clock shaped like a heart, the scarecrow a diploma, and the lion a medal for courage. They are satisfied with the gifts. They are no longer lacking the main components of their existence. His remedies cannot help Dorothy, however. Finally she realizes that she can send herself back home by clicking the heels of the magic shoes she took from the witch upon whom Dorothy's house landed and summarily killed.

Baum's idea that each individual "carries within him the solution to his own problems"[4] is a central axiom of the American (and Texan) ideal. The story of the wizard and his false identity also fits neatly with the history of early Texas and Stephen F. Austin's settlers, many of whom took on new identities as they marked out their future plantations.

Sugar Land—April 2005

The discussion that follows had its origin in what can only be called re-vision. First there was the recall of my own youth in Louisville, Kentucky, a turning back to earlier days that is part and parcel of a memoir I am presently writing (Baker 2001, 14).

In April 2005, nine years after beginning the project on San Isidro Cemetery, I asked my colleague Juan García to join me for the day while I visited and photographed the cemetery and different sites in the county. I had known Juan for about thirteen years. We had met in photography class when we were both studying with photographer George Krause. In a strange coincidence, it turned out that Juan was from Fort Bend County and grew up in Richmond. His grandparents, who raised him, knew my parents very well. At a church bazaar in 1982 at Saint John Fisher Catholic Church (one of the Basilian missions in the county), when I was first doing black-and-white photography, I photographed his grandparents. I had the negatives of two stunning portraits, one of his grandfather alone and one of both grandparents together. I remember that, when I took the picture, his grandmother seemed a little irritated with me for asking if I could take it. She must have been wondering, *why would the rich daughter of the local mortician want a photograph of me and my husband?* Juan later told me that I was correct in interpreting his grandmother's response to my request. She did not like the idea of the picture but let me take it anyway. When I met Juan in 1992, it had not been long since his grandfather had died. I gave him the negatives. The connection provided by the portrait of his grandfather forged a solid, productive friendship and a lifetime collaboration.

In April 2005 I had returned to Houston for a funeral. Juan had seen my father the day before I arrived and told him that it was urgent I call him. His grandmother had just died. He had lived with her and had been her sole caretaker for more than fifteen years. I called him and went over to their home, where we spent the day talking about many things, including my cemetery project. In all the conversations we had over the years he had never told me that his grandfather had also worked for Imperial Sugar before the family moved to Richmond. The family considered themselves to be from Sugar Land. Before they moved to Richmond, his grandfather had worked for Imperial Sugar for more than thirty years, laboring in the boiler room, where the sugar was cooked.

Juan's memories of Sugar Land were placed from his home in Richmond, but he was aware (as was I) of the strange company town, the convicts working in groups alongside the highway, and the history of racial divisions that controlled the county before the Civil Rights era. The day after the funeral we decided to visit Sugar Land and the cemetery. Juan has always been very attuned to the sensitivities of time and place and very aware of the consequences of history while not developing a polarizing hatred toward people involved in past injustices. I wanted his opinion on the project. We both took our cameras.

The Fountain

The Sugar Land Town Square had been completed for several years before I finally was able to go see it. It helped that Juan was just as interested in visiting the place. We arrived, and the first thing we saw was a magnificent fountain crowned by a larger-than-life statue of Stephen F. Austin, father of Texas. He has one hand in the air holding his rifle, the other holding the reins of his pack mule. He appears to be struggling to cross a waterway. Sharon Wallingford, who has published a pictorial history of the county, explains that the water surrounding Austin and the undulating road of bricks symbolize the Brazos River.[5]

In an interview with the *Houston Chronicle,* the mayor of Sugar Land explained the significance of the Brazos; he said it is "the very river that gave life to Fort Bend and Sugar Land." Written into the road of bricks is a "historical narrative that tells of the discovery of Texas, its earliest settlers and the perils they faced."[6] The designers of the fountain and plaza, SLA Studio Land Planners and Architects, accurately assessed the significance of the Brazos River. The idea of tangibly embedding the narrative of the county into the river (as they did in the road of brick) may have been an indication of their awareness of how the river "contains" the county's history.

The designers had chosen well; the "river" of bricks with the imbedded narrative is a powerful landmark. After looking at Austin's statue for a while, I began reading the story and walking the numerous curves of the brick road. It had a mesmerizing effect. I had my digital camera with me and took a photograph every few steps. In the meantime, Juan walked over to the main office of the Town Center to ask if there was a printed version of the narrative on the brick road. He was directed to the tall, imposing city hall at the foot of the brick road/Brazos River.

In the meantime, I found a short explanation next to the foundation that told of the square's design and intention. Yet this did not explain why the Karankawa (Native Americans), early Spanish explorers, and slaves who worked the plantations were given only a phrase or two in the account. The primary focus was on discoveries and settlements made by the legendary Old Three Hundred, Austin's colonists who settled Fort Bend County.[7]

It was not until seven months later that I recognized the connection between the brick road of the Brazos and Baum's yellow brick road. When it finally came together in my mind, I was surprised at the numerous similarities of Baum's version not only to the brick road of Sugar Land but also to the history and identity of the entire county. The river itself parallels Baum's yellow brick road in several ways. It is a conduit of travel and was used to transport goods and people throughout much of the nineteenth century. The land along its banks, called the Brazos River bottoms, is extremely fertile. Travelers also found themselves inside a frontier of barbarism, sometimes emanating from savage groups that lived along the "road." At other times, savagery erupted among the settlers themselves. The territory the river delineated was known as a place where a man could either get rich or be killed or both. It was a frontier where a white family could transform itself from hardscrabble pioneers to genteel planters within one generation.[8]

The brick road traveled with the river from the arrival of Austin to the establishment of the county's base of economic and political power in the 1990s. Imagining the river as living history, we know that the Brazos carried its white settlers through bloody encounters with Native Americans. Austin was determined that indigenous populations had to be eliminated. Regular expeditions were organized for the purpose of exterminating Indians.[9] Ethnic Mexicans were living among the white settlers in the colony, in addition to having regular contact through interactions in Nacogdoches, San Antonio, and New Orleans. Yet these relationships were often violent or subversive. A number were "retained" after the Texas Revolution and used as unpaid laborers to do the same work as the plantation slaves.[10] As Chapter 5 mentions, a formerly neutral group of ethnic Mexican men from East Texas revolted two years after San Jacinto, in what became the Cordova Rebellion. Mirabeau B. Lamar, president of the republic, along with other Texas leaders, effectively banned Mexicans from the region even if they were native-born Texans.[11] However, even with this animosity, a number continued to live in the new Texas.

African Americans were obviously not banished because they were in bondage (controlled) and their labor was needed. The expression "being sent down the river" was a euphemism associated with a slave's being sold to a plantation in Louisiana or Texas and then being sent down the Mississippi or the Brazos.[12] Folklorist John Mason Brewer explains in the introduction of *The Word on the Brazos*[13] that the lives of slaves living in the Brazos bottoms were brutal and depriving. Brewer maintains that, by the mid-twentieth century, their descendents had less education and knew less about the world than ever because the whole region kept the black people in terrible circumstances.[14] According to Brewer, the bottoms were a terrible place for black people to live.

The large farms (later called plantations), sometimes in the thousands of acres, required many laborers. Slaves were purchased in New Orleans and Galveston, as well as on Market Square in Houston.[15] A number of settlers brought slaves with them when they migrated from other Southern states. In the new territory, more slave children were born. The uncle and guardian of Confederate hero Frank Terry also imported slaves from Cuba (as did Alamo hero Jim Bowie) and once got lost in a winter storm after arriving at Matagorda Bay, where he and the slaves nearly froze to death.[16] It could be said that a few planters treated their slaves decently; yet, even in the best of circumstances, bondage still constituted an atrocity.

Theft of the Body and the Lost Meaning of Kinship

In the context of the United States . . . enslaved offspring . . . become under the press of a patronymic, patrifocal, patrilineal, and patriarchal order, the man/woman on the boundary, whose human and familial . . . status . . . had yet to be defined. I would call this enforced state of breach another instance of . . . where "kinship" loses meaning (Spillers 1987, 74).

A sense of tragedy is endemic in narratives about the separation of a parent from a child. In nineteenth-century Fort Bend, separation and death occurred frequently. A woman who grew up in the far western side of the county recently told me the story of her great-grandfather and his infant daughter. A baby girl was born in Southeast Texas, near the town of Egypt, just outside the western edge of Fort Bend. It happened that the mother and the baby had to travel away from the plantation. The baby's father walked them a few miles down the road away from the plantation. He carried the baby until it was time for him to turn back. The woman was not able to tell me more about that particular incident, but I was left wondering. Was he holding the baby to help the mother with her luggage or because he had some feeling for the child? My first thought was that, in the nineteenth century, mothers carried babies. How did the father feel as he walked those two miles? Was there a sense of relief or abandonment when he handed the infant to the mother? Did he want to walk farther with her, perhaps even accompany the mother to her new home?

The father of the baby was in an untenable position. He was a married man, the master of the plantation, and the baby's mother was his slave. Hortense Spillers,[17] in her essay "Mama's Baby, Papa's Maybe," references a few words from Frederick Douglass's graphic narrative. Yet, for this particular story, I present more of Douglass's story: "The children of slave women shall in all cases follow the condition of their mothers; and this is done too obviously to administer to their own lusts, and make gratification of their wicked desires profitable as well as pleasurable; for by this cunning arrangement, the slaveholder, in cases not a few, sustains to his slaves the double relation of master and father."[18]

Perhaps the father experienced some feeling as he carried the baby down the two miles of road away from the plantation. Yet, the baby's story began in a much more violent moment when her father "administered" his "own lusts." The baby's mother was a young slave woman, younger than twenty. She worked in the master's kitchen. At a certain moment, the master entered the room and raped her. His name was Borden. His family was one of Austin's Old Three Hundred. She became pregnant. A few months after the baby was born, he manumitted both mother and child, but they had to leave the plantation. It was during their departure that he walked with the mother, carrying *his* baby for the first few miles after they left their home. The baby's name was Betty Elizabeth Lewis.

That act of violence allowed for freedom that greatly affected the history of Betty Elizabeth and her descendants, who were part of a group of freedmen who established the town of Kendleton in southwest Fort Bend County. Two centuries later, the trauma has oddly paired itself with the pride connected to being a light-skinned African American with long, soft hair. The attractive and articulate eighty-one-year-old Honey Humphrey Owens is a direct descendant of one of Kendleton's founders, Stephen Humphrey. As I sat in her living room, she graciously told me her family narrative. She also mentioned that she no longer kept her hair as long as she did when she was younger. For many African Americans, having long, soft hair is a very desirable trait, yet its mere existence within the group is a marker of the unspeakable acts of rape and seduction.

The mother of Betty Elizabeth Lewis "lost" her body in a situation that Spillers proposes has no "hint or suggestion of a dimension of ethics, or relatedness between human personality and its anatomical features." The "procedures for the captive flesh" reduced the young mother to an object of lust, freed yet ejected, possibly at the insistence of a "jealous mistress." However, as Spillers realizes, the banishment of mother and child—a mad, unreasonable response—results from the will of the powerful (and publicly unacknowledged) father, given further authority by the madness of his wife's jealousy. Unfortunately for the mother-child pair and for U.S. history in general, the madness is co-opted by a "tale writ between the lines and in the not-quite spaces of an American domesticity."[19] Even though great African American

Geese in San Isidro Cemetery (2001).

intellects (male and female) continually address the issue of these violent, asymmetric sexual relationships in our (American) history, a blindness continues and keeps us from pulling the narrative out of its hidden space between the lines.

The necessary blindness that mediates the trauma continues into the generations. The denial of kinship between the white planter father and the mixed race daughter, I believe, is at the center of the exaggerated violence toward blacks that prevailed until the mid-twentieth century. Spillers cites Claude Meillassoux in her discussion of the consequences of slavery and its resultant violent sexual encounters between master and female slave. What is created is "an economic and social agent whose virtue lies in being outside the kinship system." In the case of Betty Elizabeth Lewis, the child did not have to leave her mother. Yet, in many situations, babies and mothers were separated because: ". . . under the conditions of captivity, the offspring of the female does not 'belong' to the Mother, nor is s/he 'related' to the owner, though the latter 'possesses' it . . . often fathered it . . . without whatever benefit of patrimony."[20]

Patrimony generally means economic resources. The denial of patrimony removes the possibility (at least most of the time) of inheritance. As Spillers eloquently explains, it removes the transfer ". . . of titles and entitlement, of real estate and the prerogatives of 'cold cash,' from father to sons,"[21] making it possible for the wealth of a slave holding county to remain in the hands of very few individuals.

The Emerald City as a Place of Illusions

In a fascinating piece that elaborates the relationship between Baum's *Wizard of Oz* and nineteenth-century American politics, Gretchen Ritter proposes that the author used the emptiness of the Emerald City and the Wizard's false self to discuss the corruption and guile within American government.[22] The tangible presence of Sugar Land's seat of local government (for me) is entwined with the untenable history I had found in the eight years I had been researching the book. The missing narratives make the Emerald City/Sugar Land City Hall seem like an empty shell of power. Never mind that, as Ritter reminds her readers, the Wizard was a "very good man;" unfortunately he was a "very bad Wizard."[23]

The history of the county is further confused if the planters/slave masters were indeed "really good men." With the ability to diminish the human form through violence and bondage, they built their own yellow brick road. It now leads to the seat of local government with its elegant columns that face the statue of their original father whose patrimony is sought and acknowledged.

Spectacles for Greener Communities

The narrator in Baum's novel tells of the protagonists' entry into the Land of Oz: "The road was smooth and well paved, now, and the country about was beautiful, so that the travelers rejoiced in leaving the forest far behind, and with it the many dangers they had met in its gloomy shades."[24] The description of a smooth and well-paved road that carried travelers into a beautiful country could be the metaphor of desire for new communities such as those in Sugar Land. The travelers/ residents have left the forest, danger, and "gloomy shades."[25] Through the efforts of their real or symbolic ancestors, the wild land has been tamed . . . the roads are now smooth and well paved, the land is beautiful. This trajectory is symbolized in the story carved into the brick road outside the Sugar Land City Hall—Austin and his determined followers cleared out the dangers of the frontier.

Similar to the requirements for residents of the different subdivisions in Sugar Land, which restrict either property or behavior, as is common in most master-planned communities,[26] Baum's protagonists are required to wear green eye-glasses while they are inside the city walls. Once Baum's characters arrive at the gate and inform the guard of their wish to see the wizard, they are told they have to "put on spectacles."[27] Anyone who enters without them would be blinded by the "brightness and glory" of the Emerald City. Even with the green eyeglasses on, the protagonists were still "dazzled by the brilliancy of the wonderful City."[28]

The brilliance of Sugar Land and indeed the entire eastern section of the county is magnificent. The area has been noted repeatedly (throughout the nation) for the economic and social success of its architectural designs.[29] For proponents of these types of communities, the design of most of East Fort Bend's "Greener Communities" include what one developer explained as an incorporation of the advantages offered by the natural landscape of the property, compatibility of building motifs, and "concern for personal safety and ease of residential movement."[30]

The reports of success do not exaggerate: Sugar Land and its multiple master-planned communities have gained the notice of the entire nation.[31] Yet the insulation required to create such an idealized space has had its price. To maintain the elevated position of the ideal, anything different in value has to be made invisible. An additional example is given by Michel de Certeau in *The Practice of Everyday Life*. In the chapter titled "Walking in the City," he writes of the ill-fated World Trade Center in New York. The buildings hovered at such an extreme height that they seemed to touch the heavens. Here de Certeau invokes the myth of Icarus, the son of Daedalus (Icarus is the boy who wore wings made out of feathers and wax but flew too close to the sun; he died when the wax melted and he plummeted into the sea). Daedalus constructed the wings for Icarus. The father has a past, as does Fort Bend County and Sugar Land. For the residents of the Emerald City, the use of green spectacles increases the wizard's influence over them. They are already content because they know he has created a green community that is aesthetically pleasing and serves as a safe haven from the wild beasts beyond its borders.

Amnesia

Michel de Certeau is warning those in the World Trade Center (and other skyscraping institutions built by excessive capitalism). He says the inhabitants at the top may look outside and find that everything below is a blur. While the privilege of height allows a spectacular view of the world, what the naked eye can see consists of flowing dots of color as individuals and cars move about on the sidewalks and streets below. He does not predict the actual destruction of the towers, yet his reference to Icarus is telling.

What de Certeau does not mention is the story of Icarus's cousin, Talos. Daedalus was initially a very successful architect and inventor. He took as an apprentice his nephew Talos, who was as talented as his master. Fearing that Talos would threaten his success, Daedalus threw him from the top of the Acropolis. When Daedalus was tried and banished for the murder, he fled to Crete, where he worked in the court of King Minos. Was the allegory of Icarus, Daedalus, and the ill-fated Talos a morality tale simply about punishment? Was Icarus's death a way for the gods to punish his father for the sins of envy and murder?

The narrative of homicide is diminished in the grandeur of the gorgeous young man flying by means of his genius father's invention. His dramatic fall to the sea captures our attention. We do not notice the fall of Talos. The young body of the apprentice was thrown from the Acropolis. His screams must have been heard all around. When his body hit the side of the mountain, the jagged rock cut into his skin, crushing his head and breaking his limbs. The uncanny aspect of the story is the mind of Daedalus himself. As he assists (and later betrays) King Minos and as he invents yet another new form of technology that enables men to fly, does he ever think of Talos and his fall? Can his memory recognize the bloodied body at the bottom of the mountain?

As I proceeded through this project, the delays became longer and longer as I kept finding information that seemed too difficult to incorporate in the green-spectacled environment of Fort Bend County. The incongruence of so many bloodied bodies that I have found within the communities there (such as Telfair, a new subdivision that describes itself as "green") made it difficult to complete the book. I searched for a way to present the information fairly, attempting not to judge, as any competent academic should. I hoped to find some answers to the inconsistent pairings of idealized fame and brutal violence, of individualized freedom for some and widely accepted bondage for others, of good and evil within the same space inside the same people. The only conclusion I finally came to was that people have forgotten. Bits of information are scattered about the county, indicating that not everything is green, but few acknowledge the tarnish. When a newspaper article on the cemetery was published, a Sugar Land city council member responded by saying that the focus on San Isidro *mistakenly* renewed old conflicts.[32] Perhaps this was true and needed. At the least, I found a startling amnesia not only among the residents of the newly constructed city but also among the others who had lived there for decades or whose families had made the county their home even longer. The amnesia is also mine.

In a 1993 interview in the journal *Belles Lettres,* Toni Morrison, who won the Nobel Prize for literature, commented on the amnesia she had addressed in her novel *Beloved.*[33] She had retrieved forgotten antebellum narratives in the form of a ghost. It seemed that at least a few American people were beginning to allow themselves to remember the tragedy and violence of slavery and its impact on the history and identity of the United States. As Morrison explains, "Nobody wants to do it. Nobody wants to go back and try to remember all that stuff. You think that you might go under, that you might be devastated. When I was writing the book I thought that some parts were going to be too difficult to deal with. But in those moments I kept saying to myself: 'All I have to do is to think about the people who lived there, who lived through it. If they could live it, I could write about it.'"[34]

Men in White

In October 2005 Fred Salazar accompanied a former student of mine on a visit to my home. Salazar is in his fifties. He grew up in Baytown, an industrial city northeast of Houston. He had learned from my student that I was writing about Fort Bend County and was curious as to what I had found. He said that his family had lived there for a while in the 1930s, working as sharecroppers on a farm named Sartatia. He did not remember much about the place, but one event stayed in his mind. As a small boy, he was riding in the car with his family as they traveled along Highway 90 southwest of Houston, where he would see groups of men dressed in white, working the fields. A man in a brown uniform with a shotgun would be sitting on a tall horse close by. On one occasion when the family drove to Sugar Land in the winter, they passed a Texas Department of Corrections truck with the back full of men in white, sitting in the open air. It was very cold, and Salazar became quite upset because the men did not have coats or blankets to cover them. Some were using pieces of cardboard to cover their legs. Salazar insisted that the family stop and lend them blankets or something, but his father did not stop the car.

The men in white played a significant, if invisible, role in the economic success of the county. Michel de Certeau would propose that the repressed history of their incarceration, torture, and forced labor has not disappeared. It has been transformed and placed in spaces that are, at the moment, hard to reach. Individual moments of history are remembered in scenes like the one Fred Salazar described. The convicts were cold and had no blankets or coats. They used pieces of cardboards to cover their legs. Surely Salazar was not the only person who saw these men.

The county became the home of prisons in the 1880s, when two entrepreneurs named Cunningham and Ellis purchased a contract with the entire Texas prison system to lease prisoners for labor on plantations. On some unknown date, it is said that, after the death of a convict, the guards had to find a burial place. They decided to put the body in a casket and float it down Oyster Creek. The burial ground would be decided by wherever the casket would land. Glen Clover told me the casket landed at San Isidro Cemetery.

When I visited the cemetery as an adult, I often heard of the undeveloped section called the "prison cemetery" or the "black cemetery." Prisoners were scattered throughout the county's large plantations. Once slavery ended, the planters were desperate to find cheap labor. The large workforce needed for the sugar and cotton crops was not available in the regular population. Interestingly, the Texas prison population skyrocketed in the last decades of the nineteenth century. Men were imprisoned for years for stealing a loaf of bread, a ham, or an article of clothing. At first they were mostly African American; then, after the start of the twentieth century the percentages of ethnic Mexicans grew. The prison system abolished convict leasing in 1912 (on paper) and purchased several thousand acres just south of the sugar refinery.

Robert Perkinson, author of a dissertation on the history of Texas prisons, told me that after leasing was outlawed, the local system found two different ways of dealing with the labor problem. One was by using convicts who were paroled to local farmers and expected to work for meager wages, with the threat of reimprisonment if they misbehaved. The second was a business arrangement between county prison farms and Imperial Sugar. There was no convict leasing, but through these "convict farms," the state of Texas would produce the sugar, which would then be sold to the sugar refinery.

Prison labor as another form of slave labor is a frequent subject in academic texts. Texas is known for its prisons and exaggerated executions.[35] Fort Bend County is known as the place for prisons. While convict farms are scattered throughout the state, in the early twentieth century, the county's fertile Brazos bottoms encouraged prison officials to buy most of the available land.

The Story of Telfair and the Panopticon

In 2004 local historian Tim Cumings told me that the state of Texas was taking care of its budget troubles by selling prison land. In the largest sale of state-owned land in the history of the Texas General Land Office, two thousand acres were sold to a corporation named Newland Communities. The corporation's press release does not mention the prison history.[36] The land was part of the original Harlem and Cunningham plantations that were purchased by the prison system in the 1890s. The names changed over the years, but in the early twentieth century it was known as Imperial Farm.

The *Houston Chronicle* announced the new subdivision and its historic connection to the prison. The name is Telfair, "after one of the oldest oak-lined squares in downtown . . . Savannah . . . with its landscaped . . . neighborhood[s] . . . shady live oak trees, colorful gardens, and fountains."[37] The prison farm was morphing into a quaint, Southern neighborhood. While seeking additional information on the Southern theme in Newland's projects, I searched the Internet for the words "Georgia" and "Telfair." I thought I was going to find information on the Savannah neighborhood and any famous individuals who might have lived there. Telfair is the name of a city and a county in rural central Georgia. It is also the name of a prison, the Telfair State Prison in Helena, Georgia, which houses a little more than a thousand inmates. Perhaps the Newland Corporation knew of the Telfair prison and decided that, since it was a small facility and there were cities and counties also named Telfair, the coincidence of giving a master-planned subdivision the name of a prison would not be noticed.

In a morbid form of recycling, Newland announced that it was studying ways to "conserve" the main prison building "for civic or commercial uses." Constructed in 1939, the Greek Revival building was used as a prison dormitory as recently as the year 2000. Even if the dormitory is later demolished, traces of the prison remain. Recently, as I was traveling through Sugar Land on the U.S. Highway 59 freeway (I was not driving, which gave me ample time to observe the landscape), I passed the new building of the University of Houston system at Sugar Land and noticed some architectural aspects that surprised me: it looked like a prison building. Perhaps it was because I was pondering the Telfair project and the old prison dormitory or maybe, because

I had been rethinking the work on prisons by Michel Foucault, his idea of the Panopticon was on my mind. The building is large, about three stories high, with few windows. Its brick is a color between dark rose and dark red. The width of the building and its moderate height give it the appearance of an educational institution. It stands out in landscape that very recently was cleared farmland. There are no large trees or other buildings nearby. What seemed so striking to me was the glass tower at the top. It rose a few feet over the roof, providing the image of a watchtower. At this point I immediately thought of the prison and Jeremy Bentham's Panopticon as described by Foucault: "an annular building; at the centre, a . . . tower . . . pierced with wide windows that open onto the inner side of the . . . ring. . . . All that is needed, then, is to place a supervisor in the central . . . tower . . . make[ing] it possible to see constantly and to recognize immediately."[38]

The university building in Sugar Land was completed in 2002. Searching for additional information, I contacted a campus administrator, who informed me that it was designed by the firm B2HK Architecture, who based the design on one that was originally used at the University of Houston, Victoria campus. It is named the Albert and Mamie George Building. Most of the funds needed for construction were donated by the George Foundation, which is based in Fort Bend County and oversees the George Historical Ranch. I asked about the roof design, carefully avoiding calling it a watch tower. She described it as a cupola. I had not thought of that description because most cupolas that I knew of are at the top of domes on state capitols or churches.

The roof of this building is flat, with large eaves on each side. The administrator was enthusiastic in her description. One of her last comments reminded me of de Certeau's remark that abandoned memory can result in sporadic moments. She said that, in the evening, when the light is turned on inside the cupola, it gives the semblance of a lighted beacon at the top of the building. I almost shuddered. In her enthusiasm for this new institution, which is greatly appreciated and sorely needed by residents on the west side of the county, she could not have known that her description of the beacon tied her current pursuits (and those of the institution) to the unspeakable events that occurred on the land watched over by the cupola on the roof of the Mamie and Albert George Building.[39]

The property sold for the Telfair subdivision is located a few miles to the north, facing U.S. Highway 90A. The land belonging to the University of Houston system is farther south, close to the new First Colony mall, which houses major retailers Dillard's and J. C. Penney and upscale stores such as Abercrombie and Fitch, Godiva Chocolatier, and Williams-Sonoma. The University of Houston news release announced the new campus location had been purchased from the Texas Department of Transportation.[40] When I first read the statement I thought, yes, this makes sense, the new campus borders U.S. Highway 59, called the Southwest Freeway. After hearing the administrator describe the beacon of light over the university building, I decided to search out the transaction. The information was technically correct: the transaction was with the Texas Department of Transportation. However, in an effort to correct budgetary problems, the land had been transferred from the Texas Department of Corrections in 1987. This was explained in a footnote of a report dated January 2001 and titled "Paving the Way: A Review of the Texas Department of Transportation," under the section "Improve Asset Management." The Texas Department of Transportation sold the land to the University of Houston sometime between 1996 and 1999 . The following quote provides additional information to more clearly display the trajectory of the land sale:

> Two major transactions at the Leander Rehabilitation Center and the Sugar Land Prison Farm accounted for much of the decrease in land value. 446 acres of the Leander property were sold for over $18 million. Some of the Sugar Land property was transferred to the University of Houston (approximately 275 acres) and the city of Sugar Land (approximately 400 acres). The value of the land was also changed to take into consideration the development costs needed to prepare the land for sales. TxDOT [the Texas Department of Transportation] still owns 233 acres at Leander and 5,107 acres at Sugar Land Prison Farm. In 1999, the two properties together represented $62.7 million or 39 percent of the $161 million value of all land (excluding the value of facilities) owned by TxDOT.[41]

In an uncanny way, my project on San Isidro Cemetery was appearing more and more like my work in Monterrey, Nuevo León, México. Similar to Sugar Land, Monterrey had become an economic powerhouse with a convoluted and often occulted history. The downtown plaza of Monterrey, built in the 1980s appeared to be (in a sense) a precursor of the Sugar Land Town Square. A large concrete and brick expanse covered a "new square" exhibiting Monterrey's wealth and power. The construction of the new plaza destroyed a centuries-old neighborhood that contained many narratives that would have clarified the history of Nuevo León. The concrete of the plaza seemed to be a symbolic lid on the stories, covering them over and in effect smothering them into silence.[42]

Whether the Sugar Land Town Square was built on prison land or land owned by Imperial Sugar, there is no doubt that these acres of rich Brazos River bottom land were farmed by prison convicts. Many of these convicts were buried in San Isidro Cemetery.

Between What We See and What We Know

. . . ghostly things kept cropping up (Gordon 1997, 8).

In Avery Gordon's conclusion to *Ghostly Matters: Haunting and the Sociological Imagination,* she explains that the "heart" of the book's "meditation on haunting is an engagement with the novels by Luisa Valenzuela and Toni Morrison." Valenzuela has written on the *desaparecidos* ("disappeared") of Argentina, and

Morrison on slavery. Gordon's commentary on how these two novelists assisted her in finding a voice to discuss the haunting in our social fabric resonates with my experience in researching this project: . . ." They have helped me to better articulate what were initially stammering and inchoate suspicions and disappointments. The completion of this project confirms my belief that Valenzuela['s] and Morrison's way of seeing—their way of negotiating the always unsettled relationship between what we see and what we know—has tremendous significance for social analysis and for those who write with critical intentions and, at least in part, to effect social and political change."[43]

My own "stammering and inchoate suspicions and disappointments" began when I decided that a traditional ethnography of the culture and traditions of the ethnic Mexicans associated with San Isidro was not a suitable way to study the meaning of the cemetery. As I began to study the history of the land, as well as the slaves and prisoners who worked the fields, I found myself stammering and disappointed at the inchoate violence that followed the narratives. Conversations with Marjorie Adams, who knew many stories about Fort Bend's slavery and post-Reconstruction years, were troubling. Hayden White, who was advising me at the time, encouraged me to question the need of writing the graphic details of the lynchings, rapes, and burnings, believing that the sensational nature of the narrative would exoticize the experiences of the people involved. Yet I had to address the occurrence of the violence: To avoid doing so would be to continue the myth of the Emerald City and its illusory image of perfection.

A significant moment of decision occurred when I found the archives of the *Dallas Morning News* online. Suddenly I had immediate access to newspaper articles reaching back to 1882. A request for the *San Antonio Express* archives brought a series of articles that focused on allegations of prisoner abuse in the Texas Prison System. They did not contain much specific information regarding the conditions of the prisons or the treatment of the prisoners. I had gone through the local papers but had not found very much information, attributing the lack to either the paper's avoidance of controversy or my own inability to decipher the microfilm. When I discovered the Dallas newspaper archives I thought I would attempt at least one more time to find information on the post-Reconstruction period or the prison system. I assumed that there would not be much information because of the distance from Fort Bend to Dallas, approximately 200 miles, a very long distance in the nineteenth century. Instead I found more information than I ever expected; hundreds of articles on the Fort Bend prison farms, details on the severe prisoner abuse that occurred on a daily basis, charges and counter charges of corruption.

Stark inconsistencies in the resulting narrative emphasized the violent nature of the information I was finding and the historical information provided by Sugar Land and the county. The entanglement between the prison horror stories and the magnificently wealthy and powerful county ("the Land of Oz" and the "Emerald City") created a project full of "renegade ghosts."[44]

There are too many ghosts to adequately address the prison narrative in this manuscript. Suffice it to say that many men were illegally incarcerated for years on charges of stealing a loaf of bread or a chicken. They were mostly black until the twentieth century, when the percentage of ethnic Mexicans increased due to immigration. In one year, over two hundred prisoners out of a population of only 1,000 died . In 1913, thirteen black prisoners were stuffed into a room called a "dark cell" as punishment for not working hard enough. Twenty-four hours later the door was opened and eleven were dead. Investigations would occur after newspapers publicized sensational incidents, but the violence continued. Men were "disciplined" in an oddly homoerotic manner with something called the "bat": they were stripped naked with their hands and legs held down by prisoners while a guard would hit them with a leather strip that was about four inches wide. Men would maim themselves, sometimes cutting their own hands off in order not to be forced into the fields. While operating on a convict, a prison physician decided to cut one side of his scrotum. When the prisoner complained, the physician stated that he better be quiet because if he kept talking he would cut more.[45]

As late as the 1980s my father, in his role as undertaker, went to one of the Sugar Land prison units to pick up a prisoner who had been killed by a guard. He says that the guard was not reprimanded and the death was seen as another inconvenience.

The newspaper articles do not state the exact location of the "dark cell," where the eleven inmates suffocated. Yet, when I travel on U.S. Highway 59 past what was once prison land, I do not wonder *whether* the space is haunted but rather *how* it is haunted. The "renegade ghosts" of these men travel about the Brazos bottoms, occasionally visiting those families who have purchased homes on land once used to raise cotton and sugar. They may walk the halls of the university campus. They certainly inhabit the space of San Isidro Cemetery. Perhaps that is why the cemetery has been able to maintain its geographic integrity throughout all of the land development and suburban growth. It is the last space that has not been transformed into a false front of history.

In April 2005 I visited San Isidro Cemetery with Juan García. We thought about entering the "black section," but it is always locked. As I played with the lock I remembered the words of John de la Cruz: "There are rattlesnakes in there. It's dangerous. You can't go inside." In a flash of intuition I moved the combination to a variant of the main lock (whose numbers my father had given me nine years before). It worked, and we were able to enter easily. We sat on an old tree inside the black section of San Isidro and talked for a long time.

Five months earlier John de la Cruz had finally let me in the space. While we walked around, he kept remarking that a number of gravestones that he had previously found were gone. He counted at least seven missing. The city of Sugar Land had offered to purchase the cemetery from the African American church that held the land title. At first it appeared that San Isidro would be able to buy the land instead, which would have been wonderful; the entire cemetery would retain its original boundary. The disappearance of the gravestones made me wonder whether someone was trying to remove evidence.

After a long conversation with Juan, I got up to look around and take some photographs. I was hoping to find some remaining gravestones, thinking that anything from slavery times would probably not be there. Yet I found another link to slavery. It was a stone made of concrete. Time had worn away the words; they were barely visible. Juan and I decided to make a rubbing. It said, "Robert Goodman 1832–1935."

Once we completed the image in pencil, we stood up to photograph the stone, thinking we would probably not get much detail. I stood at the foot of Robert Goodman's gravestone and was surprised that I was able to see all of the letters very clearly.

Monticello in Texas

When I spoke with Fort Bend County district attorney John Healey in 2002, he recommended that I locate a copy of *Fort Bend County, Texas: A Pictorial History,* by Sharon Wallingford.[1] It was a helpful suggestion since very little history has been published on the county. *Pictorial History* was released as a fund-raising project for the Exchange Club of Sugar Land the same year that I first returned to visit the cemetery, in 1996. Nine years later, as I write the conclusion of this book, I finally look at Wallingford's work. It was easier to search the National Archives in Washington, D.C., or the New York Public Library than it was to open the book and see which narratives were emphasized and which were missing.

Pictorial History provides an indication of how the historical producers of the county place the significance of their project. After the acknowledgements and before the foreword is a reproduction of a painting of Jefferson's Monticello. Next to the painting is an epigraph by Jefferson that speaks of "multiple testimony, multiple views" that give "solid establishment to truth." It continues: "Much is known to one that is not known to another and no one knows everything."[2] Perhaps the multiple testimony and views presented by Wallingford are of the Czech community and the German prisoner of war inmates in the western part of the county. Otherwise, the multiple testimony and views are missing. I would like to think this is because the author was not aware of alternative sources of information. As I searched though the history of the county I could not help but see that the mythologies of Texas and the county have overpowered the historical narratives. Jacqueline Rose proposes in *States of Fantasy* that a place can be emptied of its history, with nation-building mythologies appropriating its stories.[3] Texas history has been overtaken by the mythology of the Alamo, greatly overshadowing the rich and complex story of San Antonio, Bexar County, and the rest of Texas. In Fort Bend, the idealizing narrative of the Old Three Hundred has grown into a Texas-sized myth while effectively erasing the stories of their slave laborers and slave mistresses.

The county's founding fathers have been given a status similar to that shown in the placement of Jefferson's home at the beginning of Wallingford's text. It is a revealing association. Monticello is reminiscent of nineteenth-century Fort Bend plantations. At Jefferson's home, there is little mention of his slaves. Tour guides become uncomfortable when asked about the children Jefferson had with his slave Sally Hemings.[4] While there is a tour through the slave section, the only remnants are rocks used for the foundations of the slave cabins. The cemetery where Jefferson is buried is locked and guarded with a tall wrought-iron fence. People throw coins on his large grave-stone.

In contrast, the slave cemetery at Monticello is mentioned in a small brochure with a map of the buildings and parking areas. "Discovered" in 2001 during an archeological dig, it is surrounded by a rustic wood fence that is located in the middle of the parking lot, next to one of the plantation's gift shops. There are no gravestones, but a sign at the site states that large rocks were used to mark the graves of the slaves, and one can see a number of boulders in the cemetery. Someone has made two fallen branches into a cross. Three miniature U.S. flags have been placed next to a boulder.

Monticello is a national shrine to the establishment of the American nation-state. Jefferson designed the plantation and the nation. With a closer reading of his œuvre, it becomes clear that his idea of freedom did not include people of color.[5] Yet, he chose to have children with his slave and certainly was aware that Monticello would never have been possible without slave labor (some of whom were his own children). The tour guide's stammering after a visitor asks about Sally Hemings's children reflects the uncomfortable nature of this public secret. Wallingford's book begins her story of the county with the image of Monticello, but slaves, prisoners, and sharecroppers are barely mentioned in her text.

This pairing of the national and the local is similar to what I found while researching this book. The location of Washington, D.C., in an area that consisted mainly of plantations (indicated by frequent signs in the capital indicating that a plantation was once nearby) and thousands of slaves (many owned by early American leaders) provides a strong connection to the Southern history of Fort Bend County. Even in the present this pairing continues. It seems no accident that one of the former most powerful people in Congress is from Sugar Land.[6]

They Are Religious, Earnest, Sincere, and Devoted, and They Hate . . .

Evil: malevolence; bad intent . . . unkindness . . . bad blood; enmity, hate . . . spite (Roget's Thesaurus).[7]

The word "evil" has an intense connotation that weighs heavily in this book. *Roget's Thesaurus* equates "evil" with words that in our world have less distinctive effects, such as "bad intent" and "unkindness." The idea of evil existing in the county's "rich heritage" is a polar opposite to the nostalgic presentation of Wallingford's text, which states that her book will "educate old and new residents about the county's rich culture." It also states that gathering information from the 1950s forward was "like having a family reunion and talking about the 'good old days.'"[8] This paradox is exemplified in an essay by Mark Twain that sets forth his observations of the Viennese parliament:

> If I have reported the behaviour of the House intelligibly, the reader has been surprised by it, and has wondered whence these law-makers come and what they are made of. . . . As to the make-up of the House, it is this: the deputies come from all the walks of life and from all the grades of society. There are princes, counts, barons, priests, peasants, mechanics, labourers, lawyers, judges, physicians, professors, merchants, bankers, shopkeepers. They are religious men, they are earnest, sincere, devoted, and they hate the Jews.[9]

The inconsistency of having what most people consider fine moral virtues (e.g., piety, earnestness, sincerity, devotion) while harboring unabashed hatred (enough to maim and kill) is the central question behind the research for this book. Silenced narratives are traced, and conjectures are made about historical events that were not documented. More significantly, there is a renegade haunting to this text. It questions how unimaginable evil can emanate from (what in the county would be called) "fine, upstanding people." The editor of *A Pictorial History* lists the qualities of Fort Bend's early settlers: They had "vision and courage . . . were leaders . . . followers and their helpers . . . [were] willing to take risks for their dreams and . . . beliefs . . . [had] an entrepreneurial spirit . . . and . . . gave . . . [the county] character. . . ."[10]

The more sinister aspects appear in unexpected places. The Fort Bend County jail, built in 1897 had three levels. One photograph of the building shows a family with six children standing in front of the main gate (the jail had living quarters for the sheriff and his family). Most notable was the third floor. The jail actually had its own gallows in what appears to be a tower at the front of the building. Only two documented hangings took place in the building, both in 1898.[11] They were black men: Manuel Morris from Wharton County and Peter Autry from Fort Bend.[12] It is unlikely that the gallows would have been built to be used only twice.[13] In the documented history of the county, the number of lynchings is reported as only a handful at a time when most of the South had an epidemic of lynchings. It is probable that the county had more rigid control over its sheriff's department and newspapers, so that most deaths remained unreported.[14]

To Wallingford's credit (and that of the staff at Monticello), they acknowledge that that the plantations needed slave labor to survive. Unfortunately, Wallingford says little more. Her book shows a photograph of a large cotton-picking machine; the caption states that migrant laborers worked on local farms. Another photograph shows a group of ethnic Mexican children standing together at an employer-sponsored festival.

What remains as I complete this ethnography are those shadowy stories going back to Austin's first colony of settlers, where so much violence seemed to sink into the landscape.[15] This is not to imply that the Spanish government was much less brutal. The caveat in this situation is found in the constantly repeated narratives of outstanding settlers and idealized heroes. These stories create a dilemma, making it nearly impossible to understand the positioning of the cemetery and the general situated-ness of Texas history. Wading through savagery so extreme, that continued through much of the twentieth century, pressed me to analyze the entire positioning of not only county history but also of the state of Texas and its implications for the symbolic construction of the American nation-state. Recalling Susan Buck-Morss' essay "Hegel and Haiti," I pondered how the inconsistencies between a brutal history and a "triumphant" history (which gave birth to a success that has been noted throughout the United States) resonate with her treatise of Hegel and his enlightened counterparts' desire for freedom. The freedom Hegel proposed was circumscribed for a particular group. The line between those with freedom and those without was delineated by the mark of race.[16] The erratic narrative of identity placed Austin's new Texans and their descendants in an anxious position as keepers of the boundary.

The Production of Heroism and the Creation of Bondage

*Historiography changes according to the place occupied by its agent
(Costa Lima 1993, 13).*

In an analysis of the madness and irony of Don Quixote, Luiz Costa Lima
surmises that the gallant knight loses his rationality because he cannot "make
a distinction between the world of the feats of his favorite heroes and that of
quotidian existence. . . . Quixote is mad in that he imposes on quotidian reality a kind of thematization that disturbs it"; it is a disturbance that charac-
terizes "the fictitious."[17] It does not take a great deal of imagination for one to
envision the Southern planter as a grand knight after reading the classic *Mind
of the South,* by W. J. Cash.[18] When I first spoke with Marjorie Adams, she
told me that many of the chivalrous Southern slave owners were overtaken
by madness because of "what they had done." The polemic arising from the
inconsistency between the poetics of the gracious gentleman planter and the
daily misery of his slaves (or sharecroppers or leased prisoners) creates a *mad*
discourse. According to Foucault, the diagnosis of madness has always been
subjective.[19] In this way the diagnostician and the historian are similar. How
they administer their tasks is not contingent upon their competence or discipline; it is their political, ideological, and philosophical background that most
heavily influences their conclusions.[20]

　　The historical narrative of Fort Bend County embedded in the brick road
of the Sugar Land Town Center was the solution to the difficult problem; the
story of the hero was divided from (or polarized with regard to) its companion,
the everyday. According to the officially produced history, the heroes became
heroes because they were special, which implied an almost divine genealogy
(attributed to the Old Three Hundred), extraordinary courage, and inordinate
physical beauty. A particular example is Colonel Frank Terry, as described by
Wharton.[21] The reality is that the hero could not have become a significant
figure without the scores of people who served him and worked his land.

　　None of the hero's characteristics are associated with the laborers and
domestic servants who produced the crops and maintained the plantations.
Their descriptions contained the opposite: an embarrassing genealogy related
to the oversexualization of the black female by the white slave-holding society, cowardice, and ugliness. All of the negative associations are displaced onto
those in bondage. The ultimate responsibility for keeping people in bondage

(so that the planter could be served) and torturing escaped slaves (and, later, supposedly unmanageable prison convicts) remained on the Other side of the boundary between the hero's imaginary and the reality of his actions. What I found in my research evoked this principle in almost everything associated with the history of the cemetery and the county. The Texas (and county) historian has contracted the madness of Don Quixote; the shadow of the hero is so large that the historian cannot see the necessity of the everyday.

The idea of Don Quixote is forgivable and nostalgically chivalrous. His trajectory can be approached without emotional difficulty because its irony smoothes the ride. He is only insane, not savage and murderous. Perhaps this is a less controversial approach to the good/evil gentleman planter. He sounds like the Wizard of Oz after his real identity is discovered: He is not a bad man, he says, only a bad wizard. His greatest crime, according to some, is that he is only a common man seeking to do extraordinary things. Societal rules in the United States until the mid-twentieth century allowed for black people to be subjugated and controlled. Scholars like Houston Baker Jr. propose that these allowances were conveniently transformed into the constantly mutating U.S. prison system, which now holds hundreds of thousands of black men in involuntary servitude.[22]

For the planter, assistance given by slaves and servants allowed him to be the gentleman. This was evident at Monticello. Jefferson's constant writing and inventing were possible only because everyone else around him provided for all of his needs and those of his plantation. Ownership of slaves provided not only inexpensive labor and constantly available domestic help but also status.

In 1982 I visited the Fort Bend County library to search their genealogical records for my great-great-grandfather Jesús Paredes, who lived on the Texas-Mexico border near the end of the twentieth century. I found his name in a book of Texas Confederate veterans. Paredes was part of a group that fought off border raiders during the Civil War. As I was preparing the microfilm machine to search the old census records, I explained Paredes's history to the librarian assisting me. She said excitedly, "You might even find that your family owned slaves!"

The Ethics of Terror

William Faulkner's novel *Absalom, Absalom!* centers on Thomas Sutpen, a wealthy Southern planter. Sutpen's experience of poverty and dismissal shapes

his obsession of becoming a rich Southern planter, the master of a plantation. He is from Kentucky, and his family is poor. His father sends him to a
rich neighbor to ask for money. Sutpen is turned away at the front door by a
well-dressed slave. He is told to approach the house through the back door.
This incident propels Sutpen to create his "grand design," which leads him to
Haiti, where he marries and later abandons a wife and a son.

He eventually lands in Mississippi and marries again, this time the daughter of a well-respected gentleman. Everyone involved with Sutpen throughout
his lifetime is only a character to him, a momentary necessity or digression in
reaching his goal of attaining wealth and establishing a lineage. He is dismis-
sive of his wife and children (both from the marriage and from his slave). He
treats his employees savagely and his slaves even worse. His first child, named
Charles Bon, whom he left behind in Haiti, returns like a renegade ghost. The
abandonment is Sutpen's attempt to disassociate himself from his new family after he finds out that his wife's mother is of mixed blood. In the ultimate
tragedy, Sutpen's white son kills his mixed-race son. Eventually the grand design collapses upon itself.

Sutpen's story carries a segment of explanation. His need to command
and control in the service of economic success relates to being turned away by
a well-dressed slave at the front door of a rich man's house. The people around
him become pawns in his quest to complete his economic and genealogical
design. The arrival of Charles Bon (the mixed-blood son born in Haiti) provokes the beginning of the destruction.

In the case of the county planters, even as Sharon Wallingford expresses
her admiration for the strong and determined settlers in Austin Colony (as
well as the later arrivals), her superlative narratives on the quality of this
group become complicated when other sources of information are used.
Gregg Cantrell, in his biography of Stephen F. Austin, notes that a popular expression in the 1820s was that the "dregs of American society" went to
Texas.[23] These were people who could not find success in their home states.
Many took on an alias (such as Austin's assistant Samuel Williams) and owed
substantial amounts of money (as did Austin and Williams, among others).
Moreover, a number abandoned their wives (as did Alamo hero William Bar-
rett Travis).[24]

In the twentieth century, William Eldridge, in partnership with Isaac
Kempner, purchased the Imperial Sugar Company. By the time Eldridge
moved to Sugar Land, he had already killed five people. He never served time
in prison, and the records of his last trial disappeared.[25] In the late 1990s there
was a move to establish a museum at the Eldridge mansion. Cemetery asso-

ciation members told me that strong opposition to the plan existed in Sugar Land because of Eldridge's violent history.

Destroying the Image of Heroes

A painted portrait of Macario García in uniform was placed on display at the Fort Bend Courthouse in 1982. In 1997, it was moved to the main rotunda of the building by request of then-justice of the peace, Jim Adolphus. In 2002, county judge Jim Adolphus and district attorney John Healey hosted a celebration commemorating García by presenting a plaque that detailed the heroism at the German front that earned him the Congressional Medal of Honor. At least one hundred people were in attendance, including García's brother, his widow, children, and grandchildren. A number of people from Sugar Land sat in the crowded chairs lined up in the rotunda of the courthouse. My father had informed me of the upcoming ceremony. I went with my camera, hoping to get photographs of what seemed like a momentous occasion. A reception for an ethnic Mexican in the main space of the Fort Bend courthouse was an exemplary event. His attainment of the medal had not been significant enough for Wallingford's book; she mentioned his name in an insert next to large photographs of the county's German prisoners of war, who by several accounts were welcomed and very well liked by county residents.[26] The page facing the one-sentence insert is a 5x7 portrait of Houston developer Gerald Hines standing in front of a plane with a by-line noting that he took his flying lessons in Fort Bend in 1942. There is no photograph of García.

Just as García's confrontation at the Richmond Drive-In was not reported in the Houston papers, there was a second incident regarding the war hero that was lost to the general public. Sometime in the 1990s, García's portrait was ripped apart by an unknown, knife-wielding vandal. Its location inside the main rotunda of the county courthouse was not the likely location for adolescent perpetrators (although that remains a possibility). The portrait was restored and perhaps the reception and memorializing was an attempt at creating or restoring respect for García as a war hero. In the speeches that day there was no mention of the formerly damaged portrait or of the unfortunate circumstances of his death. The vandalism was never reported in the papers.[27]

The slashing of the painting is not surprising, considering the county's history of antagonism toward ethnic Mexicans. There are individuals whose attitudes continue to be structured by a Jim Crow perspective (a significant number in the county). The destruction of García's portrait may have been seen as an acceptable way to exhibit disgust towards its presence in the court-house. The slashing occured with (perhaps) no witnesses. The portrait has been restored. No one has been accused. There is no evidence. The public response (if there is one) is to blame the unnamed, delinquent vandal. The charge of racism evaporates with the evidence. García is again disrespected, this time a few blocks from the site of the old Richmond Drive-In. The differ-ence this second time is that it is kept a secret. All that is now remembered is the apparently good faith of a thoughtful county judge and a friendly district attorney, with the product of their efforts in place next to the image of the hero and a narrative forever circulating through newspaper archives on the Internet. The image of the destroyed canvas remains invisible.

The last time I spoke with John de la Cruz he was concerned about the potential purchase of what is called the "black cemetery" across the chain-link fence from San Isidro. The title of the two-and-a-half acres had been transferred from Sugar Land Industries to an African American church in the 1980s. The church initially agreed to a symbolic amount of $25,000, but something went wrong. The city of Sugar Land is currently interested in the property, now worth millions. City representatives tell de la Cruz they want to make it a city cemetery, which does not seem likely since, in the past, so many nearby residents were against any type of cemetery near the subdivi-sion. It sounds like a ruse. The negotiations with the church have stalled, and a number of gravestones have disappeared from the black section.

If San Isidro is unable to purchase the additional acreage, the graveyard may soon be bordered by opulent homes instead of an overgrown cemetery. The graves of the prisoners and slaves would be lost. I am hoping that de la Cruz and other association members will resort to new technologies that can identify a grave without excavation. It is unfortunate that the black cemetery is at such risk.[28] At the least, the San Isidro Association secured the Mexican cemetery's future. It is unlikely that the San Isidro Cemetery will be disman-tled or displaced.

Additional factors may also be protecting the cemetery. If the black cem-etery (where slaves were buried, as some people told my father) is lost but San Isidro remains, the detritus will remain, albeit in tidy and compact form. John de la Cruz and other association members are slowly clearing the brush in the black cemetery, but San Isidro has been "beautified" for decades. The care and attention given the individual and family spaces has in a sense cleansed the cemetery of its brutal past. There is nothing ugly within view; even the large black-and-white geese that inhabit the place are beautiful. San Isidro's reconditioned existence is perfect as a space that contains a less revolting form of detritus. Perhaps one of the nearby residents would say, "At least it looks good." The graves of ethnic Mexicans in Sugar Creek represent the symbolic notion that the depreciated Other needs to be present in order for the dominant to remain powerful. In what would seem irrational to residents who prefer to have the dirty past completely obliterated, Derrida's often-used concept of *différence*[29] tells us that San Isidro must remain because its outline produces the form and identity of Austin's settler heroes, who are so important to this city that has learned so well to engage in a historiography that carefully selects only its ideal self.

Notes

Introduction

1. In Fort Bend County, before the 1980s, the term *mexicano* was most often used by people of Mexican descent when speaking about themselves. Other descriptors include Mexican American, Latino, Hispanic, ethnic Mexican, and Chicano.

2. John B. Judis, "Home Invasion: DeLay of the Land," *New Republic* 232 (May 16, 2005): 18–21. I thank my colleague Alessandro Carrera for suggesting this article.

3. The official name of the corporation is Sugar Land Industries.

4. Houston Baker Jr., *Turning South Again: Re-thinking Modernism/Re-Reading Booker T.,* Durham: Duke University, 2001, 15.

5. bell hooks, *Yearning: Race, Gender, and Cultural Politics,* Boston: South End Press, 1990.

6. Ibid., 124.

7. In using the term "identity" I am referring to a perception rather than actual fact since I am aware that perception is reality in the minds of many people. Michel Foucault addresses this concept in *Archeology of Knowledge and the Discourse on Knowledge* (1982), in which he proposes that discourse (i.e., what is written or discussed) forms the public's perspective of a person, group of people, or an event. The *idea* of who and what people are is constructed by the information (written and oral) that swirls around them.

8. W. J. Cash, *The Mind of the South* (1941, repr. Vintage Press, 1969).

9. Ann Laura Stoler, *Carnal Knowledge and Imperial Power: Race and the Intimate in Colonial Rule,* Berkeley: University of California, 2002, 13.

10. "The Affective Grid of Southern Politics" is a variation of the phrase "affective grid of colonial politics" that Stoler uses (Ibid., 7).

11. Michel de Certeau, *The Writing of History,* trans. by Tom Conley. New York: Columbia University, 1988, 5.

12. Stoler, 2002, 11.

13. Judis, "Home Invasion," p. 18.

14. Stephen Tyler, *The Unspeakable: Discourse, Dialogue, and Rhetoric in the Post-Modern World,* Madison: University of Wisconsin, 1987, 140.

15. Bill Harvey, *Texas Cemeteries: The Resting Places of Famous, Infamous, and Just Plain Interesting Texans,* Austin: University of Texas, 2003, 4. Also worth noting is Berlin and Harris's *Slavery in New York,* a fascinating account of the history of slavery in Manhattan that begins with the discovery of the city's "Negro burial ground." Established in the late 1600s, the cem-

etery was vast, encompassing a "five- to six-acre plot—about five city blocks"—on Wall Street. More than four hundred burials were excavated. "Archeologists estimated that as many as ten thousand [people] may be buried underneath nearby parks and buildings" (Sherrill D. Wilson, "African Burial Ground," p. 7). "The discovery of the slave cemetery began a process through which New Yorkers have begun to learn that slavery was central—not peripheral—to New York's history" (Berlin and Harris, *Slavery in New York,* p. 3) While *Slavery in New York* begins with a narrative on the burial ground, after two pages in the introduction, the story quickly shifts to a history of slavery in New York.

16. Terry Jordan, *Texas Graveyards: A Cultural Legacy,* Austin: University of Texas, 1982.

17. Meredith Watkins, "The Cemetery and Cultural Memory: Montreal, 1860–1900," *Urban History Review,* 21, no. 1, Fall 2002, p. 52–62.

18. The erased material culture that Watkins considers equivalent to "erased memory" resonates with Walter Mignolo's writing on what he terms "border gnosis or border thinking." Mignolo discusses Michel Foucault's idea of the repression of "historical contents" and their subjugation into silence—"buried behind disciplines and the production of knowledge" ("Lecture One: 7 January 1976," in Foucault, *Power/Knowledge: Selected Interviews and Other Writings, 1972–1977,* 78–92).

19. Baker, 2001.

20. Hayden White (*The Content of the Form,* 3) cites Roland Barthes's *Image, Music, Text,* 79.

Chapter 1

1. Stephen Tyler. "Vision Quest in the West or What the Mind's Eye Sees." *Journal of Anthropological Research.* (40, 1984): 23–40.

2. Ann Laura Stoler places reproduction and genealogy at the center of order in a environment where one or more groups are severely oppressed. *Race and the Education of Desire: Foucault's History of Sexuality and the Colonial Order of Things.* (Durham: Duke, 1995).

3. In the essay titled "Montaigne's 'Of Cannibals: The Savage "I,"'" Michel de Certeau proposes that the foreign, exotic, and barbaric may be present in "civilized" society, yet remain masked and hidden (de Certeau, *Heterologies: Discourse on the Other* trans. by Brian Massumi (Minneapolis: University of Minnesota): 67–79. Although we often look for savagery elsewhere, when it occurs within our own surroundings, it is difficult for us to define or even discern. Thus suicide, corporate and political corruption may be difficult to categorize as "barbaric," but they can surely be deemed "wrong, illegal, and/or violent." None of these designations fits with the moral, stable, family environment presented by the Sugar Land area.

4. As I wrote this section on the San Isidro Cemetery, I could not help but think of Gaston Bachelard's *Poetics of Space,* in which he explains that it is "on the plane of the daydream and not on that of facts that childhood remains alive and poetically useful within us. Through this permanent childhood, we maintain the poetry of the past. To inhabit oneirically the house we were born in means more than to inhabit it in memory; it means living in this house that is gone, the way we used to dream it" (Gaston Bachelard, *Poetics of Space,* trans. by Maria Jolas [1964, repr. Boston: Beacon Press]) 16. My visits to the cemetery (whether past or present) felt like daydreams, past memories that seemed palpable and real. Walking among the graves gave me a feeling of timelessness. Even though things had changed significantly—the fields gone, big houses now nearby—something central to the space seemed extremely familiar.

5. According to John de la Cruz (former president of the San Isidro Cemetery Associa-

tion), an agent from the Texas A&M Agricultural Extension Service examined the trees and stated they were from the sixteenth century.

6. A number of narratives describe the cemetery across the fence. Depicted at different times as the "black," "slave," or "prisoners" cemetery, it has been next to San Isidro as long as anyone alive can remember. In the early 1950s, when José F. Hernández asked why the cemetery on the other side of the fence was not used, people would respond that they did not want to be buried there because it had been a cemetery for slaves. In the 1970s Sugar Land Industries transferred ownership of the black cemetery to a local church, which held the title for more than thirty years but was not involved in its upkeep. The church later sold it to the San Isidro Cemetery Association.

7. The term *el labrador* means someone who works farmland. In Reyes's poem and in the work of Lope de Vega (mentioned later), a labrador is a person who works for the landowner. In Sugar Land, mexicanos commonly used the term for someone who worked for the sugar company. In Texas censuses of the nineteenth century, however, "labrador" designated someone who owned land. I thank Andres Tijerina for pointing out the alternate meaning of the term.

8. Lope de Vega, *San Isidro labrador de Madrid,* Acta 1, linea 905 (1598, repr. Alicante: Biblioteca Virtual Miguel de Cervantes, 2002). http://www.cervantesvirtual.com/servlet/SirveObras/01349419788793385422802/p0000001.htm#I_2_ (accessed March 26, 2007).

9. Tomas Morales, *Semblanzas de Testigos de Cristo Para los Nuevos Tiempos.* (Madrid: Editorial Encuentro, 1994).

10. *Réel:* what is said to be real, but cannot be proven.

11. The term "making do" relates to Michel de Certeau's concept of the tactics employed when individuals initiate minor transgressions while appearing to conform to the rules of their society, employer, and so on (Michel de Certeau, *The Practice of Everyday Life,* trans. by Steven Rendall, Berkeley: University of California, 1984): 32.

12. Those who lived in the former slave quarters behind the sugar refinery were locked in after midnight. The entire neighborhood was bordered by Oyster Creek on one side and closed in by the refinery on the remaining boundaries. A guard stood on duty at the only bridge over the creek that led outside the neighborhood. The name "quarters" came from slavery times, but in the twentieth century it was the home of both black and Mexican workers. Even though the company assisted its workers in purchasing homes in the quarters, the neighborhood had no running water until the 1960s.

13. Robert Armstrong, *Sugar Land Texas and the Imperial Sugar Company,* (Houston: privately printed, 1991): 167.

14. Rudy Cruz, interviewed by the *Houston Chronicle,* November 15, 1998.

15. Avery Gordon, *Ghostly Matters: Haunting and the Sociological Imagination* (Minneapolis: University of Minnesota, 1997): 166.

16. Ibid.

17. Francis Hodgson Burnett, *The Secret Garden* (1911, repr. New York: Grosset and Dunlap, 1983).

18. Walter James Hoffman, "The Travels of Manabush," *The Menomini Indians* (New York: Johnson reprint, 1970), 91, 171. Referenced in Michael Pomedli "Owls—Images and Voices in the Ojibwa and Midewinin Worlds."*American Indian Culture and Research Journal.* 26, 2 (2002): 47–48Michael Pomedli, "Owls—Images and Voices in the Ojibwa and Midewinin Worlds," *American Indian Culture and Research Journal,* (26, no. 2 2002): 47–48.

19. Gordon, 1997, 10.

20. Elizabeth Fox-Genovese, *Within the Plantation Household: Black and White Women of the Old South* (Chapel Hill: University of North Carolina, 1988): 203

21. Ibid., 29.

22. Pauline Yelderman, *The Jaybirds of Fort Bend County* (Waco: Texian Press, 1979): 49.

23. Lori Rodríguez, "Homes vs. Heritage: The Relationship between a Subdivision and a Cemetery Is Side-by-Side but Hardly Eye-to-Eye," *Houston Chronicle,* November 15, 1998.

Chapter 2

1. de Certeau, *Writing of History,* 1988, 69,

2. Since its inception, the offices of the Texas State Historical Association have been located on the campus of the University of Texas–Austin.

3. Ada Louis Huxtable, "Remember the Alamo."

4. According to the Institute of Texan Cultures.

5. de Certeau 1988, 47.

6. Lori Rodríguez, "Homes vs. Heritage," *Houston Chronicle,* Nov. 15, 1998.

7. Oscar Villalón, "Remember the Alamo: Sure, as Long as We Remember It for What It Really Is: A Symbol for Many, of Something Sinister"; David Drury, "No Small Affair: The Fall of the Small Garrison Gave Birth to Texas and an Enduring Symbol of Sacrifice."

8. Texas historian Gregg Cantrell often makes note of Austin's view of Mexico as a barbarous nation in *Stephen F. Austin: Empresario of Texas* (New Haven: Yale University Press, 1999).

9. Lester Bugbee, "Slavery in Early Texas I," *Political Science Quarterly,* 13, no. 3 (1898): 390.

10. Clarence Wharton, *Wharton's History of Fort Bend County* (San Antonio: Naylor Co., 1939); Gregg Cantrell, *Stephen F. Austin: Empresario of Texas.*

11. Eugene Barker, *Handbook of Texas Online,* s.v. "Mexican Colonization Laws."

12. Wharton, *Wharton's History,* 1939.

13. Stephen F. Austin, speech at the Second Presbyterian Church of Louisville, Kentucky; cited in Cantrell, *Stephen F. Austin,* p. 340.

14. Cantrell, *Stephen F. Austin,* 1999, 2.

15. Ibid., 340.

16. Ibid.

17. The son of Dutch colonials, the Baron de Bastrop was born Philip Hendrik Nering Bögel. In 1793 he was accused of embezzlement and left the Netherlands for Spanish Louisiana, where he then invented his baronial title (Cantrell, *Stephen F. Austin,* p. 86). The city of Bastrop, Texas, is named after Bögel.

18. Ibid., 86.

19. Ibid.

20. Ibid.

21. Bustamante was president of the republic from 1837 to 1841. Gómez Farías was president of Mexico five different times, from 1833 to 1834 and from 1846 to 1847. Lorenzo de Zavala was a legislator and colonization committee member and later a Texas revolutionary and the first vice president of the Republic of Texas. Between 1828 and 1832 General Mier y Terán was a congressman, general, and secretary of war and the navy (Sons of the Dewitt Colony). Ramos Arizpe is known as the father of Mexican federalism. Servando Teresa de Mier is considered one of the foremost Mexican intellectuals of his day. For having influenced the establishment of the Republic of Mexico in 1824, he is also known as *el abuelo de la patria mexicana* (the grandfather

of the Mexican republic) (Adolfo Arrioja Vizcaino, *Fray Servando Teresa de Mier: Confesiones de un guadalupano federalista*).

22. Mier is known for his international adventures. He was imprisoned in Mexico and Europe for heresy against the church, sedition against the Mexican government. It is said that in Baltimore, Maryland he took on the role of a Bishop. Servando Teresa de Mier, *Obras completas. IV. La formación de un republicano*, pp. 91–94; Servando Teresa de Mier, *Escritos inéditos*, pp. 335–52, cited in Ilona Katzew, *Casta Painting: Images of Race in Eighteenth-century Mexico*, p. 204.

23. Adolfo Arrioja Vizcaino, *Fray Servando Teresa de Mier: Confesiones de un Guadalupano Federalista*. (Mexico: Plaza y Janes, 2003).

24. Marie-Theresa Hernández, *Delirio: The Fantastic, The Demonic, and The Réel. The Buried History of Nuevo León* (Austin: University of Texas, 2002).

25. Ilona Katzew, *Casta Painting: Images of Race in Eighteenth-Century Mexico*, (New Haven: Yale University Press, 2004): 202.

26. Ibid., 204.

27. Servando Teresa de Mier, *Obras completas. IV. La formación de un republicano*, pp. 91–94; Servando Teresa de Mier, *Escritos inéditos*, pp. 335–52, cited in Ilona Katzew, *Casta Painting*, 204.

28. Ibid.

29. Austin, letter to J. E. B. Austin, June 13, 1823; cited in Cantrell, *Stephen F. Austin*, 115.

30. Cantrell, *Stephen F. Austin*, 1999.

31. Austin, letter to Sen. Lewis F. Linn, May 4, 1836; cited in Cantrell, *Stephen F. Austin*, 344. Cantrell states that the letter was published in the *Saint Louis Commercial Bulletin* on June 3, 1836, and in the *Baltimore Republican and Commercial Advertiser* on May 10, 1836, as well as in other newspapers. Austin's concerns about slave insurrection were mentioned in several of his letters.

32. Ibid., 344.

33. Roberto Blum, "Para conquistar el futuro: Al 100 años de la independencia mexicana," *El Economista* (Mexico) (September 14, 2000).

34. Evelia Trejo, *Los Limites de un Discurso: Lorenzo de Zavala, Su "Ensayo Historico y la Cuestion Religiosa en México,"* (México: Fondo de Cultura Economica, 2001), 21.

35. Lorenzo Zavala, *Ensayo Critico de las Revoluciones de México desde 1808 Hasta 1830*, (1831, repr. México: Porrua, 1969): 7.

36. Ibid.

37. Trejo, 2001.

38. "Minister of Hacienda" is the equivalent of "Minister of the Treasury."

39. Margaret Swett, Henson, *Lorenzo Zavala: The Pragmatic Idealist* (Fort Worth: Texas Christian University, 1996).

40. Trejo, 2001.

41. Ibid.

42. Ibid.

43. Cantrell, 1999, 128.

44. Ibid., 129.

45. Ibid., 130.

46. Austin, letter to Mary Holley, August 21, 1835; cited in Cantrell, *Stephen F. Austin*, 130.

47. Henson, 1996; Cleaves, 1931.

48. Cantrell, 1999, 7.

49. Hayden White, *Tropics of Discourse: Essays in Cultural Criticism*, (Baltimore: Johns Hopkins University, 1978), 167.

50. Cash, 1969, 3.

51. *Arkansas Gazette*, September 12, 1822, and *Missouri Republican*, October 16, 1822; cited in Cantrell, *Stephen F. Austin*, pp. 132–33.

52. Austin left a debt of $10,000 in Arkansas, Williams owed $700 in New Orleans, and Bastrop was accused of embezzlement in the Netherlands (Cantrell, *Stephen F. Austin*, 133).

53. Cash, 1969, 13.

54. Cantrell, 1999, 179.

55. Ibid.

56. Wharton, 1939.

57. Ibid., 30.

58. Ibid., 46.

59. *Caldwell vs. State of Texas*, 28 Criminal Appeals 566, ide. 137 U.S. 693. Caldwell's case is addressed in a subsequent chapter.

60. Wharton 1939, 199.

61. Ibid., 8.

62. S.A. McMillan, *The Book of Fort Bend County* (privately printed: S. A. McMillan and Phillip Rich 1926), 31.

63. A.J. Sowell, *History of Fort Bend County* (Houston: W.H. Coyle Stationers and Printers, 1904), x.

64. John de la Cruz of the San Isidro Cemetery Association told me about the helmet.

65. McMillan, 1926.

66. Sowell, 1904.

67. Pauline Yelderman, *The Jaybirds of Fort Bend County*, (Waco: Texian Press, 1979).

68. Anderson et al., 2003.

69. Yelderman, 1979, iv.

70. George B. Handley provides significant insight into the subject of the genealogy and position of these masters in the post–Civil War South (Handley, *Postslavery Literatures in the Americas: Family Portraits in Black and White* (Charlottesville: University of Virginia, 2000).

71. White, 1978, 73.

72. Cash, 1969.

73. Elizabeth Fox-Genovese describes the domain of the master on his plantation: "The households largely circumscribed the lives of women and slaves. The masters who presided over them constituted the principal, although never exclusive mediators between the inhabitants of the household and the larger world" (Fox-Genovese, *Within the Plantation Household: Black and White Women of the Old South*, 92–93).

74. Stoler, 1995, 105.

75. N. Doran Maillard. *The History of the Republic of Texas: From The* Discovery of the Country to the Present Time, and the Cause of Her *Separation from Mexico*. (London: Smith, Elder, 1842):iv.

76. Ibid., 222.

77. Wharton, 1939.

78. Old Three Hundred settler Francis Bingham was "not certain" if his name was Bigham or Biggam, even land documents stated Bingham. He would spell his name Biggam on some documents and Bigham on others. Bingham (Bigham/Biggam) was born in Ireland, immigrating to the United States in 1798 after an "Irish uprising." Wharton does not reference his source, but states that Bingham had two lawsuits pending in Mississippi after arriving in Texas.

"One of them he [Bingham] wrote, was against 'the killer of one of my negroes,' and the other 'against a villain for altering one of my hogs.' He manifests more wrath against the villain who 'altered' his hog than the killer of his negro (*sic*)." Bingham brought to Texas letters of introduction from numerous prominent people, including the governor of Georgia. Bingham (Bigham/Biggam) was the father-in-law of the County's Confederate hero, Colonel Frank Terry, who will be discussed in a subsequent chapter. Wharton states Bingham's (Bigham/Biggam) given name as Asa, while other documents use the name Francis. Clarence Wharton, *The History of Fort Bend County* (San Antonio: Naylor Co., 1939), 34–35.

Chapter 3

1. The portrait of Terry is no longer on display at the high school.
2. Wharton, 1939, 160.
3. de Certeau, *The Practice of Everyday Life,* 1984, 108.
4. Ibid.
5. Wharton, 1939; Sowell, 1904; Yelderman, 1979.
6. Hobbs, 2001.
7. Armstrong, 1991, 13.
8. Ibid.
9. *Herald Coaster* (Rosenberg, Texas), sesquicentennial edition, June 1, 1972. Armstrong's conclusion regarding the source of Terry's wealth is incongruent with the serious tone of his book. Based on the fact that Terry invested an exorbitant amount in the recently purchased Oakland Plantation (later renamed the Sugar Land Plantation), Armstrong is convinced that the money came from a California gold mine (Robert Armstrong, 1991, 13).
10. Ibid.
11. Leslie Lovett cites the county's statistics as given in the U.S. censuses of 1850 and 1860. In 1860 the county was home to 2,007 white inhabitants and 4,127 slaves. She notes that in 1860 Fort Bend ranked thirty-fourth in population, yet its slave population ranked eighth. The "percentage of slaveholders living in Fort Bend far outstripped the total percentage for the state . . . [and] over twice the average for the entire South" (Lovett, "The Jaybird-Woodpecker War: Reconstruction and Redemption in Fort Bend County, Texas 1869–1889," 10–11, 14).
12. Wharton, 1939; Yelderman, 1979.
13. Hobbs, 2001; Wharton, 1939. The sum of $300,000 in 1860 is equivalent to $6,600,000 in 2003. Economic History Services. See http://eh.net/hmit/compare/result.php ?use%5B%5D=DOLLAR&use%5B%5D=GDPDEFLATION&use%5B%5D=UNSKILLED &use%5B%5D=GDPCP&use%5B%5D=NOMINALGDP&amount2=3&year2=1860&year _result=&amount=&year_source= (accessed January 3, 2005).
14. Importation of Slaves into Territories, HR 77, 9th Cong., 2nd sess., 2 stat., sec. 2. This act of the U.S. Congress prohibited the importation of slaves to the United Status after January 1, 1808.
15. Hobbs, 2001; Wharton, 1939.
16. de Certeau, 1988.
17. Even thought no direct connection exists between Terry's Texas Rangers and the later famous (or infamous) Texas Rangers, the two are often associated because of their similar names.
18. Wharton, 1939, 170–71.
19. de Certeau, 1984, 107.

20. Ibid., 109.

21. Wharton, 1939, 171.

22. Yelderman, 1979, Lovett, 1994.

23. Conley, 1988, xii.

24. The idea of "silent dead" evolves from Holland's statement regarding the "boundaries between living and dead, silent and vocal. In this case, black female slaves could be described as those who are dead and silent. See *Raising the Dead: Readings of Death and (Black) Subjectivity* (Durham: Duke University Press, 2000), 98.

25. Ibid., 98.

26. Holland, 2000, 28.

27. A Sir Francis Bingham (1863–1935) actually existed: He was a major general in the British Royal Army. Among the many positions Bingham held was that of deputy director of artillery, War Office, from 1913 to 1916 (University of London, King's College, Liddell Hart Centre for Military Archives). Armstrong's confusion of Francis Bingham (Bigham/Biggam) of Texas with Sir Francis Bingham of the United Kingdom continues the pattern of overvaluing individuals connected to the Old Three Hundred, as shown by Wharton, Yelderman, and other Texas historians. Clarence Wharton notes that Francis Bigham/Biggam did not know which was the correct spelling of his own name.

28. Kenneth Hobbs, "Benjamin Franklin Terry," *Handbook of Texas Online,* 2001. http://www.tsha.utexas.edu/handbook/online/articles/TT/fte28.html (accessed February 4, 2006).

29. The Sandy Point Cemetery in Brazoria County lists "Francis Bingham, b. 1772, d. 1854. A Texas Veteran." http://www.interment.net/data/us/tx/brazoria/sandypoint/sandypoint.htm (accessed January 8, 2007).

30. Slavoj Zizek, *The Fragile Absolute—or, Why is the Christian Legacy Worth Fighting For?* (London: Verso, 2000), 3.

31. Wharton, 1939.

32. Margaret Walker, *Jubilee* (Boston: Houghton Mifflin, 1966).

33. Marjorie Melton Adams spoke about this in one of our first conversations in 2004.

34. Jenny Sharpe, *Ghosts of Slavery: A Literary Archaeology of Black Women's Lives;* Deborah Gray White, *Ain't I a Woman?: Female Slaves in the Plantation South.* Sharpe and White (among others) both present a thorough analysis of the sexual pressures and frequent violence experienced by female slaves in the South.

35. Eric Sundquist, *Faulkner: The House Divided* (Baltimore: Johns Hopkins University, 1983), 100.

36. Ibid.

37. Andrew Burstein, "Jefferson's Rationalizations," *William and Mary Quarterly* (57, No. 1, January 2000), 193.

38. Sundquist, 1983, 100.

39. Joshua Rothman, "James Callender and Social Knowledge of Interracial Sex in Antebellum Virginia," in *Sally Hemings and Thomas Jefferson: History Memory and Civic Culture,* ed. Jan Ellen Lewis and Peter S. Onuf (Charlottesville: University Press of Virginia, 1999), 87. Quoted in Elise Lemire, *Miscegenation: Making Race in America* (Philadelphia, University of Pennsylvania Press, 2002), 87.

40. Wharton, 1939, 76.

41. Yelderman, 1979,76; Wharton, 1939, 207.

42. Wharton, 1939, 207.

43. Sonnichsen mistakenly states that Gibson was killed in January 1889. The actual month was June (C. L. Sonnichsen, *I'll Die before I Run: The Story of the Great Feuds of Texas,* (New York: Devin-Adair, 1962), 255.

44. Wharton, 1939, 255.

45. Ibid.

46. Sonnichsen, 1962. 256.

47. Ned Gibson's obituary in the *Richmond Democrat,* June 28, 1889, cited in Yelderman's *The Jaybirds,* 1979, 80.

48. Ibid., 210.

49. Ibid., 251.

50. Ibid.

51. Faulkner, 1936, 20.

52. American and French Research on the Treasury of the French Language (ARTFL) Project: *Roget's Thesaurus.*

53. Hale, 1998.

54. Ibid., 114.

55. Ibid.

56. Handley proposes that planters found that a "pure" genealogy became increasingly necessary as the identification of racial markers diminished due to miscegenation (George Handley, *Postslavery Literatures in the Americas*).

57. Ibid.

58. Godden, 1994, 711.

59. William Faulkner, *Absalom, Absalom!* p. 220; cited in Richard Godden, "Absalom, Absalom!, Haiti and Labor History: Reading Unreadable Revolutions."

60. Yelderman, 1979, 98.

61. Sonnichsen, 1961, 253; Yelderman, 1979, 78.

62. Yelderman, 1979, 79.

63. Wharton, 1939.

64. Wharton, 1939, 251.

65. For an excellent analysis of the relationship between horse breeding and human breeding read, Arnd Krüger, "A Horse Breeder's Perspective: Scientific Racism in Germany, 1870–1933." In *Identity and Intolerance: Nationalism, Racism, and Xenophobia in Germany and the United States,* Norbert Finzsch and Diemar Schirmer, eds. German Historical Institute and Cambridge University Press, 1998, 171–96.

66. Documentation abounds on the frequency of these relationships. In her seminal essay on African American slave women, Spillers writes of the sexual encounters between the white men on slave ships and the female slaves in transport. She suggests that these incidents were not what these men would have documented in their letters home to their mothers (Hortense Spillers, "Mama's Baby, Papa's Maybe." Other scholars dealing with this issue include Patricia Yeager, bell hooks, Toni Morrison, Elise Lemire, and Debra White. Nonacademic narratives about concubinage are numerous. Their sources are memoirs, newspaper accounts, literature, and oral histories (recorded in WPA narratives from former slaves living in or near Fort Bend).

67. The official web page for Puerto Rico tourism describes the Serrallés Castle Museum as "a magnificent Spanish Revival mansion, built in 1930 for the Serrallés family, owners of the Don Q rum distillery. The antique furnishings recall the era of the sugar barons. A short film tracing the history of the rum and sugar industries enhances your visit." The distillery was named after Don Quixote.

68. After reading the expression "first families" many times in the Wharton, Yelderman, Sonnichsen, and Sowell texts, I find that I must qualify its meaning. The Serrallés family of Ponce appears to have been considered the city's first family because of its immense wealth, power, and whiteness. The many photographs exhibited in their former residence were images of fair-skinned people. The meaning of "first" would therefore

designate "first" only in externals, not in their actual quality as human beings. See http://
64.233.161.104/search?q=cache:8xY811yXDWwJ:welcome.topuertorico.org/city/ponce.shtml
+serralles+castle+ponce&hl=en&client=safari (accessed October 10, 2003).

69. Burstein, 2000.

70. Armstrong, 1991, 22.

71. Ibid.

72. Wharton, 1939.

73. Wharton, *History of Fort Bend County,* p. 177; cited in Armstrong, *Sugar Land, Texas, and the Imperial Sugar Company.* See also *Handbook of Texas Online,* s.v. "Wharton, Clarence Ray."

74. Yelderman, 1979.

75. Lemire, 2002, 4.

76. See American and French Research on the Treasury of the French Language (ARTFL) Project: *Roget's Thesaurus,* http://machaut.uchicago.edu/?resource=Roget%27s, s.v. "fuse."

77. Ibid., 346.

78. Laws passed during the time of the Texas Republic made it illegal to imprison a man for monetary debt (Cantrell, *Stephen F. Austin*). The county hero of the 1880s, Henry Frost, murdered a number of people but was never arrested on any charges (Wharton, *History of Fort Bend County,* 1939). Before William Eldridge became part owner and overseer of the Imperial Sugar Company, he was known to have murdered five people but never served prison time (Diane Ware, "Creating a Company Town: William T. Eldridge, Isaac H. Kempner, and Sugar Land, Texas [1906–1947]").

79. Joan Dayan, *Haiti, History, and the Gods* (Berkeley: University of California, 1995).

80. John Irwin, *Doubling and Incest/Repetition and Revenge: A Speculative Reading of Faulkner* (Baltimore, Johns Hopkins University, 1996), 20.

81. At least twice, Stephen F. Austin noted his concern that slave rebellions similar to those in Haiti might occur in Texas; cited in Cantrell, *Stephen F. Austin* (June 13, 1830). In an October 7, 1861, diary entry, Mary Chestnut writes of her concern about slave revolts similar to those in Haiti (*Mary Chestnut's Civil War,* Edited by Vann Woodward, New Haven: Yale University, 1981).

82. David Geggus, *Haitian Revolutionary Studies,* (Bloomington: University of Indiana, 2002).

83. Dayan, 1995.

84. Leslie Lovett, "The Jaybird-Woodpecker War: Reconstruction and Redemption in Fort Bend County, Texas 1869–1889," (Master's thesis, Rice University, 1994).

85. Abigail Curlee, "A Study of Texas Slave Plantations, 1822 to 1865," (PhD dissertation, University of Texas, 1936). MacMillan.

86. Alenka Zupančič, *Ethics of the Real: Kant and Lacan* (London: Verso, 2000), 191.

87. Grace Elizabeth Hale, *Making Whiteness: The Culture of Segregation in the South, 1890–1940,* (New York: Vintage, 1998).

88. Mark Twain, *Pudd'nhead Wilson and Those Extraordinary Twins,* (Hartford, Conn: American Publishing, 1894), 52–53.

89. Ibid., 188.

90. Martha McCulloch, "Review of *The Tragedy of Pudd'nhead Wilson,* (*Southern Magazine,* February, 1894).

91. Ibid.

92. Yelderman, 1979, 142–43.

93. A decision to erect a statue of the Mexica/Aztec god Quetzalcóatl provoked national controversy. The location was the most highly visible city park in San Jose, California. The

chair of the city's planning commission fought the decision vehemently because, he contended, the statue represented a pagan culture. An article in the *San Francisco Chronicle* on September 30, 1993, stated: "Bernal Diaz del Castillo, one of Cortes' soldiers, witnessed these sacrifices when he saw captured Spanish soldiers dragged up to the top of a pyramid, their chests sawed open and their palpitating hearts pulled out. Their bodies were then kicked down the pyramid steps, and attendants flayed them."

94. de Certeau, *Heterologies,* 1986, 71.

95. Yelderman, 1979, 97.

96. A photograph of the Fort Bend Ku Klux Klan appears in Sharon Wallingford's *Fort Bend County, Texas: A Pictorial History* (Fort Bend Publishing Group, 1996), 85. Wallingford does not provide commentary to the images, making it difficult to ascertain the motive behind her choice of photographs. As an editor, she may be seeking a bit of sensationalism or implying that the presence of the KKK is an accepted and significant part of the county's history. Other documentation on the KKK in Fort Bend is almost nonexistent.

97. de Certeau, *The Writing of History,* 1988, 300.

98. Yelderman, 1979.

99. Wharton, 1939.

100. de Certeau, *The Writing of History,* 1988, 301.

101. Ibid., 305.

Chapter 4

1. de Certeau, *The Writing of History,* 1988.

2. Cantrell, 1999.

3. Brewer, John Mason, *Dog Ghosts, and Other Texas Negro Folk Tales; The Word on the Brazos: Negro Preacher Tales from the Brazos Bottoms of Texas* (Austin: University of Texas, 1958).

4. Harold M. Hyman, *Oleander Odyssey: The Kempners of Galveston, Texas, 1854–1980's* (College Station, Texas: Texas A&M University, 1990).

5. de Certeau, *The Writing of History,* 1988, 323.

6. For more information on the white primaries, see Darlene Clark Hine, *Black Victory: The Rise and Fall of the White Primary in Texas* (Millwood, N.Y.: KTO Press, 1979).

7. Lovett, 1994.

8. Litwack, 1979 (rpr 1980, New York: Vintage): 277

9. Ibid.

10. Wang, Xi, "Black Suffrage and the Redefinition of American Freedom, 1860–1870," *Cardozo Law Review* vol. 17 (1995): 2153–2223.

11. Wharton, 1939.

12. Gordon, 1997, 172.

13. Wayne Gard, *Handbook of Texas Online,* s.v. "Vigilantes and Vigilance Committees."

14. Sonnichsen, *I'll Die before I Run,* 244 cites the *Houston Post,* August 7, 1888, and August 22, 1888.

15. Sonnichsen, 1962.

16. Wharton, 1939.

17. Sonnichsen, 1962, 242.

18. Ibid.

19. Ibid.

20. Wharton, 1939, 197.

21. Sonnichsen, 1962, 242.

22. Wharton, 1939, 137.

23. Sonnichsen, 1962, 244.

24. Ibid.

25. Sonnichsen, 1962, 244.

26. Wharton, 1939.

27. Sonnichsen, 1962, 245.

28. Yelderman, 1979, 70

29. Sonnichsen, 1962, 247.

30. Wharton, 1939, 199.

31. Ibid., 246

32. Ibid.

33. Sonnichsen states that Frost retaliated by having Bearfield arrested on perjury charges and that "whatever happened to Bearfield has never been revealed" (*I'll Die before I Run,* p. 247). The connotation of "whatever happened" alludes to the possibility of Bearfield's disappearance or death.

34. According to the Rev. John Collins, CSB, "It took me from eight until eleven in the morning to make the trip. A stretch of bad road . . . caused the delay." It is less than ten miles from Rosenberg to Clodine, and Collins was traveling by car. Collins to the Very Rev. Henry Carr, CSB, April 2, 1942, Archives of the Congregation of the Society of Saint Basil, Toronto, Canada.

35. Sonnichsen states that the county residents gathered on September 5 (*I'll Die before I Run,* 248), whereas the date Yelderman gives is September 4 (*Jay Birds,* 71).

36. John Leffler states that the town was "[n]amed after Richmond, England" (*Handbook of Texas Online,* s.v., "Richmond, Texas"), which differs from Wharton's assertion that it was named after Richmond, Virginia (*History of Fort Bend County,* 85).

37. Sonnichsen, 1962, 235.

38. Lovett, 1994.

39. Sonnichsen 1962, 233–34.

40. Ibid.

41. Wendel Addington, "Slave Insurrections in Texas." *Journal of Negro History,* vol. 35 (3, October, 1950).

42. The slave revolt in Haiti (San Domingue) at the end of the eighteenth century plays a significant part in William Faulkner's *Absalom, Absalom!*

43. Sowell, 1904, 183.

44. Yelderman, 1979, 72.

45. Ibid.

46. Wharton (*History of Fort Bend County,* 1939, 201) lists Charles Ferguson, district clerk; J. D. Davis and H. G. Lucas, school teachers; Peter Warren, restaurant owner; C. M. Williams, barber; Tom Taylor, county commissioner; and Tom Taylor's brother, Jack Taylor.

47. Sonnichsen (*I'll Die before I Run,* p. 248) states that ten men were involved, whereas Yelderman contends that six took part (*Jay Birds,* 71).

48. Yelderman, 1979.

49. Yelderman (*Jay Birds,* p. 72), in contrast, lists three hundred men riding double file to the homes of blacks in Richmond.

50. Yelderman, 1979, 72–73

51. Sonnichsen, 1962; Wharton, 1939.

52. Sonnichsen, 1962, 248.

53. Wharton, 1939.

54. Ibid.

55. Yelderman, 73.

56. Foucault, 1977.

57. Sonnichsen, 1962.

58. Yelderman, 1979, 73.

59. Sonnichsen, 1962, 322–23.

60. Ibid.

61. Foucault, 1977, 57.

62. Sonnichsen, 1962, 249.

63. "African Americans in Texas: Historical and Cultural Legacies by the Texas Historical Commission," http://www.thc.state.tx.us/publications/brochures/AfrcnAmrcn.pdf (accessed January 6, 2007). Adams, who is a committee member of the Texas Historical Commission, has been working with the Kendleton Historical Society to make the Green house a museum. Adams told me that some connection might have existed between the Turkey Creek feud and a violent confrontation in Pittsville that occurred in July 1888. Pittsville no longer exists, but it was located in Fort Bend County. According to Wharton, problems cropped up during a barbecue and led to angry confrontations between whites but no killing. This is the incident during which Randal (who was white) was called a black man.

64. The number of white men killed in the Turkey Creek story changed slightly every time I spoke with someone from Kendleton.

65. "Many Negroes Massacred," *New York Times,* March 1, 1888.

66. Trouillot, 1995.

67. Frederick Law Olmsted, *A Journey Through Texas: Or, a Saddle-Trip on the Southwestern Frontier.* 1857 (rpr Austin, University of Texas, 1978): 362–63

68. Roland Barthes, *Image, Music, Text,* trans. by Stephen Heath (New York: Hills and Wang, 1977).

69. Michel-Rolph Trouillot describes a fact or an event that a society cannot even conceive of because its occurrence seems completely implausible. Although Trouillot does not reference Michel de Certeau, his theses are very similar to de Certeau's theory as presented in *The Writing of History* (1988) (Trouillot, *Silencing the Past: Power and the Production of History*).

70. Macmillan/McGraw-Hill, formal response to written comments, textbook hearing #2, http://www.tea.state.tx.us/textbooks/adoptprocess/aug_macmillan2.pdf (accessed January 6, 2007).

71. The official website of the George Ranch Historical Park describes its mission as the safeguarding of historical resources, including preservation, education, community involvement, and communication. At the end of this list is "Identity: To maintain a reputation of integrity and stability." See http://www.georgeranch.org/about/mission/ (accessed January 6, 2007). The park is maintained by an affiliation between the Fort Bend County Museum Association and the George Foundation. It is funded by the latter.

72. Naomi Carrier Grundy, *Social Politics in Victorian Texas, 1890: A Living Interpretation of African Americans and Their Responsibilities in the Home of JHP Davis, Rancher/Farmer, Fort Bend County, Texas.*

73. Ibid., p. 4.

74. Ibid., p. 9.

75. Ibid., p. 5.

76. De Certeau, 1988, 245–46.

77. Ibid., 246.

78. Tristan Tzara, *Où boivent les loups* (Paris, 1932), 161; cited in Gaston Bachelard, *Water and Dreams: An Essay on the Imagination of Matter,* 193.

79. A notation on a monument to Stephen F. Austin at a memorial park in the city he founded on the banks of the Brazos, just north of Fort Bend County, states: "If he who by conquest wins an empire and receives the world's applause, how much is due to him who by unceasing toil lays in the wilderness the foundation for an infant colony and build therein a vigorous state?"

80. Hyman, 1990.

Chapter 5

1. Tere Romo, "The Chicanization of Mexican Calendar Art." Paper presented at Smithsonian National Conference: The Interpretation and Representation of Latino Cultures: Research and Museums (Washington, D.C. 2000).

2. Ibid.

3. Rodríguez gave three of his children indigenous names: Tizoc, Tonatiuh, and Cuitláhuac. See Elizabeth Hernández, "Preparan más homenajes para Ismael Rodríguez," *El Universal* (Mexico City, August 11, 2004).

4. Harry Gilroy, "Movie Fete Postscript," (*New York Times,* July 7, 1957).

5. Trejo, *Los Limites del Discurso,* 2002.

6. Even with solid relationships with early Texas heroes, Seguín was forced to leave Texas for New Orleans after he was branded a traitor to the republic. He eventually supported Mexico in the U.S.–Mexican War of 1846. Juan Seguín, *A Revolution Remembered: The Memoirs and Selected Correspondence of Juan N. Seguín.* (Austin, Texas Historical Association, 2002).

7. Maillard, *The History of the Republic of Texas,* 1842.

8. Walker, 1988.

9. Montejano, 1987.

10. Kay Almere Read, "Sacred Commoners: the Motion of Cosmic Powers in Mexica Rulership," *History of Religions,* vol. 34 (August, 1994): 49.

11. Ibid.

12. Read, 1994, 42.

13. Ibid., 42–43.

14. Ibid., 49.

15. Kay Almere Read, "Binding Reeds and Burning Hearts: Mexica-Tenochca Concepts of Time and Sacrifice," 287

16. Michel-Rolph Trouillot, *Silencing the Past: Power and the Production of History,* (Boston, Beacon, 1995).

17. Flores, 2002; Bost, 2003.

18. Hardin is a journalist for *Texas Monthly* magazine. Gregg J. Dimmick is a physician and historian who has published a book on Santa Ana's presence in Southeast Texas (which includes Fort Bend County).

19. Richard Flores, *Remembering the Alamo: Memory, Modernity, and the Master Symbol* (Austin, University of Texas, 2002).

20. Richard Flores, Introduction to *History and Legends of the Alamo and Other Missions in and Around San Antonio* by Adina de Zavala (Houston, Arte Publico Press, 1996).

21. Arnoldo De León, *They Called Them Greasers: Anglo Attitudes Towards Mexicans in Texas* (Austin, University of Texas, 1983).

22. In *The Adventures of Big-foot Wallace, the Texas Ranger and Hunter,* John Duval quotes his subject as saying that the "[Mexican] inhabitants of this ranch were certainly the [most]

wretched-looking specimen of humanity I had ever seen. . . . Men, women, and children were squalid beyond description" (pp. 189, 199). Wallace's comment that Mexican General Barragán had the misfortune to be born a Mexican is quite telling of Texan attitudes toward Mexicans at the time (1870). Duval's book is described by Luke Warm as "the first best-selling book on a Texas personality" (Warm, "'Bigfoot' Wallace," *TexasEscapes.com, A Texas Travel History and Architecture Magazine*).

23. William Fairfax Gray, diary entry, February 1, 1836. In Gray, *The Diary of William Fairfax Gray: From Virginia to Texas, 1835–1837,* ed. by Paul Lack (Dallas: Southern Methodist University, 1997): 78.

24. Benjamin Johnson, *Revolution in Texas: How a Forgotten Rebellion and Its Bloody Suppression Turned Mexicans into Americans* (New Haven, Yale University, 2003).

25. Johnson, *Revolution in Texas,* 2003, 3.

26. Gray, *The Diary of William Fairfax Gray,* 1997, 82.

27. Neil Foley, *The White Scourge: Mexicans, Blacks, Poor Whites in Texas Cotton Culture* (Berkeley, University of California, 1997): 35.

28. Ibid., 37.

29. Edward Everett Davis, "King Cotton Leads Mexicans into Texas," *Texas Outlook* 9 (April 1925), 1–3; cited in Neil Foley, *The White Scourge: Mexicans, Blacks, and Poor Whites in Texas Cotton Culture,* 11.

30. Richard J. Schiefen, CSB, *Mission Notes* (1968). Schiefen was associate professor of history at the University of Saint Thomas in Houston.

31. de León, *The Tejano Community* (Austin, University of Texas, 1983).

32. John G. Bourke relates his perception of the savagery of ethnic Mexicans in South Texas (south of the Nueces River) in "The American Congo," *Scribner's* 15(5) (May 1894): 590–610.

33. Gray explains the similarity between slavery in the United States and the debtor system in Mexico: "Many families become enslaved, and are held by the large proprietors as part of their estate. They are generally bought and sold with the land, sometimes sold individually, by the debtor procuring some one to pay his debt. He then changes masters and serves him who paid for him. Some estates in Mexico are said to have several thousand of these *debtor slaves* on them, and instead of dying in despair or repining at their lot, they are said to be submissive and content, and much attached to their masters. The practice has obtained but little in Texas" (Gray, *Diary of William Fairfax Gray,* 57).

34. Bob Bowman, "A Tough East Texan," *TexasEscapes.Com,* (October 10–17, 2000).

35. Sowell, *History of Fort Bend County,* 1904.

36. Trouillot, *Silencing the Past,* 1995, 48.

37. Ibid.

38. Walter Benjamin, "The Storyteller," in *Illuminations,* ed. by Hannah Arendt (New York, Schocken Books, 1968), 83–110.

39. Sowell, *History of Fort Bend County,* 1904, 55.

40. Ibid.

41. Information obtained from John Molleston, Texas General Land Office, Archives Division (May 2005). In view of the fact that the land office information states that Gonzales owned property in Victoria before the Texas Revolution, he was very likely a member of the De León colony. For more information on the Victoria settlement, see Ana Castillo Crimm, *The De León Family: A Tejano Family History,* (Austin, University of Texas, 2003).

42. Bob Bowman, "A Tough East Texan," 2000.

43. Mary Varner Meryweather and Donald Raney, *Handbook of Texas Online,* s.v. "Varner, Martin."

44. Texas General Land Office, State of Texas, http://www.glo.state.tx.us/ (accessed Jan. 13, 2007).

45. I am reminded by my colleague Laura Helper-Ferris that in 1904 lynchings of African Americans occurred frequently in Texas and throughout the South. This, however, does not explain the tone of Bowman's article, which was published in the year 2000.

46. Texas Historical Commission, Bob Bowman Biography.

47. Robert B. Blake, *Handbook of Texas Online,* s.v. "Cordova, Vicente."

48. In "The Córdova Rebellion," Wallace L. McKeehan cites A. J. Sowell, *Early Settlers and Indian Fighters of Southwest Texas: Facts Gathered from Survivors of Frontier Days* (Austin: B. C. Jones, 1900).

49. Paul Lack, "The Cordova Rebellion," In *Tejano Journey, 1770–1850,* ed. by Gerald Poyo, (Austin: University of Texas, 1996): 99.

50. Sowell, *History of Fort Bend County,* 1904.

51. A. J. Sowell, *Early Settlers and Indian Fighters,* 1900. Paul D. Lack, "Cordova Revolt," 89–109.

52. Ibid.

53. Harriet Matilda Jamison Durst in "Early Days of Texas," Durst Family Collection, Stephen F. Austin University, no date or page number given; cited in Lack, "Cordova Revolt," 97.

54. Seguin, *A Revolution Remembered,* 1996, 154.

55. John Milton Chance, *After San Jacinto: The Texas-Mexican Frontier, 1836–1841* (Austin, University of Texas, 1963).

56. Robert Blake Research Collection, Steen Library, Stephen F. Austin State University. xliii, 251; cited in Lack, "Cordova Revolt."

57. Lack, "The Cordova Rebellion," 1996, 109; Ibid., 109.

58. Johnson, *Revolution in Texas,* 2003.

59. de Certeau, 1986, 227.

60. Ibid.

61. de Certeau, 1984, 32.

62. From the transcript of remarks by Judge James DeAnda, given on November 19, 2004, at the "*Hernández v. Texas* at 50" conference in Houston. George I. Sánchez Lecture, Institute for Higher Education Law and Governance, University of Houston Law Center,

63. War Department, Citation G.O. 74, September 1, 1945; cited in Raúl Morín, *Among the Valiant: Mexican Americans in WWII and Korea,* 144.

64. Morín, *Among the Valiant,* 1963.

65. Ibid., 146.

66. Ibid.

67. Ibid., 147.

68. *New York Times,* "Twenty-eight Army Men Get Medals of Honor: Ceremony at White House Conducted by President Is Largest of Its Kind," (August 24, 1945).

69. Maria-Cristina García, *Handbook of Texas Online,* s.v. "García, Macario"; Kenneth Hobbs, *Handbook of Texas Online,* s.v. "Terry, Benjamin Franklin."

70. Hobbs, "Terry, Benjamin Franklin."

71. *Houston Chronicle,* "Sugar Land Hero to Be Honored in City Tonight," (September 6, 1945).

72. From the 1940s to the 1960s Robert E. ("Bob") Smith was considered one of the wealthiest and most powerful men in Houston. He built the Galveston Yacht Basin and was instrumental in constructing the Astrodome and bringing a national baseball team to the city.

At the time of his death in 1973, he was worth an estimated $500 million (more than $2 billion in 2005 dollars) (Diana J. Kleiner, *Texas History Online,* s.v. "Smith, Robert Everett").

73. George N. Green, *Handbook of Texas Online,* s.v. "Good Neighbor Commission."

74. Eddie Barr, *Houston Press,* "Honor Medal Winner Gets Lost in City," (September 7, 1945).

75. Texas History Online lists the incident at the Richmond Drive-In in addition to García's WWII exploits.

76. Shaeffer was Jewish and a leader in the local B'nai Brith; information provided by José F. Hernández.

77. DeAnda, "*Hernández v. Texas* at 50."

78. Alford, *The Proud People,* 1972.

79. Ibid., 168–70.

80. Enrique Castillo, *Los Veteranos: A Legacy of Valor.*

81. Michael Olivas found additional information on the Macario García case at the Fort Bend County Courthouse. Although García was arrested, his case was ultimately (and quietly) dropped. I thank Olivas for sharing this information with me.

82. *New York Times,* August 23, 1945.

83. Walter Winchell Papers, T-Mss 1991–019, Billy Rose Theatre Collection, New York Public Library for the Performing Arts. See Walter Winchell, "The Jergens Journal," Series II, Scripts and Writing; subseries Radio Scripts, September 23, 1945 (Sunday), broadcast pages 4–5. Winchell mistakenly writes García's given name as "Marcio" instead of the correct "Macario."

84. Willard Hotel, http://washington.intercontinental.com/ (accessed January 6, 2007).

85. It also resonates with William Faulkner's *Absalom, Absalom!,* in which Thomas Sutpen is greatly affected when an elegantly dressed Negro slave turns him away at the door of the grand home of a Kentucky planter. This rejection serves as a decisive motivator in Sutpen's subsequent plan to establish a large plantation.

86. "South Carolina Newspapers" by Robert Altman, http://www.scpress.org/newshistory .htm/ (accessed October 25, 2005). Altman writes that "Quillen's columns were syndicated in more than 400 newspapers, and he was writing for *The Saturday Evening Post* and other magazines. Under Quillen's editorial direction, [the column] . . . was one of the nation's best-known weeklies during the 1920s and 1930s." Quillen was known for his commonsense quotes (in the style of Will Rogers) and a long-running comic strip titled "Aunt Het." Quillen's obituary in the December 9, 1948, issue of the *Greenville News* describes him as a "humorist, a columnist, an editorialist, a publisher," and "a friend to the unfortunate, a counselor to the unwise, a protector to the unwary" (Ibid.).

87. Robert Quillen, "Not the Tyrant Himself but Slave Who Cracks Whip," *Dallas Morning News,* (September 10, 1945).

88. Ibid. Quillen does not designate Hendrix's racial background, which in almost all instances indicates "white." See the photograph of Hendrix posted at the "Home of the Heroes" website: http://www.homeofheroes.com/photos/6_ww2/hendrix_recent_small.jpg (accessed January 6, 2007).

89. Clarence Wharton criticized black politicians, such as Charles Ferguson, for being overly aggressive. Similarly, he praised Ferguson's brother Henry for always being polite and well mannered. The behavior of the county's official hero, Col. Frank Terry, was perceived differently. According to Wharton, "His aggressive nature did not irritate, but by common consent gave him a leadership which the County folks were ready to acknowledge" (Wharton, *History of Fort Bend County,* 1939, 160).

90. Enrique Castillo, "Los Veteranos, 2002."

91. Studies show that WWII veterans continued to experience stress and/or emotional discomfort for as long as fifty years after their combat experience. See Bas J. N. Schreuder, Wim C. Kleijn, and Harry G. M. Rooijmans, "Nocturnal Re-experiencing More than Forty Years after War Trauma," *Journal of Traumatic Stress* 13(3) (2000): 453–63. Also see N. Hunt and I. Robbins, "The Long-term Consequences of War: The Experience of WWII," *Aging and Mental Health* 5(2) (2001): 183–90.

92. De Certeau, 1988, 58.

93. *Houston Chronicle,* "Hero Refused Service in Café," (September 20, 1945).

94. *Houston Chronicle,* (September 20, 1945). During the Civil Rights movement of the 1960s, the Houston newspaper took more of an interest in the community's diverse population. By 2001 the article on García would have brought praise for the newspaper since it was honoring the war hero by showing how García had struggled during the Jim Crow era. Even so, the newspaper's statement that the article was republished verbatim on July 20, 2001, is incorrect. The citation at the *Chronicle*'s website states that the original article contains 112 words and that the current article is "From Our Files, taken verbatim from the pages of the *Houston Chronicle.*" http://proquest.umi.com.ezproxy.lib.uh.edu/pqd link?index=0&did=75667676&SrchMode=1&sid=1&Fmt=3&VInst=PROD&VType=PQD& RQT=309&VName=PQD&TS=1139104609&clientId=86 (accessed February 4, 2005).

Chapter 6

1. When John de la Cruz and other members of the San Isidro Cemetery Association told me about Bodame, I could not quite understand the name of the village. In the summer of 2005 my father and I drove from the city of Sugar Land to the banks of the Brazos River. He wanted to show me the location of a small community he had often visited in the 1950s and 1960s. He called it "Bodame." Surprised to hear the name again, I asked him what it meant. He said it mean the Brazos River "bottoms."

2. Hyman, 1990, 347.

3. Until 1986 the neighborhood had neither a sewer nor a water system (*Houston Chronicle,* "Fifth Street/Water, Sewage Woes Plague Unincorporated Neighborhood," August 17, 1986; "Fifth Street Residents to Get Water," October 12, 1986).

4. Eunice Collier is a pseudonym.

5. Fort Bend County Deed Records, vol. 627, 694, 1974.

6. Gloria Anzaldúa, *Borderlands/La Frontera: The New Mestiza,* 1987, 8.

7. A number of lawyers were among the early Anglo Texans. Stephen Austin was studying law in New Orleans when he left to establish his colony in Texas. Others were Sam Houston; William Barrett Travis (Cantrell, *Stephen F. Austin,* 81–82, 256); David Burnet (Margaret Swett Henson, *Handbook of Texas Online,* s.v. "Burnett, David Gouverneur"); and Sam Houston (Kreneck, Thomas H. *Handbook of Texas Online,* s.v. "Houston, Samuel").

8. Sugar Creek manager Gary Stanford provided this information. The first few years after Sugar Creek was constructed, no one was allowed past the guard station without specific permission from registered residents. This practice ended when the mayor of Sugar Land was refused permission to enter the subdivision to pick up his son after a party the boy had attended. After a lawsuit, the subdivision relaxed its restrictive policy somewhat.

9. Mary Douglad, *Purity and Danger: An Analysis of the Concepts of Pollution and Taboo* (rpr 1966, London: Routledge, 1995).

10. Patricia Yeager explains the practice of "throwing away" in her analysis of Kate Chopin's 1894 novel, *La Belle Zoraïde* (Yeager, *Dirt and Desire: Reconstructing Southern Women's Writing, 1930–1990*, 69–70).

11. Alan Lomax (*The Land Where the Blues Began,* 217) states that the importance of people and animals was based on their material value. Lomax is describing southern Louisiana, but he could just as well be characterizing Southeast Texas: "Lomax . . . describes the delta levee world of the turn of the century as the last American frontier, even more lawless than the far west in its palmiest days because there was so to speak open season on blacks, considered less valuable than the mules they drove" (cited in Yeager, *Dirt and Desire,* 72).

12. Rodríguez, "Homes versus Heritage," 1998.

13. Brian Gaston, letter to the editor, *Houston Chronicle,* November 25, 1998.

14. Brian Gaston is a strong supporter of former congressman Tom DeLay, who is known as Sugar Land's most important elected official (Bob Dunn, "DeLay's Lawyers Turn Table on Prosecutors," *Fort Bend Now,* October 11, 2005). Gaston's blog response was posted on October 12, 2005, and is available at http://www.fortbendnow.com/news/253/new-evidence-led-to-latest-delay-indictments-earle-says (accessed January 6, 2007). Shortly after DeLay's indictment for alleged money laundering, Gaston placed a message on the *Fort Bend Now,* an online periodical about the county. Gaston, who is a former four-term city councilman, stated that the district attorney who brought the charges against DeLay was acting like a "keystone kop" with an "agenda . . . to smear DeLay during the political season." According to Gaston, the charges had "little chance" of being proven.

15. *State of Texas vs. Aniceto Sánchez,* District Court of Fort Bend County, Texas, 23rd Judicial District, no. 25496, appeal from Fort Bend County, opinion of Judge Beauchamp, p. 1.

16. John J. Herrera, *Handbook of Texas Online,* s.v. "Herrera, John J." See also José Francisco Ruiz, *Handbook of Texas Online,* s.v. "Ruiz, José Francisco," as well as Adolfo Casias Herrera, *Handbook of Texas Online,* s.v. "Herrera, Blas María."

17. DeAnda, "*Hernández v. Texas* at 50."

18. *State of Texas vs. Sánchez,* social science brief, James DeAnda and John J. Herrera, p. 2.

19. Alonso Perales, *El México americano y la política del sur de Texas* (San Antonio: Artes Gráficas, 1931, 4); cited in Benjamin Márquez, "The Politics of Race and Assimilation: The League of United Latin American Citizens, 1929–1940," *Western Political Quarterly* 42(2) (1987): 355–75.

20. Marquez, "The Politics of Race and Assimilation," 1987.

21. *State of Texas vs. Sánchez,* appeal from Fort Bend County, opinion of Judge Beauchamp.

22. DeAnda, "*Hernández v. Texas* at 50."

23. Ibid.

Chapter 7

1. L. Frank Baum, *The Wonderful Wizard of Oz,* (Chicago, G.M. Hill, 1900): 59.

2. Henry M. Littlefield, "The Wizard of Oz: Parable on Populism," *American Quarterly,* vol. 16 (no. 1, 1964): 48

3. L. Frank Baum, *The Wonderful Wizard of Oz,* 1900, 4.

4. Henry M. Littlefield, "The Wizard of Oz: Parable on Populism," 1964, 57

5. Sharon Wallingford, "Sugar Land Sculpture Honors Texas Pioneer," *Houston Chronicle,* (Jan. 15, 2004).

6. Ibid.

7. Ibid.

8. Clarence Wharton's descriptions of numerous settlers often begin by recounting the severe physical hardships they endured, yet soon they became the best families of the county. Wharton, *History of Fort Bend,* 1939.

9. Gregg Cantrell, *Stephen F. Austin,* 1999.

10. Dilue Rose Harris, "The Reminiscences of Mrs. Dilue Harris, Part II," *Southwestern Historical Quarterly* 4(3) (Jan., 1901).

11. Paul Lack, "The Cordova Rebellion," 1996.

12. With regard to "going down the river," Mark Twain explains in *Pudd'nhead Wilson:* "If at the end of that time, you have not confessed, I will not only sell all four of you, BUT—I will sell you DOWN THE RIVER!" It was equivalent to condemning them to hell. No Missouri Negro doubted this. Twain, *Pudd'nhead Wilson and Those Extraordinary Twins,* 1890, 39.

13. John Mason Brewer, *Dog Ghosts, and Other Texas Negro Folk Tales,* 1976.

14. Ibid.

15. Randolph Campbell, *An Empire for Slavery: The Peculiar Institution in Texas, 1821–1865,* (Baton Rouge, Louisiana State University, 1989).

16. Wharton, *History of Fort Bend County,* 1939.

17. Ibid.

18. Frederick Douglass, *Narrative of the Life of Frederick Douglass,* (Oxford, UK, Oxford University, 1999, 16. written work.

19. Hortense Spillers, "Mama's Baby, Papa's Maybe," *Diacritics* 17(2) (Summer 1987): 77.

20. Claude Meillassoux, "Female Slavery," in *Women and Slavery in Africa,* Ed. by Claire Robertson and Martin Klien (Madison: University of Wisconsin–Madison, 1983): 50, cited by Hortense Spillers, "Mama's Baby, Papa's Maybe,"1987, 74.

21. Ibid., 74.

22. Gretchen Ritter, "Silver Slippers and a Golden Cap: L. Frank Baum and the Wonderful Wizard of Oz and Historical Memory in American Politics," *Journal of American Studies Journal of American Studies* 31(2) (1997).

23. L. Frank Baum, *Wonderful Wizard of Oz,* 1900, 60. cited by Gretchen Ritter, "Silver Slippers," 1997, 183.

24. L. Frank Baum, *Wonderful Wizard of Oz,* 1900, 33.

25. Ibid.

26. Evan McKenzie, *Privatopia: Homeowners Associations and the Rise of Residential Private Government,* (New Haven, Yale University, 1996).

27. L. Frank Baum, *Wonderful Wizard of Oz,* 1900, 35.

28. Ibid., 37.

29. Sugar Land demographics for 2004 show that 56.8 percent of the city's residents are employed in professional and managerial positions (http://www.sugarlandecodev.com/2–5 _workforce.htm; accessed January 16, 2007). From 1990 to 2000 the city's population increased 158 percent, to 63, 328 (http://www.sugarlandecodev.com/2–7_demoInfo.htm; accessed January 16, 2007).

30. Jim Jenkins, "Today's Master-planned Community Developers Must Apply Expertise," Newland Communities. Jenkins is president of the Texas division of the Newland Communities, which is building the new Telfair subdivision on land formerly owned by the Texas prison system.

31. Doug Adolph, "Sugar Land Town Square Plaza/City Hall Awarded Best Community Impact," *Public Management* 87(11) (Dec., 2005): 31. Sugar Land Town Square was given the Best Community Impact award by the *Houston Business Journal.* Judges remarked that the

"three-story city hall and historically themed plaza, in all its grandeur, symbolizes the past, the present, and the future of a city that has set itself apart from others. The new location of the city hall enables the city of Sugar Land to centralize departments into one geographic center. Sugar Land Town Square is a pedestrian-oriented development that functions as the city's commercial, civic, and cultural center. In . . . the Sugar Land Town Square location, the city hall has helped in creating a sense of place and a source of community pride."

32. Brian Gaston, letter to the editor, *Houston Chronicle,* (Nov. 25, 1998).

33. Toni Morrison, *Beloved,* (New York, Knopf, 1987).

34. Angels Carabi, "Interview: Toni Morrison," *Belles Lettres* 10(2) (Spring 1995): 40.

35. Baker, 2001.

36. Telfair, Newland Communities, Sugar Land, Tex.

37. Nancy Sarnoff, "Newland Communities," *Houston Chronicle,* Feb. 25, 2005.

38. Michel Foucault, *Discipline and Punish,* 1977, 200.

39. University of Houston news release, "Newland Communities Gives $100,000 to Support New Building for UHSSL & WCJC 'Building Futures Together' Campaign to Expand Educational Opportunities in Fort Bend County."

40. Carole Keeton Strayhorn, "Paving the Way: A Review of the Texas Department of Transportation." Strayhorn, who is Texas comptroller of public accounts, cites the Texas General Land Office, *Real Property Evaluation Reports, Texas Department of Transportation* (Austin, Tex., Sept. 1, 1999), p. 69; interview with Jeff Boudreau, General Land Office, Austin, Tex., Jan. 5, 2000.

41. Texas General Land Office, *Real Property Evaluation Reports, Texas Department of Transportation* (Austin, Tex., Sept. 1, 1999).

42. Marie-Theresa Hernández, *Delirio: The Fantastic, The Demonic, and The Réel: The Buried History of Nuevo León,* (Austin, University of Texas, 2002).

43. Avery Gordon, *Ghostly Matters: Haunting and the Sociological Imagination,* (Minneapolis, University of Minnesota, 1993): 194.

44. Thulani Davis, *All the Renegade Ghosts Rise* (Washington, D.C., Anemone, 1978): 43, cited by Avery Gordon, *Ghostly Matters,* 1993, 194.

45. *Dallas Morning News,* "Legislators Hear Tale of Alleged Prison Cruelty: Ex-convict Asserts He Was Mutilated," February 8, 1925.

Conclusion

1. Sharon Wallingford, 1996.

2. Thomas Jefferson, no source given. Cited by Sharon Wallingford, *Fort Bend County, Texas: A Pictorial History,* p. 11. The major sponsor of the book is the Southern National Bank of Texas, whose building (in Sugar Land) is a replica of Jefferson's Monticello, which is reproduced as a watercolor in Wallingford's book (on the same page announcing the bank's sponsorship).

3. Jacqueline Rose, *States of Fantasy* (Oxford, Oxford University, 1996).

4. On September 29, 2005, I was on a tour through Monticello while the guide listed the accomplishments of Jefferson's children and grandchildren. A fellow tourist asked whether the guide was including Jefferson's children with Sally Hemings. The tour guide became flustered and said that the official position of the Monticello Foundation was that the DNA tests had shown that the father of Hemings's children was a Jefferson and that it was still a problem that had not been resolved.

5. Thomas Jefferson, *Notes on the State of Virginia, 1781–1782.*

6. Congressman Tom Delay's political career and the death of Enron executive Clifford Baxter have brought international notice to Sugar Land. The city is the focus of a number of articles in national and international newspapers and magazines, including the *New Republic, Washington Post, Australian, San Diego Tribune, New York Times, London Telegraph,* and *London Financial Times.*

7. *Roget's Thesaurus* (1911), American and French Research on the Treasury of the French Language (ARTFL) Project.

8. Wallingford, 1996, 1, 8–9.

9. It was first published by Twain in "Stirring Times in Austria," *Harper's New Monthly Magazine* 96(574) (March 1898): 533. Fifty-seven years later, literary critic Lionel Trilling cited Twain in the 1955 Freud Anniversary Lecture at the New York Psychoanalytic Institute. Trilling published the essay as *Freud and the Crisis of Our Culture* (1955). Jacqueline Rose referenced both Twain and Trilling when she spoke at Oxford University in 1994. This speech was published in Rose, *States of Fantasy,* 1996.

10. Wallingford, 1996, 15.

11. Ibid.

12. Peter Autry was born in Texas in 1859. In 1880 he married and lived in Fort Bend County. Manuel Morris was born in Texas in 1857. On July 8, 1878, he married Lucinda Griffin in Wharton, Texas. In 1880 he was working as a farm hand in Wharton, Texas. Both Autry and Morris are listed in the 1880 U.S. Census listings, FamilySearch.Org (Church of Jesus Christ of Latter Day Saints) http://www.familysearch.org/Eng/search/frameset_search.asp?PAGE=ancestor searchresults.asp (accessed January 18, 2007).

13. Litwack, *Been in the Storm So Long,* 1980. Many, if not most, of the lynchings were not recorded because of fear of retribution.

14. The history of the Texas prisons in Fort Bend County is barely visible, as are the sugar plantation and the company town.

15. This is the premise of Michel de Certeau's *Writing of History,* 1988.

16. Susan Buck-Morss, "Hegel and Haiti," 2000.

17. Luiz Costa Lima, *The Dark Side of Reason,* trans. by Paolo Britto (Palo Alto, Stanford University,1993): 5–6.

18. W. J. Cash, *Mind of the South,* 1969.

19. Michel Foucault, *Madness and Civlization,* trans. by Richard Howard, (New York, Vintage, 1973).

20. America's projection of hypersexuality onto the black female has been addressed by a number of scholars, including Hortense Spillers, bell hooks, Patricia Yeager, Deborah White, and Jenny Sharpe. Clarence Wharton's *History of Fort Bend County* mentions incidents in which the freedmen ran away from situations that Wharton considered banal; at one point he uses the term "baboon." In the weekly periodical *Texas Siftings,* published from 1880 to 1895 in Austin, numerous issues concerning blacks are given on the front page, drawn with exaggerated grotesque features. It is very likely that the elite of Fort Bend had access to this publication.

21. Wharton, *History of Fort Bend County,* 1939.

22. Houston Baker Jr., *Turning South Again: Re-thinking Modernism/Re-Reading Booker T.* (Durham, Duke University, 2001)

23. Greg Cantrell, *Stephen F. Austin,* 1999.

24. Ibid.

25. In "Jaybird-Woodpecker War" (1994), Leslie Lovett states that the court records for Eldridge's last murder trial have disappeared. She was told they had been moved from the Fort Bend County courthouse to the Imperial Sugar archives but were not located.

26. In *Pictorial History* (1996), Wallingford reports that, during World War II, at least 150 captured German soldiers were located in Rosenberg at the county fairgrounds. The prisoners were leased to Sugar Land Industries, the Richmond Irrigation Company, and a company that built the Clodine rice dryer. Small farmers could "sign up for up to ten prisoners at a time." John de la Cruz also remembers a POW camp at an old mill building next to the sugar refinery. Arnold P. Krammer states that the POW camps and the prisoners were well accepted in the Texas communities. Krammer, "German Prisoners of War."

27. According to José F. Hernández, this is common information in the county.

28. Much of the Phillips Memorial Cemetery was destroyed in 1991 when State Highway 3 in Galveston County was widened. Leah Caron Powell and Helen Danzeiser Dockall, "Folk Narratives and Archaeology: An African American Cemetery in Texas" in the "Public Archaeology Forum," *Journal of Field Archaeology* 22(3) (Autumn 1995): 349–53. Most significantly, between 1941 and 1942 the Housing Authority of the city of Houston removed 928 bodies of freed slaves and indigent whites from a cemetery just west of downtown Houston to make way for Allen Parkway Village. The cemetery dated back to 1865. Joe Makeig, "Workers Are Looking for Archaeological Artifacts Pre-dating 1880," *Houston Chronicle,* (July 16, 1996).

29. Jacques Derrida, *Writing and Difference,* trans. by Alan Bass, (Chicago, University of Chicago, 1978).

Bibliography

Books, Articles, and Poems

Addington, Wendell. "Slave Insurrections in Texas." *Journal of Negro History* 35(4) (October 1950): 408–35.

Adolph, Doug. "Sugar Land Town Square Plaza/City Hall Awarded Best Community Impact." *Public Management* 87(11) (December 2005): 31.

Alford, Harold J. *The Proud Peoples: The Heritage and Culture of Spanish-speaking Peoples in the United States.* New York: McKay, 1972.

Altman, Robert. "South Carolina Newspapers." South Carolina Association. http://www.sc.org/newshistory.htm. Accessed October 25, 2005.

Anderson, Adrian, Ralph Wooster, Arnoldo De León, William Hardt, and Ruthe Winegarten. *Texas and Texans.* New York: McGraw-Hill/Glencoe, 2003.

Anzaldúa, Gloria. *Borderlands/la Frontera: The New Mestiza.* San Francisco: Aunt Lute Books, 1987.

Armstrong, Robert M. *Sugar Land, Texas, and the Imperial Sugar Company.* Houston: privately printed, 1991.

Arrioja Vizcaino, Adolfo. *Fray Servando Teresa de Mier: Confesiones de un guadalupano federalista.* Mexico: Plaza y Janes, 2003.

Bachelard, Gaston. *The Poetics of Space: The Classic Look at How We Experience Intimate Places,* trans. Maria Jolas. Boston: Beacon, 1964.

———. *Water and Dreams: An Essay on the Imagination of Matter,* trans. Edith R. Farrell. Dallas: Pegasus Foundation, 1983.

Baker, Houston A., Jr. *Turning South Again: Re-thinking Modernism/Re-reading Booker T.* Durham, N.C.: Duke University Press, 2001.

Barker, Eugene. *Handbook of Texas Online,* s.v. "Mexican Colonization Laws." http://www.tsha.utexas.edu/handbook/online/articles/view/MM/ugm1.html. Accessed January 6, 2007.

Barr, Eddie. "Honor Medal Winner Gets Lost in City." *Houston Press,* September 7, 1945.

Barthes, Roland. *Image, Music, Text,* trans. Stephen Heath. New York: Hill and Wang, 1977.

Baum, L. Frank. *The Wonderful Wizard of Oz.* Chicago: G. M. Hill, 1900. www.netlibrary.com.ezproxy.lif.uh.edu/reader/. Accessed April 26, 2007.

Benjamin, Walter. *Illuminations: Essays and Reflections,* trans. Harry Zohn. New York: Schocken, 1968.

Berlin, Ira, and Leslie M. Harris. "Uncovering, Discovering, and Recovering: Digging in New York's Slave Past beyond the African Burial Ground." In *Slavery in New York,* ed. Ira Berlin and Leslie M. Harris, 1–27. New York: New Press, 2005.

Blake, Robert B. *Handbook of Texas Online,* s.v. "Cordova, Vicente." http://www.tsha.utexas .edu/handbook/online/articles/CC/fco71.html. Accessed January 6, 2007.

Blakely, Edward J., and Mary Gayle Snyder. *Fortress America: Gated Communities in the United States.* Washington, D.C.: Brookings Institution, 1997.

Blue, Carroll Parrott. *Dawn at My Back: Memoir of a Black Texas Upbringing.* Austin: University of Texas Press, 2003.

Blum, Roberto. "Para conquistar el futuro: Al 100 años de la independencia mexicana." *El Economista* (Mexico) (September 14, 2000).

Bost, Suzanne. "Women and Chili at the Alamo." *Nepantla* 4(3) (2003): 493–533.

Bowman, Bob. "A Tough East Texan." *TexasEscapes.com, A Texas Travel History and Architecture Magazine* (October 1–7, 2000). http://www.texasescapes.com/DEPARTMENTS/Guest _Columnists/East_Texas_all_things_historical/Tough_East_Texan_Martin_Varner_BB 10100.htm. Accessed January 5, 2007.

Bourke, John G. "The American Congo." *Scribner's* 15(5) (May 1894): 590–610.

Brewer, John Mason. *Dog Ghosts, and Other Texas Negro Folk Tales; The Word on the Brazos: Negro Preacher Tales from the Brazos Bottoms of Texas.* Austin: University of Texas Press, 1976.

Buck-Morss, Susan. "Hegel and Haiti." *Critical Inquiry* 26 (Summer 2000): 821–65.

Bugbee, Lester G. "Slavery in Early Texas I." *Political Science Quarterly* 13(3) (September 1898): 389–412.

Burnett, Francis Hodgson. *The Secret Garden.* New York: Grosset and Dunlap, 1996.

Burstein, Andrew. "Jefferson's Rationalizations." *William and Mary Quarterly* 57(1) (January 2000): 183–97.

Campbell, Randolph B. *An Empire for Slavery: The Peculiar Institution in Texas, 1821–1865.* Baton Rouge: Louisiana State University Press, 1989.

Cantrell, Gregg. *Stephen F. Austin: Empresario of Texas.* New Haven, Conn.: Yale University Press, 1999.

Carabi, Angels. "Interview: Toni Morrison." *Belles Lettres* 10(2) (Spring 1995): 40.

Caro, Robert. *The Path to Power: The Years of Lyndon Johnson,* Vol. 1. (New York: Vintage Press, 1982).

Cash, W. J. *The Mind of the South.* New York: Vintage, 1969.

Chance, John Milton. *After San Jacinto: The Texas-Mexican Frontier, 1836–1841.* Austin: University of Texas Press, 1963.

Chestnut, Mary Boykin. *Mary Chestnut's Civil War,* ed. C. Vann Woodward. New Haven, Conn.: Yale University Press, 1981.

Christian, Carole E. *Handbook of Texas Online,* s.v. "Herrera, John J." http://www.tsha.utexas .edu/handbook/online/articles/HH/fhe63.html. Accessed January 6, 2007.

Cleaves, W. S. "The Political Career of Lorenzo de Zavala." Master's thesis, University of Texas, 1931.

Conley, Tom. Introduction to *The Writing of History,* by Michel de Certeau. New York: Columbia University Press, 1988.

Costa Lima, Luiz. *Dark Side of Reason,* trans. Paolo Britto. Palo Alto, Calif.: Stanford University Press, 1993.

Crimm, Ana Castillo. *The De León Family: A Tejano Family History.* Austin: University of Texas Press, 2003.

Curlee, Abigail. "A Study of Texas Slave Plantations, 1822 to 1865." PhD diss., University of Texas, 1936.

Dallas Morning News. "Legislators Hear Tale of Alleged Prison Cruelty: Ex-convict Asserts He Was Mutilated" (February 8, 1925).

Dayan, Joan. *Haiti, History, and the Gods.* Berkeley: University of California Press, 1995.

de Certeau, Michel. *Heterologies: Discourse on the Other,* trans. Brian Massumi. Minneapolis: University of Minnesota Press, 1986.

———. *The Practice of Everyday Life,* trans. Steven Rendall. Berkeley: University of California Press, 1984.

———. *The Writing of History,* trans. Tom Conley. New York: Columbia University Press, 1988.

De León, Arnoldo. *The Tejano Community, 1838–1900.* Albuquerque: University of New Mexico Press, 1985.

———. *They Called Them Greasers: Anglo Attitudes toward Mexicans in Texas.* Austin: University of Texas Press, 1983.

De Shields, James T. *Border Wars of Texas: being an authentic and popular account, in chronological order, of the long and bitter conflict waged between savage Indian tribes and the pioneer settlers of Texas.* 1912. Reprint, Austin: State House Press, 1993.

DeAnda, James. Keynote address at the University of Houston Law Center Conference, "*Hernández v. Texas* at 50," Houston, Texas, November 19, 2004. http://www.law.uh .edu/hernandez50/deAnda.pdf. Accessed January 6, 2007.

Dejevsky, Mary. "Travel Texas: Big Hats, Big Park, Big Welcome." *Independent* (London) (May 8, 1999).

Derrida, Jacques. *Writing and Difference,* trans. Alan Bass. Chicago: University of Chicago Press, 1978.

Donald, David. "The Scalawag in Mississippi Reconstruction." *Journal of Southern History* 10 (November 1944): 447–60.

Douglass, Frederick. *Narrative of the Life of Frederick Douglass, an American Slave, Written by Himself.* http://library.uh.edu/search/, s.v. "Douglass, Frederick." Accessed January 5, 2007.

Douglas, Mary. *Purity and Danger: An Analysis of Concepts of Pollution and Taboo.* 1966. Reprint, London: Routledge and K. Paul, 1995.

Drury, David. "No Small Affair: The Fall of the Small Garrison Gave Birth to Texas and an Enduring Symbol of Sacrifice." *Hartford Courant* (April 9, 2004).

DuBois, W. E. B. *The Souls of Black Folk.* 1903. Reprint, New York: Signet Classics, 1995.

Dunn, Brian. "De Lay's Lawyers Turn Table on Prosecutors." *Fort Bend Now* (October 11, 2005). http:// www.fortbendnow.com/news/253/new-evidence-led-to-latest-delay-indictments-earle-says. Accessed January 6, 2007.

Duval, John. *The Adventures of Big-foot Wallace, the Texas Ranger and Hunter.* Macon, Ga.: J. W. Burke, 1870.

Faulkner, William. *Absalom, Absalom!* 1936. Reprint, New York: Vintage, 1991.

———. *Light in August.* 1959. Reprint, New York: Random House, 1932.

Flores, Richard. Introduction to *History and Legends of the Alamo and Other Missions in and around San Antonio,* by Adina de Zavala. Houston: Arte Público, 1996.

———. *Remembering the Alamo: Memory, Modernity, and the Master Symbol.* Austin: University of Texas Press, 2002.

Foley, Neil. *The White Scourge: Mexicans, Blacks, and Poor Whites in Texas Cotton Culture.* Berkeley: University of California Press, 1997.

Foucault, Michel. *Aesthetics, Method, and Epistemology,* ed. James D. Faubion and trans. Robert Hurley et al. Vol. 2: *Essential Works of Foucault, 1954–1984.* New York: Free Press, 1998.

———. *The Archeology of Knowledge and the Discourse on Knowledge. Trans. Alan Sheridan Smith.* New York: Pantheon, 1982.

———. *Discipline and Punish: The Birth of the Prison,* trans. Alan Sheridan. New York: Vintage, 1977.

———. *Madness and Civilization,* trans. Richard Howard. New York: Vintage, 1973.

———. *The Order of Things: An Archeology of the Human Sciences.* New York: Vintage, 1973.

———. *Power/Knowledge: Selected Interviews and Other Writings, 1972–1977,* ed. Colin Gordon. New York: Pantheon Books, 1980.

Fox-Genovese, Elizabeth. *Within the Plantation Household: Black and White Women of the Old South.* Chapel Hill: University of North Carolina Press, 1988.

García, Maria-Cristina. *Handbook of Texas Online,* s.v. "García, Macario." http://www.tsha.utexas.edu/handbook/online/articles/GG/fga76.html. Accessed January 5, 2007.

Gard, Wayne. *Handbook of Texas Online,* s.v. "Vigilantes and Vigilance Committees." http://www.tsha.utexas.edu/handbook/online/articles/VV/jnv1.html. Accessed January 5, 2007.

Gaston, Brian. Letter to the editor. *Houston Chronicle* (November 25, 1998).

Geggus, David. *Haitian Revolutionary Studies.* Bloomington: University of Indiana Press, 2002.

Gilroy, Harry. "Movie Fete Postscript," *New York Times* (July 7, 1957).

Godden, Richard. "Absalom, Absalom!, Haiti and Labor History: Reading Unreadable Revolutions." *English Literary History* 61(3) (Fall 1994): 685–720.

Gordon, Avery. *Ghostly Matters: Haunting and the Sociological Imagination.* Minneapolis: University of Minnesota Press, 1997.

Gray, William Fairfax. *The Diary of William Fairfax Gray from Virginia to Texas, 1835–1837,* ed. Paul D. Lack. Dallas: Southern Methodist University Press, 1997.

Green, George N. *Handbook of Texas Online,* s.v. "Good Neighbor Commission." http://www.tsha.utexas.edu/handbook/online/articles/GG/mdg2.html. Accessed January 6, 2007).

Greenville News. "Robert Quillen Obituary" (December 9, 1948).

Hale, Grace Elizabeth. *Making Whiteness: The Culture of Segregation in the South, 1890–1940.* New York: Vintage, 1998.

Hammond, Ken. "Lynchings in Texas: The Awful Violence of Frontier Justice." *Houston Chronicle* (December 1, 1985).

Handbook of Texas Online, s.v. "Wharton, Clarence Ray." http://www.tsha.utexas.edu/handbook/online/articles/WW/fwh2.html. Accessed January 5, 2007.

Handley, George B. *Postslavery Literatures in the Americas: Family Portraits in Black and White.* Charlottesville: University of Virginia Press, 2000.

Harris, Dilue Rose. "The Reminiscences of Mrs. Dilue Harris, Part I." *Southwestern Historical Quarterly* 4(1) (July 1900). http://www.tsha.utexas.edu/publications/journals/shq/online/v004/n2/article_4.html. Accessed January 5, 2007.

———. "The Reminiscences of Mrs. Dilue Harris, Part II." *Southwestern Historical Quarterly* 4(3) (January 1901). http://www.tsha.utexas.edu/publications/journals/shq/online/v004/n3/article_3.html. Accessed January 5, 2007.

Harrison, Robert Pogue. *The Dominion of the Dead.* Chicago: University of Chicago Press, 2003.

Harvey, Bill. *Texas Cemeteries: The Resting Places of Famous, Infamous, and Just Plain Interesting Texans.* Austin: University of Texas Press, 2003.

Henson, Margaret Swett. *Handbook of Texas Online,* s.v. "Burnett, David Gouverneur." http://

www.tsha.utexas.edu/handbook/online/articles/BB/fbu46.html. Accessed January 5, 2007.

———. *Lorenzo de Zavala: The Pragmatic Idealist.* Fort Worth: Texas Christian University Press, 1996.

Hernández, Elizabeth. "Preparan más homenajes para Ismael Rodríguez." *El Universal* (Mexico City) (August 11, 2004).

Hernández, Marie Theresa. *Delirio—the Fantastic, the Demonic, and the Réel: The Buried History of Nuevo León.* Austin: University of Texas Press, 2002.

———. "Reconditioning History: Adapting Knowledge from the Past into Realities of the Present." *Re-thinking History: The Journal of Theory and Practice* 3(3) (December 1999): 289–99.

Herrera, Adolfo Casias. *Handbook of Texas Online,* s.v. "Herrera, Blas María." http://www.tsha .utexas.edu/handbook/online/articles/HH/fhe73.html. Accessed January 6, 2007.

Herrera, John J. *Handbook of Texas Online,* s.v. "Herrera, John J." http://www.tsha.utexas .edu/handbook/online/articles/HH/fhe63.html. Accessed January 6, 2007.

Hine, Darlene Clark. *Black Victory: The Rise and Fall of the White Primary in Texas.* Millwood, N.Y.: KTO Press, 1979.

Hobbs, Kenneth W. *Handbook of Texas Online,* s.v. "Terry, Benjamin Franklin." http: www .tsha.utexas.edu/handbook/online/articles/TT/fte28.html. Accessed January 6, 2007.

———. *Handbook of Texas Online,* s.v. "Smith, Benjamin Fort." http://www.tsha.utexas .edu/handbook/online/articles/view/SS/fsm5.html. Accessed January 6, 2007.

Hoffman, Walter James. "The Travels of Manabush." In *The Menomini Indians* (New York: Johnson Reprint, 1970). Cited in Michael Pomedli, "Owls: Images and Voices in the Ojibwa and Midewiwin Worlds," *American Indian Culture and Research Journal* 26(2) (2002): 47–48.

Holland, Sharon Patricia. *Raising the Dead: Readings of Death and (Black) Subjectivity.* Durham, N.C.: Duke University Press, 2000.

hooks, bell. *Yearning: Race, Gender, and Cultural Politics,* Boston: South End Press, 1990.

Houston Chronicle, "Grave Access Extended," (August 21, 1993).

———. "Hero Refused Service in Café," (September 20, 1945).

———. "Sugar Land Hero to Be Honored in City Tonight," (September 6, 1945).

———. *Yearning: Race, Gender, and Cultural Politics.* Boston: South End Press. 1990.

Hunt, N., and I. Robbins. "The Long-term Consequences of War: The Experience of WWII." *Aging and Mental Health* 5(2) (2001): 183–90.

Huxtable, Ada Louis. "Remember the Alamo." *New York Times* (April 14, 1968).

Hyman, Harold. M. *Oleander Odyssey: The Kempners of Galveston, Texas, 1854–1980s.* College Station: Texas A&M University Press, 1990.

Irwin, John T. *Doubling and Incest/Repetition and Revenge: A Speculative Reading of Faulkner.* Baltimore: Johns Hopkins University Press, 1996.

Jefferson, Thomas. *Notes on the State of Virginia, 1781–1782.* http://etext.virginia.edu/etcbin/ toccer-new2. Accessed November 1, 2005.

Jenkins, Jim. "Today's Master-planned Community Developers Must Apply Expertise." *Newland Communities* http://www.newlandcommunities.com/news_releases_details .php?ID=23. Accessed November 3, 2005.

Johnson, Benjamin. *Revolution in Texas: How a Forgotten Rebellion and Its Bloody Suppression Turned Mexicans into Americans.* New Haven, Conn.: Yale University Press, 2003.

Jordan, Terry. *Texas Graveyards: A Cultural Legacy.* Austin: University of Texas Press, 1982.

Judis, John B. "Home Invasion: DeLay of the Land." *New Republic* 232 (May 16, 2005): 18–21.

Katzew, Ilona. *Casta Painting: Images of Race in Eighteenth-century Mexico.* New Haven, Conn.: Yale University Press, 2004.

Kleiner, Diana J. *Handbook of Texas Online,* s.v. "Smith, Robert Everett." http://www.tsha .utexas.edu/handbook/online/articles/SS/fsm57_print.html. Accessed January 6, 2007.

Krammer, Arnold P. *Handbook of Texas Online,* s.v. "German Prisoners of War." http://www .tsha.utexas.edu/handbook/online/articles/GG/qug1.html. Accessed January 6, 2007.

Kreneck, Thomas H. *Handbook of Texas Online,* s.v. "Houston, Samuel." http://www.tsha .utexas.edu/handbook/online/articles/HH/fho73.html. Accessed January 6, 2007.

Krüger, Arnd. "A Horse Breeder's Perspective: Scientific Racism in Germany, 1870–1933." In *Identity and Intolerance: Nationalism, Racism, and Xenophobia in Germany and the United States.* Norbert Finzsch and Diemar Schirmer, eds. (Cambridge: German Historical Institute and Cambridge University Press, 1998), 171–96.

Lack, Paul. "The Cordova Revolt." In *Tejano Journey, 1770–1850,* ed. Gerald Poyo. (Austin: University of Texas Press, 1996). 89–109.

———. Introduction. *The Diaries of William Fairfax Gray from Virginia to Texas, 1835–1837.* Dallas: Southern Methodist University Press, 1997.

Ladd, Barbara. *Nationalism and the Color Line in George W. Cable, Mark Twain, and William Faulkner.* Baton Rouge: Louisiana State University Press, 1996.

Leffler, John. *Handbook of Texas Online,* s.v. "Richmond, Texas." http://www.tsha.utexas .edu/handbook/online/articles/RR/hfr4.html. Accessed January 6, 2007.

Lemire, Elise. *Miscegenation: Making Race in America.* Philadelphia: University of Pennsylvania Press, 2002.

Lewis, David Levering. "Refereed Reports." *Journal of American History* 83(4) (1997): 1254–67.

Littlefield, Henry M. "The Wizard of Oz: Parable on Populism." *American Quarterly* 16(1) (1964): 47–58.

Litwack, Leon F. *Been in the Storm So Long: The Aftermath of Slavery.* New York: Vintage, 1980.

Lomax, Alan. *The Land Where the Blues Began.* New York: Pantheon, 1993.

Lovett, Leslie. "The Jaybird-Woodpecker War: Reconstruction and Redemption in Fort Bend County, Texas, 1869–1889." Master's thesis, Rice University, 1994.

Maillard, N. Doran. *The History of the Republic of Texas: From the Discovery of the Country to the Present Time, and the Cause of Her Separation from Mexico.* London: Smith, Elder, 1842.

Makeig, Joe. "Workers Are Looking for Archaeological Artifacts Pre-dating 1880." *Houston Chronicle* (July 16, 1996).

Márquez, Benjamin. "The Politics of Race and Assimilation: The League of United Latin American Citizens, 1929–1940." *Western Political Quarterly* 42(2) (1987): 355–75.

McKeehan, Wallace L. "The Córdova Rebellion." Sons of Dewitt Colony Texas. http://www .tamu.edu/ccbn/dewitt/cordovavicente.htm. Accessed August 19, 2005.

McKenzie, Evan. *Privatopia: Homeowner Associations and the Rise of Residential Private Government.* New Haven, Conn.: Yale University Press, 1996.

McMillan, S. A. *The Book of Fort Bend County.* Richmond, Tex.: privately printed by S. A. McMillan and Phillip Rich, 1926.

Meillassoux, Claude. "Female Slavery." In *Women and Slavery in Africa,* ed. Claire Robertson and Martin Klein. Madison: University of Wisconsin Press, 1983. 49–66.

Meryweather, Mary Varner, and Donald Raney. *Handbook of Texas Online,* s.v. "Varner, Martin." http://www.tsha.utexas.edu/handbook/online/articles/view/VV/fva20.html. Accessed January 6, 2007.

Michener, James A. *Texas: A Novel.* New York: Random House, 1985.

Montejano, David. *Anglos and Mexicans in the Making of Texas, 1836–1986.* Austin: University of Texas Press, 1987.

Morales, Tomás. *Semblanzas de testigos de Cristo para los nuevos tiempos.* Madrid: Editorial Encuentro, 1994.

Morín, Raúl. *Among the Valiant: Mexican-Americans in WWII and Korea.* Los Angeles: Borden, 1963.

Morrison, Toni. *Beloved: A Novel.* New York: Knopf, 1987.

Muck, Patti. "Fifth Street Residents to Get Water." *Houston Chronicle* (October 12, 1986).

———. "Fifth Street/Water, Sewage Woes Plague Unincorporated Neighborhood." *Houston Chronicle* (August 17, 1986).

New York Times. "Many Negroes Massacred" (March 1, 1888).

———. "Twenty-eight Army Men Get Medals of Honor: Ceremony at White House Conducted by President Is Largest of Its Kind" (August 24, 1945).

Olmsted, Frederick Law. *A Journey through Texas: Or, a Saddle-trip on the Southwestern Frontier.* 1857. Reprint, Austin: University of Texas Press, 1978.

Pandolfo, Stefania. *Impasse of the Angels: Scenes from a Moroccan Space of Memory.* Chicago: University of Chicago Press, 1997.

Paredes, Américo. *With a Pistol in His Hand.* Austin: University of Texas Press, 1958.

Pomedli, Michael M. "Owls: Images and Voices in the Ojibwa and Midewiwin Worlds." *American Indian Culture and Research Journal* 26(2) (2002): 45–62.

Powell, Leah Carson, and Helen Danzeiser Dockall. "Folk Narratives and Archaeology: An African American Cemetery in Texas." *Journal of Field Archaeology* 22(3) (Autumn 1995): 349–53.

Quayson, Ato. *Calibrations: Reading for the Social.* Minneapolis: University of Minnesota Press, 2003.

Quillen, Robert. "Not the Tyrant Himself but Slave Who Cracks Whip." *Dallas Morning News* (September 10, 1945).

Railton, Ben. "What Else Could a Southern Gentleman Do? Quentin Compson, Rhett Butler, and Miscegenation." *Journal of Southern Literature* 35(2) (Spring 2003): 41–63.

Read, Kay Almere. "Binding Reeds and Burning Hearts: Mexica-Tenochca Concepts of Time and Sacrifice." PhD diss., University of Chicago, 1991.

———. "Sacred Commoners: The Motion of Cosmic Powers in Mexica Rulership." *History of Religions* 34 (August 1994): 39–69.

Reyes, Alfonso. "El Descastado," *Obras Completas de Alfonso Reyes,* Tomo X, *Constancia Poesia,* (Mexico: Fondo de Cultura Economica, 1959), 70.

Ritter, Gretchen. "Silver Slippers and a Golden Cap: L. Frank Baum and the Wonderful Wizard of Oz and Historical Memory in American Politics." *Journal of American Studies* 31(2) (1997): 171–202.

Rodríguez, Lori. "Homes vs. Heritage." *Houston Chronicle* (November 15, 1998).

Romo, Tere. "The Chicanization of Mexican Calendar Art." Paper presented at Smithsonian National Conference: The Interpretation and Representation of Latino Cultures: Research and Museums. Washington, D.C., November 20–23, 2002. http://latino.si.edu/researchand museums/presentations/romo.html. Accessed January 5, 2007.

Rose, Jacqueline. *States of Fantasy.* New York: Oxford University Press, 1996.

Rothman, Joshua. "James Callender and Social Knowledge of Interracial Sex in Antebellum Virginia." In *Sally Hemings and Thomas Jefferson: History, Memory, and Civic Culture,* ed. Jan Ellen Lewis and Peter S. Onuf (Charlottesville: University Press of Virginia, 1999); quoted in Elise Lemire, *Miscegenation: Making Race in America* (Philadelphia: University of Pennsylvania Press, 2002).

Rubio, Abel G. *Stolen Heritage: A Mexican-American's Rediscovery of His Family's Lost Land Grant,* ed. Thomas H. Kreneck. Austin: Eakin, 1986.

Ruiz, José Francisco. *Handbook of Texas Online,* s.v. "Ruiz, José Francisco." http://www.tsha .utexas.edu/handbook/online/articles/RR/fru11.html. Accessed January 6, 2007.

Sarnoff, Nancy. "Newland Communities." *Houston Chronicle* (February 25, 2005).

Schiefen, Richard. "When You Think 'Missions' . . . Think 'Basilian Missions.'" *Mission Notes.* Archives of the Congregation of the Society of Saint Basil, Toronto, Canada. Sugar Land, Tex.: Basilian Fathers Home and Foreign Missions, June 1968.

Schreuder, Bas J. N., Wim C. Kleijn, and Harry G. M. Rooijmans. "Nocturnal Re-experiencing More than Forty Years after War Trauma." *Journal of Traumatic Stress* 13(3) (2000): 453–63.

Sebald, W. G. *Austerlitz,* trans. Anthea Bell. New York: Modern Library, 2001.

Seguín, Juan. *A Revolution Remembered: The Memoirs and Selected Correspondence of Juan N. Seguín,* ed. Jesús de la Teja. Austin: Texas State Historical Association, 2002.

Sharpe, Jenny. *Ghosts of Slavery: A Literary Archaeology of Black Women's Lives.* Minneapolis: University of Minnesota Press, 2004.

Sonnichsen, C. L. *I'll Die before I'll Run: The Story of the Great Feuds of Texas.* New York: Devin-Adair, 1962.

Sowell, A. J. *History of Fort Bend County.* Houston: W. H. Coyle Stationers and Printers, 1904.

Spillers, Hortense. "Mama's Baby, Papa's Maby." *Diacritics.* Special issue: *Culture and Countermemory: The American Connection* 17(2) (Summer 1987): 64–81.

Stoler, Ann Laura. *Carnal Knowledge and Imperial Power: Race and the Intimate in Colonial Rule.* Berkeley: University of California Press, 2002.

——. *Race and the Education of Desire: Foucault's* History of Sexuality *and the Colonial Order of Things.* Durham, N.C.: Duke University Press, 1995.

Strayhorn, Carole Keeton. "Paving the Way: A Review of the Texas Department of Transportation." In "Improve Asset Management," Texas Comptroller of Public Accounts, January 2001. http://www.window.state.tx.us/txdot/txdot601.html. Accessed January 6, 2007.

Strong, Bernice. *Handbook of Texas Online,* s.v. "Ruíz, José Francisco." http://www.tsha.utexas .edu/handbook/online/articles/RR/fru11.html. Accessed January 6, 2007.

Sundquist, Eric J. *Faulkner: The House Divided.* Baltimore: Johns Hopkins University Press, 1983.

Teresa de Mier, Servando. *Escritos inéditos,* ed. J. M. Miquel i Vergés and Hugo Díaz Thomé (Mexico City: Biblioteca de Obras Fundamentales de la Independencia y la Revolución, 1985), 335–52, cited in Ilona Katzew, *Casta Painting: Images of Race in Eighteenth-century México.* New Haven: Yale University Press, 2003.

——. *Obras completas. IV. La formación de un republicano,* comp. Jaime E. Rodríguez. Mexico City: Universidad Nacional Autónoma de México, 1988.

Tillinghast, Richard. *Sewanee in Ruins,* 2d ed. Memphis: University of Tennessee Press, 1983.

Trejo, Evelia. *Los límites de un discurso: Lorenzo de Zavala, su "ensayo histórico" y la cuestión religiosa en México.* Mexico, D.F.: Fondo de Cultura Económica, 2001.

Trilling, Calvin. *Freud and the Crisis of Our Culture.* Boston: Beacon, 1955.

Trouillot, Michel-Rolph. *Silencing the Past: Power and the Production of History.* Boston: Beacon, 1995.

Twain, Mark. *Pudd'nhead Wilson and Those Extraordinary Twins.* Hartford, Conn.: American Publishing, 1894.

——. "Stirring Times in Austria." *Harper's New Monthly Magazine* 96(574) (March 1898): 530–40.

Tyler, Stephen. "Vision Quest in the West, or What the Mind's Eye Sees." *Journal of Anthropological Research* 40 (1984): 23–40.

_____. *The Unspeakable: Discourse, Dialogue, and Rhetoric in the Post-Modern World\.* Madison: University of Wisconsin, 1987.

Villalón, Oscar. "Remember the Alamo: Sure, as Long as We Remember It for What It Really Is: A Symbol for Many, of Something Sinister." *San Francisco Chronicle* (April 12, 2004).

Walker, Donald R. *Penology for Profit: A History of the Texas Prison System, 1867–1912.* College Station: Texas A&M University Press, 1988.

Walker, Margaret. *Jubilee.* Boston: Houghton Mifflin, 1966.

Wallingford, Sharon. *Fort Bend County, Texas: A Pictorial History.* Stafford, Tex.: Fort Bend Publishing Group, 1996.

———. "Sugar Land Sculpture Honors Texas Pioneer: Artwork Featured in Town Square." *Houston Chronicle* (January 15, 2004).

Wang, Xi. "Black Suffrage and the Redefinition of American Freedom, 1860–1870." *Cardozo Law Review* 17 (1995): 2153–2223.

Ware, Diane. "Creating a Company Town: William T. Eldridge, Isaac H. Kempner, and Sugar Land, Texas (1906–1947)." Masters thesis, University of Houston, 1994.

Warm, Luke. "'Bigfoot' Wallace." *TexasEscapes.com, A Texas Travel History and Architecture Magazine.* http://www.texasescapes.com/TexasPersonalities/BigFootWallace/BigFoot Wallace.htm. Accessed January 5, 2007.

Watkins, Meredith G. "The Cemetery and Cultural Memory: Montreal, 1860–1900." *Urban History Review* 21(1) (Fall 2002): 52–62.

Wharton, Clarence. *The History of Fort Bend County.* New York: Naylor, 1939.

White, Deborah Gray. *Ain't I a Woman?: Female Slaves in the Plantation South.* New York: Norton, 1985.

White, Hayden. *The Content of the Form: Narrative Discourse and Historical Representation.* Baltimore: Johns Hopkins University Press, 1987.

———. *Tropics of Discourse: Essays in Cultural Criticism.* Baltimore: Johns Hopkins University Press, 1978.

Williams, Martha McCulloch. "Review of *The Tragedy of Puddn'head Wilson.*" *Southern Magazine* (February 1894).

Wilson, Sherrill D. "African Burial Ground." In *Slavery in New York,* ed. Ira Berlin and Leslie M. Harris. New York: New Press, 2005. 7.

Yeager, Patricia. *Dirt and Desire: Reconstructing Southern Women's Writing, 1930–1990.* Chicago: University of Chicago Press, 2000.

Yelderman, Pauline. *The Jaybirds of Fort Bend County.* Waco: Texian, 1979.

Zavala, Lorenzo de. *El historiador y el representante popular: Ensayo crítico de las revoluciones de méxico desde 1808 hasta 1830.* Mexico, D.F.: Porrúa, 1969.

Zizek, Slavoj. *The Fragile Absolute, or, Why Is the Christian Legacy Worth Fighting For?* New York: Verso, 2000.

Zupančič, Alenka. *Ethics of the Real: Kant, Lacan (Wo Es War).* New York: Verso, 2000.

Archival Sources

Archives of the Congregation of Saint Basil. Toronto, Canada.

Archivo general del estado de Coahuila. Ramos Arizpe, Coahuila, Mexico.

Fort Bend County Clerk, Fort Bend, Texas. Death Records.

Fort Bend County Clerk, Fort Bend, Texas. Deed Records.
Fort Bend County, Texas, District Court. 23rd Judicial District.
George Memorial Library, Richmond, Texas.
Houston Metropolitan Research Center, Houston Public Library.
New York Public Library for the Performing Arts. Walter Winchell Papers.
San Antonio, Tex. Public Library.
Texas General Land Office Archives, Austin, Texas.
U.S. Census Bureau, Census 2000.

Movies and Plays

Carrier-Grundy, Naomi. *Social Politics in Victorian Texas, 1890: A Living Interpretation of African Americans and Their Responsibilities in the Home of JHP Davis, Rancher/Farmer, Fort Bend County, Texas,* Talking Back Living History Theatre, Houston, Texas, 1998.
Gone with the Wind, directed by David O. Selznick (Selznick International Pictures, 1939).
San Isidro Labrador, directed by Lope de Vega (1958).
Tizoc—Amor Indio, directed by Ismael Rodríguez (Matouk Films S.A., 1956).

Web Pages

American and French Research on the Treasury of the French Language (ARTFL) Project. *Roget's Thesaurus* (1911). http://humanities.uchicago.edu/orgs/ARTFL/. Accessed January 5, 2007.
Center for American History. "A Guide to the Robert Bruce Blake Papers." Center for American History at the University of Texas–Austin. http://www.lib.utexas.edu/taro/utcah/00063/cah-00063.html. Accessed January 5, 2007.
Church of Jesus Christ of Latter Day Saints. http://www.familysearch.org/. Accessed January 5, 2007.
Economic History Services. http://eh.net/hmit/. Accessed April 26, 2007.
George Ranch Historical Park. http://www.georgeranch.org/about/mission/. Accessed January 5, 2007.
Home of the Heroes. http://www.homeofheroes.com/photos/6_ww2/hendrix_recent_small.jpg. Accessed January 5, 2007.
Institute of Texan Cultures. Public Communications. http://www.texancultures.utsa.edu/public/communications/about_itc.htm. Accessed January 5, 2007.
Magna Carta. British Library. http://www.bl.uk/collections/treasures/magna.html. Accessed January 6, 2007.
Ponce, Puerto Rico, City of. http://welcome.topuertorico.org/city/poncie.shtml. Accessed October 10, 2003.
Sandy Point Cemetery, Brazoria County, Texas. "Francis Bingham, b. 1772, d. 1854. A Texas Veteran." http://www.interment.net/data/us/tx/brazoria/sandypoint/sandypoint.htm. Accessed January 6, 2007.
Sons of the Dewitt Colony. http://www.tamu.edu/ccbn/dewitt/. Accessed January 6, 2007.
Sugar Land, City of. Office of Economic Development. http://www.sugarlandecodev.com/2-7_demoInfo.htm. Accessed January 30, 2006.

Telfair, Newland Communities, Sugar Land, Tex. http://www.telfair.com. Accessed January 6, 2007.

Texas General Land Office, State of Texas. http://www.glo.state.tx.us/about/landoffice.html. Accessed January 6, 2007.

Texas Historical Commission. Bob Bowman Biography. http://www.thc.state.tx.us/aboutus/commbios/biobowman.html. Accessed January 6, 2007.

Texas State Historical Association. http://www.tsha.utexas.edu/about/welcome/history.html. Accessed January 6, 2007.

University of Houston. "Newland Communities Gives $100,000 to Support New Building for UHSSL & WCJC 'Building Futures Together' Campaign to Expand Educational Opportunities in Fort Bend County." News Release. http://www.uh.edu/admin/media/nr/2005/07july/071505newlandcomm.html. Accessed January 6, 2007.

University of London, King's College, Liddell Hart Centre for Military Archives, London. http://www.kcl.ac.uk/lhcma/locreg/BINGHAM2.shtml. Accessed January 6, 2007.

Index

Absalom, Absalom, 67, 79, 190

Adolphus, Jim, 192

Adams, Marjorie: Fort Bend slavery and post-Reconstruction, 182,189; Kendleton, 86–87; murder, lynchings, disappearance, 91, 104, 109; Turkey Creek Feud, 100–101, 105

African Americans: banished, 97,99; Basilian priests and, 12; descriptive, 55; disposable, 155; freedmen, 155; intimacy, 6; political leaders, 99; post-slavery, 4; prison population, 177, 183; school principal, 55; soft hair, 171; voting power, 92

After San Jacinto, 125

ajeno, 18

agricultural worker, 18

Aguilar, Hector, 114–15

Ahuitzotl, 112–13

Alamo: Austin letters, 41; battle of, 37; docents, story of, 114–15; Latino history, 115; mythology, 185; national monument, 115; "Remember the," 115; Santa Ana, Antonio Lopez de, 113–15; space, 37; story of Texas, 48; Texas Mexicans, 114

Albert and Mamie George Building, 180

Alford, Harold Jr., 133

Allen brothers, 48

Allen, A. C., 48, 91

amalgamation, 77

American: invasion, 39; South, (*see* South, American); America's national sin, 62

amo, 18–19

"Amor Indio," 110–11

Anda, Judge James de, 127, 132, 162–63

Anderson, Benedict, 61

Andrews, William, 49

Anglos, (*see also* whites/Anglos): affluence, 10; taking land, 112; settlers, first colony of, 15, 20, 41; sources, history, 123

Annual Texian Market Days, 106

Anzaldúa, Gloria, 148–49

archives, reliability of, 11, 31, 88, 106–109, 119, 124–25, 134, 141, 182, 193

"Arcy Makes Room for Judith Martin," 106

Armstrong, Robert, 24, 56, 61, 75

Arizpe, Miguel Ramos, 44

Arkansas Gazette, 46

Ashbel Smith Papers, 125

Asian, 1, 2

Austin, Moses, 38–39, 49

Austin, Stephen F., 36; business practices, 47; land owned, 15, 36–37, 56; Mexican constitution, 44; Mexican politics, 44–45; Mexico's political elite, 41; New Orleans, 39; plan for Mexico's federal government, 44; relationship with Lorenzo de Zavala, 40, 42, 45; statue, 168; Sugar Land, 169, 174

Austin's Colony, 36, 46, 49, 108, 116, 188; business practices, 47; "dregs of the land," 47, 50; lack of civilization, 50; Oz as metaphor for, 166–69, 173–74; slaves, 47–49; stories of, 45

Aztecs, 110–12, 127, 141

Bachelard, Gaston, 30

Baker and Botts, 54, 76

Baker, Houston Jr., 2–3, 5, 9, 166, 190

Baker, James, 54

bandits, Anglo and Mexican,118

banishment, 9, 45, 97, 99, 155, 169, 171, 175

Baron de Bastrop, 39
Barthes, Roland, 13, 104–105
Basilian priests, 11–12, 117
Baum, L. Frank, 165–66, 168, 173–74
Baxter, Clifford, 1
Baytown, Texas, 176
Bearfield, Jim, 95, 99
Belasco, Mr., 28
Belles Lettres, 176
Beloved, 176
Benjamin, Walter, 119, 122
Bentham, Jeremy, 179
Berlin's Silver Bear Award, 111
Bexar County, 125
B. F. Terry High School, 54–55, 59
Billy Rose Theatre Collection, 134
Bingham, Mary, 61, 65
Bingham (Bigham/Biggam), Francis, 61–62
Blake, Robert B., 123
blacks: cemetery, (see cemetery, black); female,
    oversexualization of, 189; mammy, 60, 67;
    wealth and affluence, 1, 10
Blakely and Snyder, 148
Blue, Carroll, 161–62
Blum, Roberto, 42, 52–53
Bodame, 144
bodies, buried, 14
Bögel, Philip (see also Baron de Bastrop)
bondage, (see also slavery): acceptable solution, 41;
    impact of, 4
book, electronic, 42
Border Wars of Texas, 123
borderlands, 10
Borderlands/La Frontera, 148
Bourke, John, 118
Bowie, James, 170
Bowman, Bob, 122
Brazoria County: Gonzalez, Simon, 119–21; San
    Point Cemetery, 62; Terry, Benjamin Franklin,
    birthplace of, 56; Varner, Martin, 119–21
Brazos Bottoms: area, 1; cemeteries, 61; fertility,
    80, 85, 169, 178; terror in the, 89
Brazos River (see also Brazos Bottoms): area, 1;
    Austin, Stephen F., 37; Brazos de Dios, 85;
    Hellhole of the, 20, 86, 109; Macario Garcia,
    131; slave smuggling, 47; stories of, 87, 91;
    Sugar Land Town Center, 168
Brewer, John Mason, 169
bridge to San Isidro Cemetery, 85; access to

145–46; cemetery; deterioration, 145, 147,
    149; funeral, 26; history of, 23, 25; no longer
    there, 27
Brown vs. Board of Education, 10
Buck-Morss, Susan, 188
Bugbee, Leroy, 37
buildings, historic (see historic buildings)
Bull Run, Battle of (see First Manassas), 57–58
Burchfield, John, 149–50, 152, 154
Burnett, Frances Hodgson, 30
Bustamante, Anastacio, 40

Caldwell, William, 47–48, 91–93; little pieces of
    rope, 90–91
Canalizo, General Valentin, 124
cannibals, 48, 82–83
Cantrell, Gregg, 38, 41, 44, 46, 191
capitalism, late, metanarrative of, 5
Caro, Robert, 37
Carrier Grundy, Naomi, 105–109
Cash, W. J., 5, 46–47, 49, 189
caskets (see also coffins), 23
castas, 40
Castillo, Enrique, 134, 143
Catholic Church, 41
Catholic Diocese of Galveston-Houston, 145
cemetery (see also San Isidro Cemetery), 1, 8–9,
    14; African American, 34; black, 16, 34, 60–61,
    177, 193; detritus, 146, 152, 155; farm laborer
    buried in, 36; fence around, 28, 30, 148, 156,
    159; fire, 30–31 lawsuit, 144; narrative, 6, 36;
    opulent surroundings, 144, 145; prisoner, 61,
    145, 177; Texas Historical Site refused, 158;
    slave, Monticello, 186
Certeau, Michel de: demonic, writing on the, 107;
    ghosts, 85; Icarus and Deadalus, 174–75; mak-
    ing of history, 57; memory, 59, 126–27, 180;
    history and society, 35–36, 77, 83, 104, 126–27,
    140; "Walking in the City," 177
Chance, John Milton, 124–25
Chicano, civil rights movement, 110
Civil War, 50; in Texas, 8
Clemens, Samuel (see Twain, Mark)
Clover, Glen, 146, 150–52, 177
Coahuila y Tejas, 15, 37, 48
coffins, smuggling, 47
Cole Theatre, 111
Colonel, The (see Benjamin Franklin Terry)
Colony, The (see Austin's Colony)

Colorado River, 37

Confederacy: death of, 78, 83; remembered, 55

Confluence of Civilization, 35

Congressional Medal of Honor, 136, 143; and Macario Garcia, 128–31, 133, 141, 192

Congregation of Saint Basil, (*see also* Basilian priests) 11–12

convict farms (*see* prison farms)

Cordova-Flores Incident (*see also* Cordova Rebellion), 124

Cordova Rebellion (*see also* Cordova-Flores Incident), 122–26, 169; negroes in, 124

Cordova, Vicente, 123–27, 143

Cortez, Gregorio, 126–27

Cortina, Juan, 124

Costa Lima, Luiz, 189

Cotton: history, 5; migrant worker, 21; transport of, 56; Union blockade, 75

Court of Criminal Appeals, 48

Covarrubias, Richard, 164

Criminal District Court of Harris County, 47–48

criollos, 43

Crockett, David, 122–26, 169; as national figure, 45; theatrical works about, 45–46; as "Wildman," 45

Cruz, Guillermo, 125

Cruz, John de la: black cemetery, 34, 61, 183–84, 193; cemetery history, 31, 152; county history, 144; San Isidro Cemetery Association, 27, 32, 150

Cumings, Tim, and naming of B. F. Terry High School, 54, 59, 178

Cunningham, Edward, 75

Cunningham, William, 177

Cunningham Plantation, 178

Czech community, 185

Daedalus, 174–75

Dallas Morning News, 11, 134, 136; prisoners, articles on, 182

Davis, Edwards, 117

Davis, J. H. P., 107–108

Davis, Jefferson, 54

Dawn at My Back, 162

Day of the Dead (*see Dia de los Muertos*)

Dayan, Joan, 78

debts, colonists' unpaid, 47

DeLay, Tom, 1, 15

De León, Arnoldo, 117–18

De Loughrey, Elizabeth, 80

Democratic Political Party, Fort Bend County, 90

Derrida, 194

De Shields, James T., 123, 125

descanso, 30

Dewitt Colony, 122

Dia de los Muertos, 156–57

Diaz, Porfirio, 112

Dirt and Desire, 161

Disney, Walt, 46

diversity, racial and ethnic, 37

Donald, David, 76

Don Quixote, 189

Douglas, Ellen, 161

Douglas, Frederick, 170–71

Douglas, May, 153–54

Dubois, W. E. B., 1–2

Durst, Harriet, 125

East, Bernard, 59, 65

Eccleston, E. (*see also* Samuel Williams), 47

El Economista, 42, 52

Eldridge, William, 191, 192

Ellis, L. A., 177

emancipation, 79

Emerald City, 165–66, 173–74, 182–83

Enron, 1, 15–16

Ensayo histórico de la revoluciones de México, 42–43

ethnic Mexican: affluence, 1, 10; banishment, 9, 155, 169; Basilian priests and, 12; loss of rights, 125; migrant workers, 10; post–Civil War, 112; post–Mexican War, 112; post–slavery, 4; prison population, 177, 183; sharecroppers, 12; in the twentieth century, 4, 8, 59

ethnography, 7, 104, 182; of San Isidro Cemetery, 11

ethnographer, 7–8, 11, 27

Exchange Club of Sugar Land, 185

Farías, Valentín Gómez, 40

Faulkner, William, 67–68, 70, 73–74, 78, 190

"fearless Mexican," (*see also* Macario Garcia), 128, 131

Ferguson, Charles, 97–98

Ferguson, Henry, 94–104

Ferris, Dr., 51

fifth street neighborhood, 144

Filisola, Vicente, 124

First Colony subdivision, 27, 145, 180

First Manassas (*see* Battle of Bull Run), 57
Fleming, Arizona, 88
Flores, Richard, 115
Flush Times, 47
Foley, Neil, 117
Fordism, 5
Fort Bend County: acreage, 85; Basilian priests, 12; demographics, 70, 80, 96; economy and development, 1, 2, 10–11, 49, 54; Garcia, Macario, 130; German prisoners of war in, 185; ghosts, 6–7; history, 1, 5, 7, 8, 13, 35; Jaybird Constitution, 84, 90; Maillard, Doran, 51; Mexican descent, 10; Mexican troops, 9; Mexicans, violence against, 118–19; miscegenation, 79; museum, 108; post-Reconstruction, 80; prison, 177; race horses, 69–70; Reconstruction, 34, 100, 102; roads, 95; secret book, 88; Spanish language movies, 111
Fort Bend County, Texas: A Pictorial History, 185–87
"forty acres and a mule," 89
Foucault, Michel, 99, 179, 189
Fourth Infantry Division, 128–29
freedmen, 89; lynching of, 9; post-slavery, 4
Freeman, Elizabeth, 68
Freemason, 43
frontier, 46
Frost, Henry, 79, 93–95, 97, 103
funeral, 26, 31, 145–46, 152; home, 20–21, 23; of Colonel Benjamin Franklin Terry, 61–62

Galvan, Cosme, 31
Galvan, Guadalupe, 31–32
Galvan, Isaac, 31
Garcia, Carlos, 127–28
Garcia, Juan, 166–67, 183
Garcia, Lupe, 127–28
Garcia, Macario: birth, 130; combat, 127–29; Congressional Medal of Honor, 127–29; death, 127, 140; portrait, 139, 192–93; return home from the war, 131–36; Richmond Drive Inn (*see also* Oasis Café), 132–44, 192
Garza, Catarino, 124
Gaston, Brian, 157–76
genealogy, 49; In *Puddin' Head Wilson,* 67; Puerto Rican, 70, 72
George Foundation, 180
George Memorial Library, 160
George Ranch Historical Park, 105–107, 180
German prisoners of war, 185

Ghostly Matters: Haunting and the Sociological Imagination, 181
ghosts, 33–34, 60, 183, 191; imprints of, 27; stories about, 68, 70
Gibson, Ned, 64–66, 69, 76, 81
Gibson, Volney, 64, 69, 81, 82
Glover, Joseph, 47
Golden Globe Award, 111
Gone With the Wind, 33, 57
Gonzalez, Simon, 118, 120, 126–27, 143
Gordon, Avery: haunting and ghosts, 27, 33–34, 181–82; re-memory, 25–26
Gran Centro, 16, 22, 26, 144–45; Semersky murder, 160
grave, 23, 33
gravestone, 29–30
Gray, William Fairfax, 116
Great Depression, 20
Green, Hattie Mae, 100
Green, Henry, 100–101, 104
Groce, Jared, 47
Guadalupe, Virgin of (*see* Virgin of Guadalupe)

hagiography, 18, 78
Haitian slave uprising, 97
Hale, Grace Elizabeth, 67
Handbook of Texas Online, 90, 122–23
hangings, 188
Harlem Plantation, 178
Harrisburg (*see also* Houston), 56
Harris County Criminal Court, 93
Harvey, Bill, 8
headstone (*see* gravestone), 33
Healey, John, 139–40, 185, 192
"Hegel and Haiti," 188
Helguera, Jesús, 110–11
Hellhole of the Brazos, 20, 86, 109
Hemings, Sally, 6, 73, 186
Hendrix, SSgt. James, 136–39
Henson, Margaret Swett, 42
Hercules, the American, 46, 50
Hernández, José F. and Macario Garcia, 128, 132, 134, 142
Herrera, Blas Maria, 162
Herrera, John J., 162–64
Herrera, José Manuel de, 40
heterotopia, 36
Highway 6, State, 22
Highway 59, U.S., 22, 58, 85

Highway 90, U.S., 59

Hispanic heritage, 36

Historia de la revolución de la Nueva España

historic buildings, 35

historiography, 35–36, 105, 140, 189

history, 48; erased, 11; ethnography, 7; of Fort
  Bend County, 47–48; genealogy, 49; memory,
  2, 8–9; society, 35; subjectivity, 33; of Texas (*see*
  Texas history)

Holland, Sharon Patricia, 60–61

hooks, bell, 3

Houston (*see also* Harrisburg), 56; location of,
  16, 37

Houston Chronicle, 26,34, 36, 144; and Macario
  Garcia, 130, 138, 141–42; and Sugar Land, 144,
  157, 168

Houston Press, 131, 134

Houston's founders, 48, 91

Houston's Zavala Chapter of the Tejano Association for Historic Preservation, 42

Humphrey, Stephen, 171

Hürtgen Forest, 128–29

Hutton, Paul, 46

Icarus, 174–85

identity, 4, 195n7

imaginary, 1, 14, 22, 46, 60

immigrants, Mexican, 37–38

Imperial Farm, 178

Imperial Sugar Company, 61, 75, 167, 177, 181, 191;
  cemetery, 2, 8, 30

Imperial Sugar plantation (*see also* Sugar Land
  plantation, 16, 148, 160–61

Infante, Pedro, 111

Inquisition, The, 40

Institute of Texan Cultures, 35–36

Insurgentes, Los, 39

insurgents, 37

insurrection, Austin's fear of slave, 41

intimacy, 6

Irwin, John, 78

Iturbide, Agustín de, 39–40

Jaybird Political Party, 64, 83, 93–94, 98

Jaybird-Woodpecker Feud, 76, 82, 88, 90, 104; beginning of, 91; Ferguson, Henry, 104; Green,
  Henry, 104; punishment, 99; Shamblin, J. M.,
  91–92; Terry, Kyle, 66, 69, 76, 81; Turkey
  Creek Feud, 108

Jefferson, Thomas, and miscegenation, 56, 63, 73,
  185–86, 190

Jim Crow: colored entrance, 149; end of, 162–63;
  exclusion of Mexicans and blacks in restaurants, 132; Fort Bend County, 10, 21; Hellhole
  of the Brazos, 20; history, 10; jury participation, 162; laws, 132; lynching, 74; Mexican
  people, 21; Schaeffer's Pharmacy, 132; Texas, 8;
  years of existence, 2, 3

Johnson, Benjamin Heber, 116, 126

Johnson, Lyndon Baines, 37

Jones, Fenton, 106

Jones, Robert, 106

Jordan, Terry, 8

Jubilee, 62

Juneteenth, 106

Kamin, Jake, 25

Karankawa, 48, 50, 168

Katzen, Ilona, 40

Kempner family, 144–45, 150

Kempner, I. H., 145

Kempner, Ike, 25, 30–31

Kempner, Isaac, 191

Kendall, William, 87, 100

Kendleton, Texas, 64, 86–87, 171; Heritage Society, 87; Jaybirds and, 98; Turkey Creek, 9, 86,
  100, 104–105

Ku Klux Klan (KKK): development of, 9; lynching and torture, 82, 106; Reconstruction and,
  74

Krause, George, 167

Kennedy, John F., 21

Kyle, William, 56, 63, 75

Lacan, Jacques, 103

Lack, Paul, 123, 125

La noche triste, 110

La voz de plata, Servando Teresa de Mier as, 40

Labor: laboring classes, 11; Mexican workers from
  central Texas, 4; slave, 10

El Labrador, 17–18, 19

Lamar, Mirabeau B., 37–38

Last of the White Primary Cases, Terry vs. Adams, 87

Latino as employee, 2

League of Latin American Citizen (LULAC), 130,
  162, 164

Leal, Felipe Valdéz, 159

Lemire, Elise, 77

Lewis, Betty, Elizabeth, 171–72

Limites de un discurso, Los, 42

Linn, Lewis F., 41

Lion of the West, 45

Little, William, 49

Litwack, Leon, 89

Lively, The, 51

Long, Jane (*see also* Mother of Texas), 52

Los Veteranos: Legacy of Valor, 134, 143

Lost Cause, The, 58

Lovett, Leslie, 59, 88

Lynching, and missing narratives, 90

McMillan, S. A., 48–49

Maillard, N. Doran, 51, 72, 112

Malo (rock band), 110

"Mama's Baby, Papa's Maybe," 170

Manifest Destiny, 37–39

Marquez, Benjamin, 162, 164

Martinez, Antonio, 38–39

Martinez, Don Atanacio, 127–28

Masonic Lodge, 43

Meillassoux, Claude, 172

Melton, Willie, 87

memoir, 11, 27

memories, forgotten, 30

memory: author's, 4, 9, 15, 28; ethnography and, 7; history and, 2, 9; imagination and, 20

mestizaje, 73

mestizos as farm workers, 112

México, 111–12

Mexicans: Aztec Empire, 82; aristocrats, 40; Austin, Stephen F., 40; Austin's description of, 41 cemetery, 16; constitution, 44; invasion, Santa Ana's, 48, 50, 52; laborer, 17, 19, 22; mission, Basilian, 12; politics, 44; Revolution, 17, 112; Simon Gonzalez skinned alive, 118–21; Texas, revolt, 116; troops entering Fort Bend County, 9; upper class, 40–41; as workers, 4, 117

Mexico, 41; benighted region, 38; City, 39–40; dark, 37; independence from Spain, 39, 49; northern frontier, 38; political elite as described by Austin, 41; racial composition, 40; rebellion against, 48; separation from Spain, 43; worker from northern, 4

Michener, James, 124

Mier Expedition, 97

Mier, Fray Servando Teresa de, 40–41

Mier y Terán, General Manuel de, 40

migrant workers, 10, 21

Mind of the South, The, 46

miscegenation, 52, 73

misogyny, 51, 79, 81, 85, 105, 170

Missouri Republican, 46

Molleston, John, 121–22

Montaigne, Michel de, 82

Monticello, 63, 185, 190

Morin, Raul, 128–29

Morrison, Toni, 176, 181–82

Mother of Texas (*see* Jane Long), 52

mud alley, 68, 140

mulatto children, 78

murder, 47; not reported, 89

Museum of Southern History, 108

mythohistory, 37–38

mythology, 185

narrative: author's, 15; of Mexican cemetery, 15; Mexican descent, 10; of rape, 6; silenced, 61; of Texas, 35, 46

Nassau Bay Developers, 25

Native American, 9, 13, 52, 168–69; folklore, 32

National Association for Living History Conference, 106

National Endowment for the Humanities, 106

Negroes involved in Cordova Rebellion, 124

Newland Corporation, 178

New Orleans: Austin, Stephen F. 39; *Lively* embarked for Texas, 51; miscegenation, 73; slave market, 51

New York Public Library, 134

New York Times, 82, 103, 111, 130, 136

Nueces River, 118

Nuevo León, 39–40

Oasis Café (*see* Richmond Drive-Inn), 131

Old Three Hundred, 46, 48–49, 50, 72, 96, 168, 186, 189; descendants, 51, 132, 175; taxonomy, 50; Varner, Martin, 119, 122

Olmsted, Frederick Law, 102

Owens, Honey Humphrey, 171

owls, 32

Oyster Creek, 10, 62; cemetery, 16, 22, 27; Civil War and, 57–58; Sugar Creek Subdivision, 144

Pandolfo, Stefania, 155

Panic of 1819, 39

panopticon, 179
Paredes, Americo, 126
Paredes, Jesús, 190
passing, 21
patrimony, 173
Paul Revere of the Texas Revolution, 162
Perales, Alonso, 163
Perkinson, Robert, 177
Pittsville, 93
Pizana, Aniceto, 126
Plan of San Diego, 116, 126
plantation: ghosts on, 34; houses, 33; Jefferson's,
    186; Oakland (*see also* Sugar Land Plantation),
    156; overseer (*see also* amo), 18; prisoner labor
    and, 177; Puerto Rican, 71; slaves, 50, 55; Sugar
    Land, 56, 67, 75; in Texas, 13; Walnut Bend, 90
planters: as gentlemen, 50; sexual relationship
    with slaves, 52
Pomedli, Michael, 32
post-Reconstruction: history, 4
Powell, Elizabeth, 9
Practice of Everyday Life, The, 174
prisons: abuse of prisoners, 182–83; bloodhounds,
    94; cemetery, 1, 34, 61, 145, 177; farms, 9–10,
    22, 177–78, 181; labor, 94; labor contract, 4,
    177; laborers, 34, 58–59, 181; as labor source,
    10, 17, 177; population, 177
Proud Peoples, The, 133
prostitutes, 68
purity, 34, 45, 73
Purity and Danger, 154

Quayson, Ato, 4–5
Quillen, Robert, 136–38

Race and the Education of Desire, 50–51
racehorses, 69–70, 72
race wars, 79
railroads: first in Texas, 56; and ghosts, 33; Gran
    Centro, 26; Santa Fe, 98
Raising the Dead, 60
rape, 6, 84, 100, 169
Read, Kay, 110, 112–13
Reconstruction: backlash to, 8; Fort Bend, 34, 89;
    history, 4; miscegenation, 74; and Terry Plan-
    tation, 59
Reliant Energy, 76
Republic of Texas, 37, 38; Army, 124; Cordova Re-
    bellion and, 124; immigrants and, 52; Seguín,

Juan, 116, 118; veterans and, 118, 120; Lorenzo
    Zavala and, 116–18
Republicans: black, 93; National Convention,
    98–99; Party, 89–90
Reyes, Alfonso, 16, 18–19
Reyes, Kathy Medina, 32–33
Richmond Drive-Inn (*see* Oasis Café), 131–37,
    139–42, 163, 192–93
Richmond, Texas, 63, 76, 83, 95; history, 96;
    manual labor, 112; Rio Grande, 116, 118; site of
    first railroad, 56
Ritter, Gretchen, 173
Rodriguez, Ismael, 111–12, 117
Rodriguez, Lori, 34, 157
Rodriguez, Terri, 149
Romo, Rolando, 42
Romo, Tere, 110
Rosa, Luis de la, 126–27
Rose, Jacqueline, 185
Rosenberg, Texas: location, 20; migrant work-
    ers, 21
Ruiz, Juan Francisco, 162
Ryon, Polly, 106–107

Sabine River, 122
sacrificial blood, 113
Sade, Marquis de, 78
Saint Domingue (*see also* Haiti), 78–79
Salado, Battle of, 124
Salazar, Fred, 176–77
San Antonio Express, 182
San Antonio, Texas, 113; Hemisfair, 35; Mexican
    attack in 1842, 124
San Bernard River, 98
Sanchez, Aniceto, 160–64
Sanchez, Cuco, 159
Sanchez, George I., 134
San Felipe, Texas, 38
San Juan de Ulua, Revolt of, 43
San Isidro, 16–18; hagiography, 18
San Isidro Cemetery, 1–2, 15–16, 36, 126; access to,
    145–46; Austin land grant, 15; black cemetery
    (*see* cemetery, African American and cemetery,
    black); clean-up weekend, 146–47, 152, 156;
    Corporation, 144; disappearing tombstones,
    14; dispute with Sugar Creek Subdivision, 36,
    155; ethnography, 11; houses next to, 25; pris-
    oner, 9, 60–61, 193; restroom, 152, 154; sign,
    158, 159; slaves, 9, 19, 61

Santa Ana, Antonio Lopez de: Alamo, 113, 115; Mexican Invasion, 48, 50, 52

Santa Fe Railroad, 98

Sartatia, 95, 176

Schaeffer's Pharmacy and Jim Crow Laws, 132

scalawags, 64–65, 67, 76, 94

Secession Convention, 56

Secret Garden, The, 30

Seguin, Juan, 112, 116, 118

Selena, 159

Semersky, Hilario, 159–61, 164

Settler's Way Subdivision, 26, 146, 148

Shamblin, J. M. 47–48, 91–92, 97

Sharecroppers: Garcia family, 130 138–40; post Civil War, 75, 85

Silencing the Past, 113

Six Flags of Texas, 114

Slaves: Austin Colony, 47–49; Brazos Bottoms, 169; burial, 34; colony (*see* Kendleton); community, 4; Davis, Jefferson, 54; emancipation, 4, 75, 79, 89; freed, 4, 75, 79, 89; history, 3, 10; importation, 56; labor, 10; market, Houston, 102; Mexico, 49; number of, 50, 55–56, 63; older, 57, 62; overseer, 57; owned by Colonel Benjamin Franklin Terry, 57–60; rape, 6, 169; rebellion, 79, 97, 119; sexual relationship with owner, 52, 62–63, 68, 73, 78, 172; Texas, 37; torture, 190; unnamed woman, 59–60, 66

Smith, Benjamin Fort, 56, 100

Smith, Robert E. "Bob," 130, 141

"Social Politics in Victorian Texas, 1890,"190

Sonnichsen, C. L., 65, 91–96, 98–99, 100

South, The, 5, 60; American, 41; foundational ideology, 6; old, 49, 51; racial conflict, 70; slavery, 54; story of, 60

Southern Magazine, 81

southern way of life, 77–78

Southeast Texas and planters' rules, 69

Sowell, A. J., 48–50, 97, 104, 124; torture and murder of Simon Gonzalez, 119–22

Spanish Camp, Texas, 103

Spanish: Constitution of 1812, 44; government, 39; League, 37

Spillers, Hortense, 170–73

Stanford, Gary, 149, 152

State Theatre, 111

States of Fantasy, 185

Stoler, Ann Laura, 5–7, 50

sugar: history, 5; plantations after Civil War, 75

Sugar Creek: Subdivision, 30, 157; Boulevard, 146, 149, 159

Sugar Land Industries, 25, 144–45, 162, 193

Sugar Land Plantation, 17–18

Sugar Land, Texas, 1, 16, 18, 25, 27, 30; City Hall, 173–74; Mexican missions, 12; prisons and, 58; Town Center, 165, 168, 181, 189; wealth, 10–11

Sundquist, Eric, 62

Talking Back Living History Theatre, 109

Talos, 175

Taylor, Tom, 64, 66–67, 91

Tejano: Bexar County, 125; Cordova Rebellion, 123, 125; rebels, 124

Tenochtitlan, 112

Terry vs. Adams et. al., 10, 87, 90

Terry, Colonel Benjamin Franklin "Frank" : background, 54–57, 130; death, 57, 61–62, 77, 83; genealogy, 54–56, 72–73; leaving for the Civil War, 57–59, 66–67; mansion, 59; race horse named after, 70, 72–73; war hero memorial, 130, 189

Terry, David, 61

Terry, John, 59

Terry, Kyle: as a child, 59, 61, 66–67; background, 66, 75; death, 81; genealogy, 63, 74, 79; Jaybird-Woodpecker Feud, 63–65, 75–76, 98; murder of Ned Gibson, 64–65; whiteness of, 63, 66–69, 78–80

Terry, Rachel, 59

Terry's Texas Rangers, 57, 90

Telfair State Prison, 178

Telfair Subdivision, 175, 178, 180

Texas, 125

Texas: Civil War, 8; Department of Corrections, 85, 176; Department of Transportation, 180–81; early settlement, 1; General Land Office, 121; Good Neighbor Commission, 130, 141–42; Historical Association, 35, 87; Historical Commission, 102, 121, 122; history, 35–36; Institute for the Humanities, 122; and Jim Crow, 8; Mexicanos, 18th and 19th century, 117–18; mythologies of origin, 46; Pavilion, 36; Rangers, 90, 99, 122. 126; Republicans and, 7; violent people in, 40, 46; War of Independence, 119

Texas-Mexico border, 3

Texas Outlook, 117

Texas Revolution, 37; Fort Bend County and, 9; role of Lorenzo Zavala, 42; Southeast, 1, 58

Texians, 37

Thurmond, Strom, 5

Tizoc, 110–13, 127

Tragedy of Puddin' Head Wilson, The, 67, 80

Transylvania University, 39

Travis, William Barrett, 42, 191

Trejo, Evelia, 42

Twain, Mark, 67, 80–81, 187

Trouillot, Michel-Rolph, 102, 113, 118–19

Truman, Harry, 129, 136, 138

"Tú, Solo Tú," 159

Turkey Creed Feud, 9, 100–105, 108

Tyler, Stephen, 7

United States: census, 96; Mexican War, 53; Supreme Court, 48, 90–91; Veteran's Administration, 128; War Department, 128

Universidad Autonoma de México, 46

University of Houston, Sugar Land, 178, 180–81

University of Houston, Victoria, 180

University of Texas, 37, 125

Valenzuela, Luisa, 181–82

Varner, Martin, 118–20

Vega, Lope de, 18

Virgin of Guadalupe, 29, 31, 155

Virgin Mary, 24, 155

Volney, Comte de, 63

voters, registered, 96

Waco Tribune, 68

Wallace, David, 7

Wallingford, Sharon, 168, 185–86, 191–92

Walker, Margaret, 62

Watkins, Meredith G., 9

Wharton, Clarence: and trial of William Caldwell, 91–93; Fort Bend County history, 37, 47, 51, 54, 83, 96, 99, 105, 108; Shamblin murder, 48, 91–93; Terry, Colonel Benjamin Franklin "Frank," 54–58, 62, 79, 92, 189; Terry, Kyle, 64–67, 76

Wharton, Texas, 64–65

White, Hayden, 45–46, 49

white: Anglo, 10, 41; protection of, 41; settlement, 36; settlers, 5, 50; whiteness, 5, 6, 21, 63, 70

wild man, 45–46, 50, 81

Willard Intercontinental Hotel, 136–39

Williams, Samuel, 38, 47, 56

Winchell, Walter, 132–36, 142

With a Pistol in His Hand, 126

Wizard of Oz, 165–66, 173

Woll, General Adrian, 124

women, black: child care, 6; labor, 10; rape of , 9; sexual intimacy, 10

Wood County, 118, 120–22

Woodpeckers, political party, 63, 77

World Trade Center, New York, 174–75

Yeager, Patricia, 155, 161

Yelderman, Pauline: banishment of blacks from Fort Bend County, 97, 99; Fort Bend County history, 34, 49, 105; Jaybirds and Woodpecker political parties, 68, 77, 89, 94, 97; Terry, Colonel Benjamin Franklin "Frank," 59; Terry, Kyle, 65–66, 68, 82

Yucatan, 43

Zamora, Mr., 28

Zavala, Adina de, 115

Zavala, Lorenzo de, 112; Freemasons, 43; influence in Mexico, 42–43; positions in the Mexican government, 43; reason for leaving Mexico, 45; relationship with Austin, 40, 42, 45; Texas Revolution, 42; Vice-President of the Republic of Texas; writings, 42–44

Zizek, Slavoj, 60